Early praise for *Mazes for Programmers*

Reading the book *Mazes for Programmers* is like a fun journey through a maze. There's a good mix of simple explanations and working code, combined with ideas at the end of each chapter to inspire one to expand upon what was presented.

➤ **Walter Pullen**
   Author, "Think Labyrinth!" website

Mazes for Programmers is full of nerdy algorithmic delight and is a really fun read!

➤ **Bruce Williams**
   CTO, CargoSense, Inc.

Jamis Buck's inspired choice of mazes as a unifying theme allows him to take the reader on a deeply engaging tour of an impressive array of algorithms and programming techniques. *Mazes for Programmers* is an exemplary book of its kind, ideal for programmers looking to take a break from tuition in specific programming languages and learn something of general interest and applicability within their craft.

➤ **David A. Black**
   Author, *The Well-Grounded Rubyist*

My past 20 years as a software developer have taught me two things. First, I will probably never need to generate a maze. Second, and more important, pushing myself in new and unfamiliar ways is the best way for me to level up as a programmer. Sure, *Mazes for Programmers* will teach you how to generate mazes, but it will also give you one of the clearest step-by-step tours through algorithmic thinking you can find.

➤ **Chad Fowler**
  CTO, Wunderlist

This is a fun, playful tour of all the concepts and algorithms you'd want to know for generating and solving mazes. If only this book had existed when I was writing *Maze Crusade*!

➤ **Amanda Wixted**
  Owner, Meteor Grove Software

I starting programming because of the fundamental joy of making cool things just for the sake of making cool things. Jamis's *Mazes for Programmers* perfectly recaptures that feeling of pure, unadulterated awesomeness for awesomeness's sake. This will be a book I come back to again and again.

➤ **Corey Haines**
  CTO, Curious Nation

This book reminded me of a simple fact I sometimes forget: programming is fun.

➤ **Jeff Hardy**
  Programmer, Basecamp

Mazes for Programmers

Code Your Own Twisty Little Passages

Jamis Buck

The Pragmatic Bookshelf

Dallas, Texas • Raleigh, North Carolina

Our Pragmatic courses, workshops, and other products can help you and your team create better software and have more fun. For more information, as well as the latest Pragmatic titles, please visit us at *https://pragprog.com*.

The team that produced this book includes:

Jacquelyn Carter (editor)
Potomac Indexing, LLC (indexer)
Liz Welch (copyeditor)
Dave Thomas (typesetter)
Janet Furlow (producer)
Ellie Callahan (support)

For international rights, please contact *rights@pragprog.com*.

Printed in the United States of America.
ISBN-13: 978-1-68050-055-4
Printed on acid-free paper.
Book version: P1.0—July 2015

Contents

Part II — Next Steps

Acknowledgments

A lot more goes into a book than I had imagined—and believe me, I had imagined a lot! None of this would have been possible without the faith that Dave Thomas and Andy Hunt had in me. A huge thanks goes to them for taking a risk on a book about *mazes*, of all things!

A huge debt is also owed to Jacquelyn Carter, my tireless and (seemingly!) endlessly patient editor. I can't imagine how she didn't despair at seeing my early chapter drafts. Thanks for showing me the way, Jackie.

Thanks, too, to the wonderful army of technical reviewers who pored over my code examples and prose explanations and made numerous suggestions. It is a better book because of your help: Bruce Williams, Jeff Hardy, Nick Quaranto, Trevor Turk, Amanda Wixted, Walter Pullen, Sam Stephenson, Chris Moyer, and Nick Capito.

Also, thanks to the readers of my blog, years ago, who read my series of articles about maze algorithms and gave me such wonderful encouragement. It is because of your enthusiasm that I ever even dared to consider this book.

Lastly—and most profoundly—thanks go to my wife Tessa and my children, for the sacrifices they've made during the last eight months. Books don't write themselves (sadly!) and this one required me to be off by myself, writing, for a few hours each day. The faith of my family, and their constant support and encouragement, carried me through.

Thank you, thank you, thank you!

Introduction

Mazes are everywhere. From psychology experiments where mice scamper in search of cheese, to robotics demonstrations, to movies (*Labyrinth*, anyone?) and video games (*Pac-Man? The Legend of Zelda? Doom?*), to books and books of puzzles to be traced by finger or pencil, you've almost certainly encountered them at some point in your life.

What you're reading now is not a collection of mazes for you to solve. No, this is something much more exciting. *This is a collection of ideas to inspire you.*

You're about to learn how to generate your own mazes. *Random* mazes, unique, each one different than the one before. It's a voyage of discovery where you never know quite what you'll find when you crest the next hill.

You'll take your existing knowledge of software engineering and apply it to generating these puzzles in a variety of shapes and sizes. You'll make mazes out of squares, circles, triangles, and hexagons. You'll put them on cylinders and cubes, spheres and even Möbius strips. You'll stretch them into other dimensions, squeeze them into arbitrary outlines, weave them, braid them, print them, and fold them.

You'll discover yourself brimming with *ideas*, perhaps the most effective cure there is for programmer's block, burnout, and gray days.

About This Book

The chapters here are grouped into four parts, organized roughly around a simple progression of concepts. You'll learn about a dozen different ways to generate mazes, as well as a number of fascinating things to do with them.

Part One will introduce you to some basic techniques and will walk through the beginnings of a grid implementation that will be used throughout the book. You'll learn about Dijkstra's algorithm and see how it can be used not only to find solutions to the mazes you'll generate, but also to gain insight into the structures and patterns hiding within those mazes. By the end of

Chapter 5 you'll have learned a total of six different ways to generate these twisty little passages.

Part Two takes you to the next step and shows you some exciting ways to vary what you've done to that point. You'll see how to fit mazes into arbitrary outlines, and how to build them out radially in circles. You'll explore different grid styles based on hexagons and triangles, and even take some tentative steps toward 3D mazes by building passages that weave over and under one another.

Part Three introduces the remaining six ways to generate mazes, including some tricks for varying the algorithms to produce things like particularly dense weaves, or rooms, or even infinitely long mazes.

Finally, *Part Four* shows how to build these mazes out in multiple dimensions. You'll see how to add passages moving up and down between different levels of your mazes, and even learn ways to generate them on surfaces of 3D objects, like cubes and spheres.

What This Book Isn't

You're not going to find any mathematical proofs here. While there are definitely strong mathematical underpinnings beneath mazes and maze algorithms, you don't need to know any of that to begin enjoying them. You can do a lot without understanding any of the theory behind it, at all.

I've taken great pains to avoid using mathematical terminology in describing the algorithms in this book. If the math turns out to be your thing, or if you decide you *want* to know more about the concepts of graph theory, go for it! It'll only help make the topic that much richer.

But you certainly don't *need* to know any of that to make random mazes.

Who This Book Is For

If you've ever written software before, *at all*, then this book is for you. You don't need to have a degree in computer science, and you don't even need to have shipped any large software project before—you only need to be familiar with simple programming concepts.

Maybe you're a game designer. Your games might be visually rich and complex, graphically simplistic, or even purely textual, but mazes can still play a variety of roles in them. Nintendo's *The Legend of Zelda* or id Software's *Doom* use mazes so seamlessly as a setting that often you don't even consciously realize you're navigating one. In others, like Namco's *Pac-Man*, the maze is fully visible and acts less as a puzzle and more as an obstacle. And Will Crowther's *Colossal Cave Adventure* used mazes to invent an entire genre of interactive fiction games.

If gaming isn't your thing, perhaps *algorithms* are. Programmers—hobbyists and professionals alike—often take great delight in learning and implementing processes like random maze algorithms. Understanding these algorithms and bringing them to life is a kind of grand puzzle, all by itself, with a lot of satisfaction to be found in the journey.

And even if you don't identify with either of those categories, you may yet find value in maze algorithms. I've found that they can be very effective against burnout and "programmer's block" by providing a moderate level of challenge and a variety of visually interesting and engaging ways to play with them. Taking a bit of time each day to tinker with a different algorithm can keep your mind fresh and limber. It's great mental exercise!

How to Read This Book

How you read this book depends in large measure on your previous experience with generating random mazes.

If you've never generated mazes before, then you should probably start with Chapter 1, *Your First Random Mazes*, on page 3 and read through the book sequentially. The topics will build on each other, starting with basic concepts and projects and getting progressively more advanced.

On the other hand, if you've built a few random mazes before, you might be more interested in the things you can actually *do* with them. You could skim Chapter 2, *Automating and Displaying Your Mazes*, on page 17 to get familiar with the specific grid system that the examples use, and then jump right into topics like Chapter 6, *Fitting Mazes to Shapes*, on page 83 and Chapter 8, *Exploring Other Grids*, on page 113.

And if you've *really* been around the block a few times, you might want to skip straight to Appendix 1, *Summary of Maze Algorithms*, on page 249 to get an overview of the different algorithms, and then jump into specific chapters to learn more about those that might be new to you.

Regardless of your level of experience, there's a "Your Turn" section at the end of each chapter, with a list of suggested projects for jumping off and exploring. Take advantage of those, or explore some of your own. See what you come up with!

About the Code

The sample code and the examples in this book are all written in Ruby,[1] but the algorithms and techniques used are definitely not Ruby-specific! This book could have been written just as well in Python, or C, or Java, or C#, or any other language. I hope the examples are written clearly enough that even if you aren't familiar with Ruby, the concepts shine through. There's plenty of room for experimentation, whether or not Ruby is your thing.

If you decide to follow along in Ruby, please make sure you're using at least Ruby version 2.1, as the examples won't all run on earlier Ruby versions.

All of the code examples in this book can be downloaded from the book's website.[2] This can save you a bit of time if you'd rather not rekey an entire grid framework by hand—although that's certainly an effective way to learn something!

Online Resources

The website for this book includes a community forum, where you can post any questions, comments, or cool maze-type-things you've created. You can also submit errata if you find any errors or have suggestions for future editions of the book.

If you find this book has whetted your appetite for maze algorithms, you'll find a variety of helpful resources online. Walter Pullen's "Think Labyrinth!" site[3] has a wealth of information about the different algorithms, the psychology of mazes, and examples of mazes both large and small. I've written a series of articles on my blog[4] about these algorithms, with animations to show how they work. And if algorithm visualization is your thing, Mike Bostock has written a beautiful article about the subject[5] (including a couple of maze algorithms). It's quite mesmerizing!

As with most things, Google will be your friend. See what else you can find!

Jamis Buck

July 2015

---

1. http://www.ruby-lang.org
2. https://pragprog.com/book/jbmaze/mazes-for-programmers
3. http://www.astrolog.org/labyrnth.htm
4. http://weblog.jamisbuck.org/2011/2/7/maze-generation-algorithm-recap
5. http://bost.ocks.org/mike/algorithms/

Part I

The Basics

Maze making is probably new territory for most folks, so we'll ease into this. We'll talk about algorithms, learn about a thing called bias, and walk through some different ways to generate mazes. We'll even go a bit beyond merely generating mazes, and see some neat things we can do with finding paths through them, too.

CHAPTER 1

Your First Random Mazes

Maze-making seems magical when you're outside looking in, but don't be fooled. *There is no magic.* Starting on this very page, we'll begin demystifying the processes that drive maze generation. We'll see the scaffolding that lies just beneath their surface. We'll get specific, talking about what exactly mazes *are*, and then we'll get the ball rolling with two simple ways to create mazes, walking through them together with paper and pencil.

Eventually, this will take us to some exciting places, but like most beginnings, ours is quite humble. Here, it all starts with algorithms.

We're going to focus on those algorithms that produce mazes *randomly*. Passage length, the number of dead ends, crossroad frequency, and how often passages branch will all be determined by randomly choosing from a prescribed list of possibilities.

There is no universally ideal algorithm for generating mazes, so over the course of this book we'll explore twelve different ones. You'll learn how to choose between them depending on your project's needs, such as speed, memory efficiency, or simplicity (or even your own personal sense of aesthetics!). On top of that, most of the algorithms have little idiosyncrasies that cause the mazes they generate to share some feature, like short, stubby passages, or maybe the passages all skew a certain direction. We'll explore those, too.

But we'll get to that. By the end of this book you'll be an expert, able to nimbly switch between these different algorithms to choose just the right one for the job. You'll be pounding these out in code before you know it.

First, though, let's do it on paper.

> ### Joe asks:
> # What's an Algorithm?
>
> An *algorithm* is just a description of a process. Like a recipe in a cookbook, it tells you what steps to take in order to accomplish some task. *Any* task. Algorithms exist for everything. If lasagna is your goal, then the steps you take to make lasagna are your algorithm. Want to make your bed, or drive to work? Both can be described as a series of steps. More algorithms! Algorithms launch rockets, land airplanes, drive cars, sort information, and search the Web. Algorithms solve mazes. And if you're out to *make* a maze, like we are, your algorithm consists of the steps you take to make that maze.

Preparing the Grid

We're going to start by drawing a *grid*—just a regular crosshatching of perpendicular lines. This scaffolding will form the skeleton of the maze, the bones and sinews that will give structure and stability to our final product.

Here's what I want you to do.

Get out a piece of paper. It doesn't have to be fancy—a napkin will do in a pinch. You'll want something to write with, too, and erasability will be a plus.

On this piece of paper, draw a grid. Four-by-four ought to be plenty big enough for this first experiment, and don't worry about the lines being all neat. Anything like this figure should be fine.

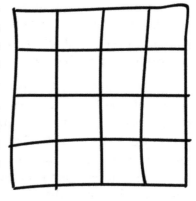

This is our starting point. We'll call the individual squares *cells*, and the grid lines around them *walls*. Beginning with this grid, our task is to erase just the right walls—*carve* just the right *passages*—in order to produce a maze.

That happens to be exactly what the algorithms in this book will do for us. Most of them create what are called *perfect* mazes, where every cell can reach every other cell by exactly one path. These mazes have no *loops*, or paths that intersect themselves. That's significant! This figure is an example of one of these perfect mazes.

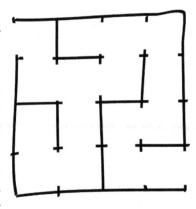

Don't mistake the name for a value judgment, though. The "perfect" bit simply refers to its logical and mathematical purity. A maze may be perfect (mathematically), and yet flawed (for example, aesthetically), at the same time!

The opposite of a perfect maze is called a *braid* maze. These are characterized by few (if any) dead ends, and passages forming loops. Here's an example of a braid maze.

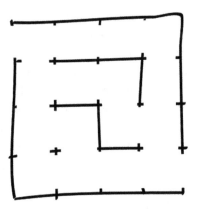

Going from one point to another in these kinds of mazes can be accomplished by multiple different paths, or solutions. We'll see more of them in Chapter 9, *Braiding and Weaving Your Mazes*, on page 129, but for now we'll focus just on their counterparts, the perfect mazes.

Let's create some!

Labyrinths versus Mazes

Some people prefer "labyrinth." Others like "maze." Some even use the word labyrinth to refer to a particular kind of maze, a single passage that never branches but winds in a convoluted path from start to finish.

Ultimately, though, it doesn't matter what they're called. Labyrinth or maze, they (mostly) mean the same thing. I'll be giving preference to the word "maze" in this book. And while those non-branching versions (technically called *unicursal* mazes) are fun to play with, they are sadly beyond the scope of this book. We'll be focusing on *multicursal* mazes—those with branching passages—which will prove to be plenty all by themselves!

The Binary Tree Algorithm

The Binary Tree algorithm is, quite possibly, the simplest algorithm around for generating a maze. As its name suggests, it merely requires you to choose between two possible options at each step. For each cell in the grid, you decide whether to carve a passage north or east. By the time you've done so for every cell, you have a maze!

This process of looking at cells is called *visiting* them. Visiting them in some order is *walking the grid*. Some walks might be random, choosing directions arbitrarily from step to step, like the ones we'll see in Chapter 4, *Avoiding Bias with Random Walks*, on page 53. Others are more predictable. For Binary Tree, it turns out that we can do it either way. The algorithm really doesn't care what order we use to visit the cells.

Let's walk this together and see how the Binary Tree comes together in practice. I'll flip a coin at each step to decide which direction we ought to carve a passage. Also, while the Binary Tree algorithm itself doesn't care where in the grid we begin walking,

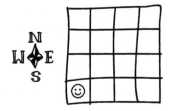

for the sake of this example we'll just go with the cell in the southwest corner.

Our choice is this: do we erase that cell's northern wall, or its eastern wall? Let's see what the coin says. If it comes up heads, we'll carve north. Tails, we'll carve east.

And...heads. Looks like we erase the northern wall.

Note that although these two cells are now linked by a connecting passage, we haven't technically visited that second cell yet. We *could* choose to visit that cell next (because Binary Tree really doesn't care which order we visit the cells) but moving across a row and visiting its cells in sequence is simpler to implement. Let's wait and hit that northern cell when this row is finished. For now, let's just hop over to the one immediately to the east of us.

Flipping the coin here, we get tails. This means we'll erase the eastern wall of our current cell.

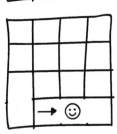

And flipping the coin for the next cell over gives us tails again.

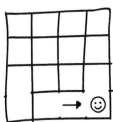

Moving east again, our current cell becomes the one in the southeast corner. We could certainly flip the coin here, too, but consider what would happen if the coin came up tails. *We'd have to carve a passage through the outer wall of the maze.* This is not generally a good idea. We'll talk more in a moment about adding entrances and exits to your mazes,

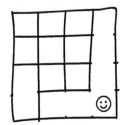

but for now we want to avoid tunneling out of bounds. Since that effectively forbids going east, north becomes our only viable option. No need to flip a coin—let's just take care of business and carve north.

In fact, that constraint exists for every cell along that entire eastern boundary. None of them can host an east-facing passage. We might as well just take care of those now by carving north on each one of them. We'll consider each of them visited as well.

Now, for the sake of demonstration, let's jump all the way to the northwest corner and see what happens next. (Yeah, this is a bit unorthodox...but remember, Binary Tree only needs us to visit all the cells—it doesn't care what order we use to do that.)

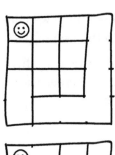

Once again, we could flip a coin, but consider what happens if the coin lands heads-up: we'd have to carve through that northern wall. We don't want that. Instead, we'll forego the coin flipping and just carve east.

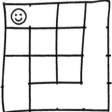

Again, notice how that constraint applies to every cell along that entire northern boundary. You can't carve north from *any* of them, so *all* of them default to going east instead.

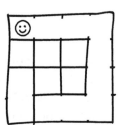

One more special case to consider. Let's jump to the northeast corner.

We can carve neither north, nor east from here. Our hands are tied. With nothing to choose from, we choose nothing. Of all the cells in our grid, this is the only one for whom nothing can be done. We shrug our shoulders and skip it.

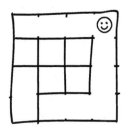

Go ahead and grab your own coin, now, and flesh out the rest of those cells that haven't been visited yet. Once a decision has been made for every cell, you should be left with a maze that looks something like the figure.

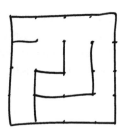

That's really all there is to it! You just learned the Binary Tree algorithm for random maze generation. Painless!

Entrances and Exits

At this point, though, you might be wondering how it can be a maze if there is no way into or out of that box. Aren't mazes supposed to have starting points and ending points? That's a fair question! The truth of the matter, honestly, is that it's entirely up to you.

Earlier we talked a bit about the idea of *perfect mazes*. It all comes back to that again. The maze you just drew is a perfect maze, and one of the attributes of a perfect maze is that there exists exactly one path between any two cells in it. Any two! You pick them, and there's guaranteed to be a path between them.

This means you can choose any two cells in your maze, make one of them the starting point and the other the ending point, and you can be confident knowing that there's a real solution to your maze. Just like that. Want to enter on one side and exit on the other? Choose two cells on the boundaries of your maze, erase the outer walls of those cells, and you're all set.

It depends on what you want your maze to do. The maze in Pac-Man, for instance, has no exit at all, because the goal is simply to eat all the pellets before the ghosts get you. Other games, like Zelda, allow you to enter a maze, but the goal is to reach a point *inside* it, so you can defeat some boss creature and obtain the treasure.

So don't be surprised when the examples in this book omit the "start" and "finish" points. Those will be up to you and your imagination!

 Joe asks:

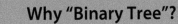

Perhaps you've heard of *binary trees*, data structures whose values are arranged hierarchically, each value having zero, one, or two child values of its own. It's not chance that this algorithm shares a name with that data structure, because *the mazes it generates are binary trees*.

It's true. Remember that one cell in the northeast corner, the one we couldn't do anything with? That's the root of the tree. It has no parent node, but it has at least one child, and possibly two, either to the west, or to the south. Follow that outward, cell to cell, and you'll see that each subsequent cell is itself either a dead end (that is, a *leaf node*), or a parent of up to two more children.

Nifty!

Understanding Texture

Looking at your maze, you might notice a few little oddities. For instance, the northern row and the eastern column are both unbroken corridors. These are completely expected, if you think about it. Remember what happened on those boundary cells, where erasing a wall would have taken us outside the bounds of the maze? We always chose the valid direction instead, north or east, forcing those boundaries to merge into a single passage.

This contributes to what we call the maze's *texture*. Texture is a general term that refers to the style of the passages of a maze, such as how long they tend to be and which direction they tend to go. Your first impression of a maze is often strongly influenced by the maze's texture.

Some algorithms will tend to produce mazes that all have similar textures. Binary Tree, for example, will always produce mazes with those two unbroken corridors on the north and east. Don't believe me? Give it a try. The following figure represents a bare handful of mazes randomly generated using Binary Tree, and notice how they all have those same long corridors on the north and east.

We might say that the Binary Tree algorithm is *biased* toward mazes with that particular texture. We'll dig more into bias and what it means for algorithms in Chapter 4, *Avoiding Bias with Random Walks*, on page 53, but for now, when we talk about bias, we're referring to the algorithm's tendency to produce mazes of certain textures.

It has another bias, too. Plant yourself in the southwest corner of your maze, and try to find your way to the northeast corner. You'll find your path looks like one of those in this figure.

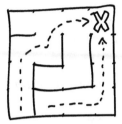

Not hard at all, is it? Even aside from the maze being small, the paths themselves are trivial. Every cell will have an exit to the north, or to the east, so you can always move northeast without any obstruction. No dead ends, no backtracking. Simple. That diagonal texture is evidence of a bias.

Now, we can't hold that against Binary Tree *too* much. Most random maze algorithms will have biases of one sort or another, though many are more subtle than this. The fact that this one is so blatant is just the price we have to pay for an algorithm as *fast*, *efficient*, and *simple* as Binary Tree.

Making Lemonade from Binary Lemons

Yes, it's true. Even with these glaring textures, there's a bright side. The Binary Tree algorithm is fast, efficient, and simple.

Think about it. You only have to visit each cell once to know how the maze will turn out. In computer-sciency terms, that means it is *O(n)*, about as fast as you can get when you have to visit every item in a collection.

It's also efficient. It only needs enough memory to represent a single cell at any given time. We'll see, later, other algorithms that are much more memory-hungry than this, some of them requiring memory proportional to the size of the *entire grid*. That's pretty limiting if you're wanting to deal with very large mazes, but it's just not an issue for Binary Tree.

Lastly, it's simple. You were able to work through it with just paper, pencil, and a coin for tossing. That can't be said for all of the algorithms we'll look at. Some would be downright painful to work out by hand!

Even the algorithm's biases aren't all bad. That diagonal texture? Sure, walking the maze from southwest to northeast might be trivial, but turn it around. What if you were to go from northeast to southwest instead?

Without an omniscient view of the
maze, you now have no clear idea
which direction will take you to the
goal. Sometimes, what seems like a
hopelessly simple maze simply needs
to be turned around. Lemonade,
indeed!

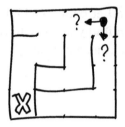

Still, a bias is a bias, and eliminating an algorithm's bias is rarely simple, or
even possible. If you can't use the texture that a given algorithm produces,
it's often easiest to look elsewhere.

So let's look elsewhere.

The Sidewinder Algorithm

Here's an algorithm called the Sidewinder, which, though closely related to
the Binary Tree, still manages to dial back the biases a notch. Recall that
Binary Tree chooses between north and east at every cell; Sidewinder, on the
other hand, tries to group adjacent cells together before carving a passage
north from one of them. Go ahead and grab another piece of paper, sketch
another grid on it, and we'll jump right in.

Now, unlike Binary Tree, the Sidewinder won't easily let us start carving
anywhere we like. It has a strong preference for beginning in the western
column, so that's where we'll start. In fact, we might as well start where we
did before, in the southwest corner. I'll just flip a coin for both of us, as before.
Once again, tails will mean "carve east," but we'll see that heads means
something a little different this time around.

Here goes!

Starting in that southwest corner, our
first flip of the coin yields tails and
tells us to erase the cell's eastern wall.
We then move to the next cell in that
direction, as in the figure.

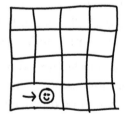

No problem. Once at this new cell, we flip the coin as before. It comes up tails again. Go ahead and erase that eastern wall and move to the next neighbor, like this.

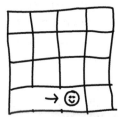

Once again, we flip our coin and...

Gasp!

Heads.

When the coin comes up heads, we look back on the path we just made, at that group of cells that were most recently joined by carving through walls. Here, it's those three cells in a row that we just visited. We'll call this

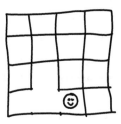

cluster a *run* of cells. We're going to randomly choose one cell from that run, and then erase its northern wall, joining it to its northern neighbor. After that, we're done with those three cells, and no further changes will be made to them. We'll call this *closing out the run*. This is shown in the preceding figure.

Note that the run here involves just those three cells, and not the cell to the north that we linked to! This is important. That cell to the north has not yet been visited, and will be fair game when the algorithm moves on to that second row.

Now, we very intentionally do *not* remove the eastern wall (because that would change those closed-out cells), and instead just move to the next cell over. When we're all comfortable the process begins again with a new run of cells, starting at our new position.

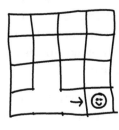

In our case, though, we've reached the eastern boundary of our grid, and no matter how much that coin of ours insists that we're supposed to keep going east, we just can't. The edge of our world is pretty immutable. When you find yourself in that situation, fall

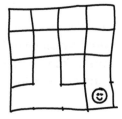

back to the same strategy we used with Binary Tree: don't bother flipping the coin. Treat that eastern boundary as an instant heads, and just close out the run. (Here, it's easy: we have only one cell in the run, so we choose it and erase the northern wall.

After closing out that row, move up to the next row and run the whole thing again. Flip, flip, flip, one after another, either adding to the run or closing it out, depending. Remember that so far, no cell in that next row has been visited. Some have been linked, *but not visited*, and Sidewinder must visit every cell in the grid exactly once. In other words, Sidewinder will look at every cell, even if it's already been linked to a cell in another row.

Bear with me a moment and let's jump up to the northwest corner. (Unorthodox again, yes, but we can do this because Sidewinder only needs us to start at the beginning of each row—we can actually do the rows themselves in any order we want.) For the sake of the demonstration, consider what would happen if the coin came up heads here, and we had to close out the run.

Yup. Just as we saw with Binary Tree, we run into an edge case in that northern row. We need to avoid erasing that northern boundary. The solution is familiar: just like we did at the eastern boundary, we disallow the direction that takes us out of bounds. We forbid heads, and force every coin toss to be tails for the duration of that row. This will have the effect of giving you an unbroken corridor across the top, just like in the Binary Tree algorithm.

Go ahead and flip your own coin for the rest, to see how the algorithm feels. When you've visited all the cells in your grid and closed out every row, you ought to wind up with something like the figure.

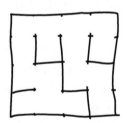

A bit more involved than Binary Tree, but not too bad. Still...yup. I'm sure you smell it, too.

A bias.

You could hardly miss it with that unbroken passage across the top. Every maze generated by Sidewinder will have that unbroken corridor. Not as bad as the two unbroken corridors of Binary Tree, but still hardly ideal. That's evidence of one of Sidewinder's biases.

The other is a bit more subtle. Put yourself in any of the cells along the southern boundary, and try to find your way to the northern row, as shown in the figure.

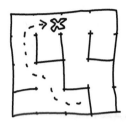

Sure enough: a nearly trivial solution. It may wind side-to-side a bit (hence the name of the algorithm), but because every horizontal run of cells will have exactly one passage north, solutions in that direction are not difficult to find.

As with Binary Tree, though, moving against the grain (north-to-south) can be more challenging.

Your Turn

By this point, you should have a decent grasp of what algorithms are, and some idea of the role they're going to play in generating random mazes. You've seen them at work with the Binary Tree and Sidewinder algorithms. You've worked through a couple of mazes on paper, and you've learned a little bit about maze textures and how they relate to algorithm biases.

Not bad!

However, as any good chef will tell you, a recipe—and here let's say, an *algorithm*—is only a place to start. Now it's your turn. Look deeper. Play around with what you've learned. If you need some suggestions to get your own idea engine running, take a look at the following experiments.

Binary Tree experiments

You'd expect an algorithm that restricts you to choosing between two options to give you very little flexibility. To some degree, that's true, but you might be surprised at what you can do simply by modifying the menu a bit. Shake up those assumptions and see what happens!

Reorient the Passages

As described, the Binary Tree algorithm produces unbroken corridors along the north and east boundaries. How might you change the algorithm to produce unbroken corridors on the south and west boundaries instead? What about north and west? South and east? What happens to the diagonal texture?

Changing the Bias

How could you change the Binary Tree algorithm to bias it toward longer horizontal runs? That is to say, how would you make the algorithm produce mazes with passages that tend to stretch horizontally? What about vertically?

Sidewinder Experiments

Now try it with Sidewinder. The same experiments apply, but the means will be a bit different. It all comes down to upsetting assumptions.

Reorient the Passages

As described, Sidewinder has a strong south-to-north texture. How would you change the algorithm to prefer paths moving east-to-west? What would happen to the unbroken northern corridor?

Changing the Bias

What could you do to bias Sidewinder toward longer horizontal runs? What about vertical runs?

You should be feeling pretty confident with both the Binary Tree algorithm, and Sidewinder. That's great! In the next chapter, we'll look at how to turn those algorithms into code, so the computer can do all the work for you.

CHAPTER 2

Automating and Displaying Your Mazes

Doodling mazes on paper is fine and all, but if that's all we had, we'd never get anything done. We're computer programmers. Let's do this right.

Let's have the computer do it for us.

Since grids are the foundation of most of what comes later, we'll start there, exploring the particular implementation used throughout the book. We'll see how it works in practice by implementing the Binary Tree and Sidewinder algorithms on top of it, and we'll work through two different ways to display it: textually (think "ASCII art"), and graphically.

Introducing Our Basic Grid

The examples in this and later chapters will all build on one particular grid implementation, so we'll spend a few pages on it here. This will be the tool we'll use to build out our mazes, either by using this Grid class directly, or by subclassing it and adding more specific functionality. Seeing how it's put together ought to make things clearer. We'll start simple, and in the next few chapters we'll add to it and extend it as needed.

What we want is to be able to instantiate the grid and operate on the cells that it contains. In pseudocode, something like this:

```
# instantiate a 10x10 grid
grid = Grid.new(10, 10)

# get the cell at row 1, column 2
cell = grid[1, 2]

# iterate over all the cells in the grid
grid.each_cell do |cell|
  # do something to the cell
end
```

Right away, we can see that the grid needs to be a container of some sort, structured—conceptually—like in the following figure.

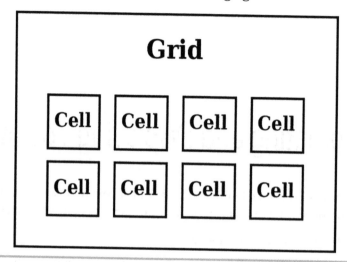

Figure 1—Grid Organization

The following implementation stays true to that architecture, with the Grid class acting essentially as a container for individual cells. It instantiates the Cell class as many times as it needs, to fill out the grid, with the individual cells each keeping track of which other cells they're next to, and which cells they're linked to via passages.

This implementation is written in Ruby,[1] but the concepts are definitely not Ruby-specific. Everything here can be adapted to your language of choice. Later examples—also in Ruby—will reuse this code, pulling it in and either drawing a maze on it (as we did by hand in the previous chapter), or extending it to add new functionality, as necessary.

Implementing the Cell Class

Since the Cell class is at the heart of this, we'll start there. Put the following code in a file named cell.rb. There's nothing too tricky here, but we'll walk through it and introduce the methods, at least.

cell.rb
```
class Cell
  attr_reader :row, :column
  attr_accessor :north, :south, :east, :west
```

---

1. http://www.ruby-lang.org

Each cell ought to know where it lives within the grid, so our class records those coordinates, row and column. It also tracks who the cell's immediate neighbors are to the north, south, east, and west.

The constructor, initialize, comes next. It accepts two parameters: the row and column within the grid where the cell is located. It also initializes a hash table called @links, which will be used to keep track of which neighboring cells are linked (joined by a passage) to this cell.

```
def initialize(row, column)
  @row, @column = row, column
  @links = {}
end
```

The next two methods are for manipulating that @links variable. The first, link(cell), connects the current cell with cell parameter. The second, unlink(cell), does the reverse and disconnects the two cells. In both cases, though, we want to make sure the operation occurs *bidirectionally*, so that the connection is recorded on both cells. An optional bidi parameter helps ensure that this happens.

```
def link(cell, bidi=true)
  @links[cell] = true
  cell.link(self, false) if bidi
  self
end

def unlink(cell, bidi=true)
  @links.delete(cell)
  cell.unlink(self, false) if bidi
  self
end
```

After those, we have two more methods dealing with cell connections. The first, links, is used for querying the list of all cells connected to this cell, and the second, linked?(cell), is for querying whether the current cell is linked to another given cell.

```
def links
  @links.keys
end

def linked?(cell)
  @links.key?(cell)
end
```

The final method, neighbors, is used to query the list of cells that adjoin this cell.

```
  def neighbors
    list = []
    list << north if north
    list << south if south
    list << east  if east
    list << west  if west
    list
  end
end
```

As we go, we'll add a few more methods to this class, but what we have here will be enough to get us started. It's not particularly useful by itself, though—we'll rarely even need to reference it directly. It's only when these cells have been bundled into a grid that they really begin to shine. Next let's look at how to make that happen.

Implementing the Grid Class

The grid class, as we saw in Figure 1, *Grid Organization*, on page 18, is essentially just a wrapper around a two-dimensional array of cells. Let's toss the following code into a file named grid.rb, making sure it's in the same directory as the cell.rb file we created earlier so the grid can find the Cell class that it needs. Once again, we'll walk through this together, one piece at a time.

First, we require the Cell class that we just wrote, since the grid depends on it. Note, also, that the grid keeps track of the number of rows and columns it comprises.

grid.rb
```
require 'cell'

class Grid
  attr_reader :rows, :columns
```

The constructor takes the dimensions of our desired grid as parameters, and sets those as attributes. It also initializes the grid by calling prepare_grid and configure_cells, which we'll implement next.

```
def initialize(rows, columns)
  @rows = rows
  @columns = columns

  @grid = prepare_grid
  configure_cells
end
```

We *could* inline these next two methods in the constructor, but doing it this way lets subclasses override the methods later, when we start playing with different types of grids.

```
def prepare_grid
  Array.new(rows) do |row|
    Array.new(columns) do |column|
      Cell.new(row, column)
    end
  end
end

def configure_cells
  each_cell do |cell|
    row, col = cell.row, cell.column

    cell.north = self[row - 1, col]
    cell.south = self[row + 1, col]
    cell.west  = self[row, col - 1]
    cell.east  = self[row, col + 1]
  end
end
```

For now, prepare_grid just sets up a simple two-dimensional array of Cell instances, and configure_cells tells each cell who its immediate neighbors are to the north, south, east, and west.

Note that the boundary cases, like the northern border where cells don't have a neighbor to the north, will be handled neatly by our custom array accessor (the [] method). That array accessor is primarily for granting random access to arbitrary cells in the grid, but it will also do bounds checking, so that if the coordinates passed to it are out of bounds, it will return nil. Let's define it next.

```
def [](row, column)
  return nil unless row.between?(0, @rows - 1)
  return nil unless column.between?(0, @grid[row].count - 1)
  @grid[row][column]
end
```

Subclasses can (and will) override this method to add some really interesting effects, like cylindrical or toroidal mazes.

While we're at it, let's take a minute to add another way to access individual cells: randomly. We'll also create a method for reporting the number of cells in the grid.

```ruby
def random_cell
  row = rand(@rows)
  column = rand(@grid[row].count)

  self[row, column]
end

def size
  @rows * @columns
end
```

These both may not seem particularly useful yet, but we'll see some algorithms soon that will use them.

Lastly, we'll implement some iterator methods for looping over the cells of the grid. Some algorithms, like Sidewinder, want to look at cells a row at a time, so we'll have an each_row method for those. Other algorithms, like Binary Tree, simply want to see the cells one at a time. We'll cover that case with each_cell.

```ruby
def each_row
  @grid.each do |row|
    yield row
  end
end

def each_cell
  each_row do |row|
    row.each do |cell|
      yield cell if cell
    end
  end
end
end
```

That's really all there is to it: a simple grid implementation that excels at demonstrating maze algorithms. Again, this is not the final product—we'll be adding to it in later chapters—but it's enough to start working through the two algorithms we already know. Let's see how this grid works in practice.

Implementing the Binary Tree Algorithm

Let's start with the Binary Tree algorithm. As you'll recall from *The Binary Tree Algorithm*, on page 6, it works simply by visiting each cell in the grid and choosing to carve a passage either north or east.

The following code does just that. We're going to put it in its own class so that we can easily reuse this code whenever we want. Save it to a file named binary_tree.rb, and make sure it's in the same directory as the cell.rb and grid.rb files we created earlier.

binary_tree.rb
```
Line 1  class BinaryTree
   -
   -    def self.on(grid)
   -      grid.each_cell do |cell|
   5        neighbors = []
   -        neighbors << cell.north if cell.north
   -        neighbors << cell.east if cell.east
   -
   -        index = rand(neighbors.length)
   10        neighbor = neighbors[index]
   -
   -        cell.link(neighbor) if neighbor
   -      end
   -
   15      grid
   -    end
   -
   -  end
```

The on(grid) method accepts a grid and applies the Binary Tree algorithm to it by iterating over each of its cells. For each cell, we collect the neighboring cells to its north and east, putting them into a list. Then, we choose one cell from that list at random, and link it to the current cell. Remember that the cell in the northeast corner of the grid has no neighbors to the north or east, so we need to make sure neighbor is valid before we try to link it up.

Not bad! With a bit of code golfing, you could probably simplify that even more (consider that a challenge, if you'd like), but this makes the point. Binary Tree is *easy*.

Choosing Random Elements from Arrays

Look at lines 9 and 10 from the listing of binary_tree.rb, where the program chooses one of the neighbors at random. That works just fine, but Ruby (at least) has a simpler way to do it:

```
neighbor = neighbors.sample
```

That one line will *sample*—or choose an element at random from—the neighbors array. We'll be using this sample method from now on.

Let's write a simple program next that we can use to put these pieces all together. Go ahead and put the following in a new file called binary_tree_demo.rb.

binary_tree_demo.rb

```ruby
require 'grid'
require 'binary_tree'

grid = Grid.new(4, 4)
BinaryTree.on(grid)
```

There's not much to it. We pull in our Grid and BinaryTree classes, instantiate a 4×4 grid, and then run the binary tree on it. Simple.

Sadly, running this little program is a bit anticlimactic. Give it a try. (Be sure to pass -I. to tell Ruby to look in the current directory for dependencies.)

```
$ ruby -I. binary_tree_demo.rb
$
```

It runs, and it finishes, but it doesn't actually *show* us anything. We kind of have to take it on faith that our maze was generated.

We could drop everything at this point and haul out a canvas API, or a graphics library, and start drawing walls and passages, but there's really no need just yet. We'll get there soon enough. Let's start simpler, with ASCII art.

Displaying a Maze on a Terminal

ASCII art is not necessarily the fanciest way, nor the prettiest, but it is often the most convenient way to display our mazes. We nearly always have easy access to a terminal, and we don't need to worry about bringing out any big guns (like external libraries or APIs). In short, it's perfect for what we need just now. Let's walk through one possible way to approach drawing our mazes using only four different characters: space (" ") for cells and passages, pipe ("|") for vertical walls, hyphen ("-") for horizontal walls, and plus ("+") to draw corners. Here's an example of a small maze drawn using these characters:

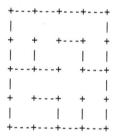

 Be careful not to think of the lines as the passages in these drawings! The lines are the walls, and the whitespace represents the corridors.

As shown, we're going to have each cell share walls with its neighbors. That is to say, the eastern wall of a cell will be the same as the western wall of its neighbor to the east. This simplifies the implementation, because when we go to draw the maze, we only have to draw the eastern and southern boundaries of each cell. We don't need to worry about a cell's northern or western boundaries (in general), because when the neighboring cell to the north or west is drawn, it will draw its own southern or eastern boundary—which corresponds to the northern or western boundary of the cell we're looking at.

The northern and western boundaries of the maze itself still need to be drawn specially, since there are no cells outside the bounds that could draw those walls for us. Still, that's a small price to pay.

Because this is something that will be generally useful, and which we'll want to use over and over again, we're going to make it so that the Grid class knows how to render itself as text. We'll put our implementation in the to_s method of Grid.

> \|/ **Joe asks:**
> ϡ **What's So Special About to_s?**
>
> In Ruby, the to_s method is what the runtime calls when it needs to convert an object into a string. (Hence the name: to_s, or *to string*.) By implementing a custom to_s method, we provide a way for an object (like our Grid) to display itself in a sane, human-readable way.
>
> Other object-oriented languages have similar facilities. In JavaScript, Java, and C#, for instance, you can override the toString() method. In SmallTalk, it's asString. In Objective-C, it's description. In C++ you actually override the << operator!

So go ahead and open up grid.rb, and add the following method just before the end keyword at the bottom of the file.

```
grid.rb
Line 1  def to_s
     -    output = "+" + "---+" * columns + "\n"
     -
     -    each_row do |row|
     5      top = "|"
     -      bottom = "+"
     -
     -      row.each do |cell|
     -        cell = Cell.new(-1, -1) unless cell
     10
     -        body = "   " # <-- that's THREE (3) spaces!
     -        east_boundary = (cell.linked?(cell.east) ? " " : "|")
```

```
-          top << body << east_boundary

15         # three spaces below, too >>--------------->> >...<
-          south_boundary = (cell.linked?(cell.south) ? "   " : "---")
-          corner = "+"
-          bottom << south_boundary << corner
-        end

20
-        output << top << "\n"
-        output << bottom << "\n"
-      end
-
25      output
-    end
```

Right off the bat, line 2 initializes the output buffer to be the top boundary of the grid. This consists of a plus character at each cell corner and three hyphens for the northern wall of each cell in that first row.

Then, starting at line 4 we begin looping over each row of the grid. As mentioned, each cell will simply use the southern wall of the cell above it as its own northern wall, so we only need to worry about the cell's body, its eastern boundary, and its southern boundary. We'll accumulate the bodies and eastern walls for each row's cells into one variable (top), and the southern boundaries into another (bottom). At the start of each row we'll prime the pump by initializing these variables to the western boundary of the grid, using a vertical pipe for the western wall, and a plus for the row's southwest corner (lines 5 and 6).

Once those variables are initialized, we'll loop over each cell in the row (starting at line 8), building the output one cell at a time, and then concatenate the two variables together when the row is done.

Some cells may (eventually) be nil, so line 9 handles that case by instantiating a dummy Cell object, as needed. Then, we concatenate the body and east wall of the current cell to the top variable, and the south wall and southeast corner to the bottom variable. Each row finishes by appending the contents of those two variables to the output, with newlines, and then we go around again until every row has been processed.

At that point, we're done, and line 25 simply returns the contents of the output buffer. Note that the return keyword is optional in Ruby at the end of a method—every method will return the value of the last expression that was evaluated.

Once we've got that new method saved to grid.rb, we can return to the binary_tree_demo.rb file and add one line to the very bottom, there:

binary_tree_demo.rb
```
puts grid
```

The puts method will automatically call the to_s method on our grid, converting it to a string, and then print it. Running our program again, we ought to see something a bit more interesting now.

```
$ ruby -I. binary_tree_demo.rb
+---+---+---+---+---+
|               |
+---+   +---+   +
|       |       |
+---+---+   +   +
|           |   |
+   +---+---+   +
|   |           |
+---+---+---+---+
$
```

It's no Mona Lisa, but it'll do in a pinch. We don't need polish for things like debugging or prototyping, and even some production applications find this sort of output plenty sufficient. (Ever played NetHack?)

Now that you've got a way to see what you're building, play around with it a bit. Change the dimensions of the grid and see how large you can make it before your terminal window starts garbling it. You might even want to revisit some of the suggestions from *Binary Tree experiments*, on page 15 and see how they come together now.

Whenever you're ready, though, Sidewinder awaits.

Implementing the Sidewinder Algorithm

The Sidewinder algorithm (from *The Sidewinder Algorithm*, on page 12) is similar in many respects to the Binary Tree algorithm. You'll recall that it has similar biases, and even a (conceptually) similar approach, randomly choosing at each step to either carve east from the current cell, or north from the current run of cells. In practice, though, Sidewinder feels like a very different beast.

In code, it looks something like this. Put the following in a file named sidewinder.rb.

sidewinder.rb

```
Line 1   class Sidewinder

           def self.on(grid)
             grid.each_row do |row|
    5          run = []

               row.each do |cell|
                 run << cell

    10             at_eastern_boundary  = (cell.east == nil)
                   at_northern_boundary = (cell.north == nil)

                   should_close_out =
                     at_eastern_boundary ||
    15               (!at_northern_boundary && rand(2) == 0)

                   if should_close_out
                     member = run.sample
                     member.link(member.north) if member.north
    20               run.clear
                   else
                     cell.link(cell.east)
                   end
                 end
    25        end

             grid
           end
    30   end
```

We begin on line 4 by looping over the grid, row by row. At the start of each row, we create a new array for our run set, and then loop over each cell in the current row. Lines 10 and 11 check to see if we're at the eastern or northern boundaries (if we are, the cell won't have a neighbor in that direction), and lines 13–15 use that to see if it's time to close out the current run. Recall that we always close the run at the end of a row (at the eastern boundary), but we also do it randomly within a row (i.e. rand(2) == 0), as long as we're not in the northernmost row (to avoid carving through the outer wall of the maze).

Once we've got that keyed in, let's try running it. Create another file, sidewinder_demo.rb, and put the following in it.

sidewinder_demo.rb

```
require 'grid'
require 'sidewinder'

grid = Grid.new(4, 4)
```

```
Sidewinder.on(grid)
```

```
puts grid
```

Running that, we should see something like this:

```
$ ruby -I. sidewinder_demo.rb
+---+---+---+---+---+
|               |
+   +---+   +   +
|   |       |   |
+---+   +   +   +
|       |   |   |
+   +---+   +---+
|   |           |
+---+---+---+---+
$
```

Piece of pie! (as my dad is fond of saying). It might be a bit more involved than Binary Tree, but that's not saying much. Play around with it some. Take another look at some of the ideas mentioned in *Sidewinder Experiments*, on page 16 and see how they come together in code.

When you're ready, we'll finish off the chapter with a look at how to render these mazes a tad more professionally.

Rendering a Maze as an Image

ASCII art is undeniably functional, but not necessarily attractive. Often, we want our products to have a bit more polish. Fortunately, APIs are available for most languages for either drawing directly to a view, or (at the very least) rendering to an offscreen canvas and saving it as an image file. We'll explore the latter of those techniques with a Ruby library called ChunkyPNG,[2] which will let us write our mazes as PNG images. (The concepts should translate readily to other UI and graphics APIs.)

If you're following along in Ruby, you'll need to install ChunkyPNG to get the code that follows to work. Fortunately, it's not hard:

```
$ gem install chunky_png
```

Now, then.

Just as we used the to_s method to render the textual representation of the maze, we'll introduce a to_png method on Grid to give us the graphical representation. The first half of it is just setup, computing the dimensions of our image

---

2. http://chunkypng.com/

and instantiating our canvas. The second half is where the meat is; it's really not too different from what we did to write our maze to a terminal.

Go ahead and open up the grid.rb file again. At the very top of the file, add the following line to make sure the ChunkyPNG library gets loaded.

```
require 'chunky_png'
```

Now, add the following method just before the final end keyword (right after the to_s method that we added earlier).

```
Line 1  def to_png(cell_size: 10)
   -      img_width = cell_size * columns
   -      img_height = cell_size * rows
   -
   5      background = ChunkyPNG::Color::WHITE
   -      wall = ChunkyPNG::Color::BLACK
   -
   -      img = ChunkyPNG::Image.new(img_width + 1, img_height + 1, background)
   -
  10      each_cell do |cell|
   -        x1 = cell.column * cell_size
   -        y1 = cell.row * cell_size
   -        x2 = (cell.column + 1) * cell_size
   -        y2 = (cell.row + 1) * cell_size
  15
   -        img.line(x1, y1, x2, y1, wall) unless cell.north
   -        img.line(x1, y1, x1, y2, wall) unless cell.west
   -
   -        img.line(x2, y1, x2, y2, wall) unless cell.linked?(cell.east)
  20        img.line(x1, y2, x2, y2, wall) unless cell.linked?(cell.south)
   -      end
   -
   -      img
   -  end
```

The to_png method accepts a single named parameter, cell_size, which we'll use to indicate how large the cells ought to be drawn (10 pixels square, by default). We'll use that value to compute the dimensions of our image on line 2. We then decide on our background color (white) and wall color (black), and instantiate our canvas (line 8).

Next, we begin iterating over the cells, drawing each one in turn. Lines 11 to 14 compute the coordinates of the northwest (x1,y1) and southeast (x2,y2) corners, which give us all the information we need to draw any of the four walls of the current cell.

This happens to be just what we do next. First, we check to see if the cell has any neighbors to the north or the west, and if not, we draw those walls (lines

16 and 17). Note that if the cell *does* have neighbors to the north or west, that neighbor will draw those walls instead, because every cell will always draw its own southern and eastern walls, as necessary. Lines 19 and 20 take care of that.

Then, when all the cells have been visited, we simply return the image object for the caller to do with as it pleases. It's trivial, for instance, to save the image to disk; simply add the following to the end of sidewinder_demo.rb or binary_tree_demo.rb.

```
img = grid.to_png
img.save "maze.png"
```

From there, it's just a matter of opening maze.png in your favorite image viewer. Voilà!

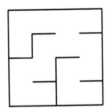

Being able to render our mazes as images enables a lot of possibilities. We'll be taking advantage of this throughout the book, and especially as we explore mazes of different shapes (Chapter 6, *Fitting Mazes to Shapes*, on page 83 and Chapter 7, *Going in Circles*, on page 97) and forms (Chapter 14, *Bending and Folding Your Mazes*, on page 223).

Your Turn

You're pretty much on the path to world domination now. Not only can you *generate* random mazes, you can *display* them, too! You've played with a few variations and tried some tricks of your own, and you're feeling pretty confident about it all.

Now for the fun part. Here's where you get to explore some on your own, seeing where your ideas take you. If you're feeling a bit starved for ideas still, browse some of the following for inspiration!

Grids

The implementation in this chapter is only one of many possible ways to represent a grid. Here are two other ways to think about the problem. Perhaps you can think of a few more as well!

Bitfield Grids

Instead of an array of Cell objects, what if you went bare metal and simply used an array of integers? Connections between cells would be represented by bits set on each element of the array. This gives you a very memory-efficient grid, but it tends to be fairly limited in what it can represent.

Edges and Nodes

Put on your computer scientist hat! If you're familiar at all with graph theory, you've no doubt noticed the connection between grids and graphs. Those perfect mazes we talked about in the last chapter? Yup, trees. Cells and passages are just other names for nodes and edges. If that connection works for you, have a go at implementing the grid that way. Each node has zero or more edges, and each edge has exactly two nodes. This gives you a more memory-hungry grid, but it can represent nearly any kind of maze!

Terminal Display

I'm not ashamed to admit that the terminal display demonstrated in this chapter is really kind of "quick and dirty." Here are a few possible ways to clean it up a bit.

Cleaner Characters

The text-based maze would look much cleaner if the plus character was only used at the junction of three or more wall segments. How might you change the display routine to be smarter about that?

Unicode Grids

Instead of standard punctuation characters, what if you were to display the maze using the Unicode box drawing characters? (That's U+2500 to U+257F.) Or you could use similar characters in any of the other terminal character sets.

Graphical Display

ChunkyPNG is a great library, but it's hardly the only option for this kind of thing. Here are a few other ways you might consider drawing your mazes, but see what else you can think of, too.

Other Graphics Platforms

Try your hand at some other graphics platforms. PDF is another great format for this, with robust support in many languages. Perhaps you'd rather render your maze to SVG, or even use JavaScript to draw it directly to an HTML canvas object! Experiment with different APIs and see what works best for you.

Thicker Walls

The method shown in this chapter creates mazes with paper-thin walls, which aren't always the most practical kind of maze. How would you render your mazes if the walls had actual thickness? (This becomes a matter of some practical application when we get to Chapter 9, *Braiding and Weaving Your Mazes*, on page 129.)

Using Tiles

Instead of drawing each cell on demand, you can prerender each kind of cell, and then lay them out like tiles. Look at all the possible combinations of exits that might exist for a cell, and then draw them all up-front. For a simple orthogonal (that is, rectangular) maze, there are 15 different cell types (16, if you include blank cells), ranging from the four-way intersection, to four distinct three-way intersections, and so on all the way to dead ends.

Next up, we're going to make you truly unstoppable. We're going to see how to actually *solve* these mazes you've been creating!

CHAPTER 3

Finding Solutions

As fun as it is to generate maze after maze after maze, eventually someone's going to ask you how to actually *solve* these puzzles. Once or twice is fine, but the last thing you want to do is perpetually put pencil to paper and manually work out the solution to each one, case by case. You'd never have time for making more mazes! Since the computer generated these, surely it can solve them, too, right?

You bet it can.

It turns out that we can choose from among an entire *host* of algorithms to solve mazes—so many, in fact, that this book would turn into at least *two* books if we tried to cover them all. Some, like the Pledge or Trémaux algorithms, are useful when you can't see the entire maze. Others, like dead-end filling and the shortest-path algorithms, require a more omniscient view. Seriously, there are far too many to cover here. Instead, we'll concentrate on just one, the Swiss Army knife of path-finding algorithms: Dijkstra's.

\\//   **Joe asks:**
‿   ## Who Is "Dijkstra?"

Edsger Dijkstra (1930–2002) was a Dutch computer scientist. Aside from inventing his eponymous algorithm, he was active in many different areas within computer science, fields like formal verification and distributed computing. He also wrote many papers and articles, including a well-known letter from the late 1960s called "Go To Statement Considered Harmful."

Like any Swiss Army knife, it won't always be the best fit for the job. Other algorithms might solve some mazes faster, or more efficiently, but Dijkstra's algorithm has a lot going for it in spite of that. First, it's not picky about the mazes you give it. Some algorithms only work on certain kinds of mazes, but not Dijkstra's! It'll solve anything we throw at it. Second, the byproducts of Dijkstra's algorithm will let us do some fun things, like increase the difficulty of our mazes, or give us insight into their textures and the biases of the algorithms we're using to generate them.

We'll look at a simplified version of Dijkstra's in this chapter, walking through it step-by-step, and then we'll see how it's implemented in code. We'll also see some of these byproducts in action when we try to find longer paths through our mazes, or color them to better visualize textures.

Dijkstra's Algorithm

Dijkstra's algorithm measures the shortest distance between some starting point (which we specify), and every other cell in the maze. In a nutshell, it works by flooding the maze, starting at that point we chose. The longer it takes the flood to reach a cell, the farther that cell is from our starting point.

The version of the algorithm that follows is a bit simplified. The full algorithm can find a shortest path through any configuration of cells and passages, regardless of how those cells are connected, and we'll see that version later in the book. For now, the simplified version is all we need.

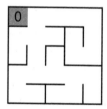

The algorithm begins when it is given a starting point. This is usually the cell at the start of the path we want to find, like the entrance to the maze. The algorithm marks it with a zero, because the path from that cell to itself is exactly zero cells long. Dijkstra's hasn't yet figured out the distance between this cell and every other cell in the grid, so it sets the distance for all other cells to be blank, or undefined. The figure uses the northwest corner as the starting point.

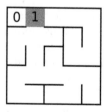

Next, it looks at all of the unvisited (white, unnumbered) neighbors linked to that cell. We'll call this set of cells the *frontier*. The algorithm assigns the value 1 to each of the cells in the frontier, because they are all exactly one cell away from the starting point. Here we see that the first cell has only a single accessible neighbor, so the new frontier set contains only that cell.

The algorithm does it all again for that cell in the new frontier set, the one just marked with 1. It visits each of the cell's unvisited, accessible neighbors and makes the distance for each of them 2, because they are each one step farther from our starting point. Those cells now become the new frontier set, as shown.

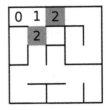

This process repeats until every cell in the maze has been visited (that is, assigned a distance). The figure gives you an idea of what we're left with: a matrix showing the distance of every cell in the maze relative to that initial starting cell.

With this matrix, we can do a lot of really neat things, not least of which is to find the path from any cell in the maze, back to the starting cell. To do so, we position ourselves at the *endpoint* of our path—we'll call it the goal—and then look at neighboring cells. The cell whose distance is one less than the current cell will be the next stepping stone on our path. We make that cell the current cell, repeat the process until we reach the initial cell (the one with distance zero), and we're done! The figure shows one such path, if the southeast corner were selected as the goal.

This is always guaranteed to be the shortest path between those two points. That's a pretty useful guarantee! Next, let's look at one way to implement this.

Implementing Dijkstra's

To bring this simplified version of Dijkstra's together, we're going to lean on a new class, called Distances, which will keep track of how far each cell is from the reference cell (the cell where we start counting from). Once we've implemented that class, we'll add our actual implementation of Dijkstra's to the Cell class, which will let us apply it pretty much anywhere we need to.

So, first off, let's add that Distances class. For now, it's just a simple wrapper around a Hash instance, but we'll be making it more useful soon. Create a new file named distances.rb, and add the following to it.

```
distances.rb
class Distances
  def initialize(root)
    @root = root
    @cells = {}
    @cells[@root] = 0
  end

  def [](cell)
    @cells[cell]
  end

  def []=(cell, distance)
    @cells[cell] = distance
  end

  def cells
    @cells.keys
  end
end
```

We will use this class to record the distance of each cell from the starting point, @root, so the initialize constructor simply sets up the hash so that the distance of the root from itself is 0.

We also add an array accessor method, [](cell), so that we can query the distance of a given cell from the root, as well as a corresponding setter, []=(cell, distance), for recording the distance for a given cell.

Finally, we add a cells method to get the list of all of the cells that are present.

Easy enough.

Next, let's use that new class. We'll add a distances method to Cell, which will implement Dijkstra's algorithm and return a Distances instance containing that matrix of distances we talked about previously.

First, we need to make sure our new Distances class gets loaded. Add the following line to the very top of cell.rb.

```
require 'distances'
```

Now, add the following method at the end of that file, just before the final end keyword.

```
Line 1  def distances
   -      distances = Distances.new(self)
   -      frontier = [ self ]
   -
   5      while frontier.any?
   -        new_frontier = []
   -
   -        frontier.each do |cell|
   -          cell.links.each do |linked|
  10            next if distances[linked]
   -            distances[linked] = distances[cell] + 1
   -            new_frontier << linked
   -          end
   -        end
  15
   -        frontier = new_frontier
   -      end
   -
   -      distances
  20    end
```

On line 2 we instantiate our new Distances class, which we'll use to store all the distances that we are about to compute. The current cell is the root, since that's what all the distances will be relative to. We also initialize our frontier set to be an array of just one element: this cell, our starting point.

Line 5 begins the loop that drives the algorithm. We're going to keep looping until there are no more cells in the frontier set, which will mean that we've measured the distance of every cell to our root cell.

On every pass through that loop, we create a new frontier set (line 6) which will hold all of the unvisited cells that are linked to cells in the current frontier set. These will be considered on the *next* pass through the algorithm. The current pass will populate that set by iterating over the frontier cells (line 8), and considering every neighbor that is linked to them (line 9).

Since our map initially returns nil if a cell hasn't been visited yet, line 10 can use that to detect cells that have been visited, skipping them. Otherwise, line 11 computes the linked cell's distance to be one more than the frontier cell's distance (because it's one step further away), and then adds the cell to our new frontier set (line 12).

After all of the frontier cells have been considered, we make the new frontier set the real frontier (line 16), and go around again. When the algorithm finishes, we return our map of distances, just as promised.

Whew!

We're almost ready, but we don't yet have a way to see what Dijkstra's algorithm returns. We'd like to be able to display the corresponding distance value *in the cell itself,* but our existing Grid#to_s is not very extensible. We'd either have to change the version in the Grid class directly (not too appealing, since most grids won't need this feature), or we'd have to copy and paste most of it into another class so we could change it.

Instead, let's take a minute to step back and fix the root problem. Let's make Grid#to_s a bit more extensible. We'll add a method, called contents_of(cell), that subclasses may override, which will describe what text may be used to label any given cell. By default, it will just render a space, which is the behavior of our existing implementation. Open up grid.rb and add this new method just before the to_s method.

```ruby
def contents_of(cell)
  " "
end
```

Now, with grid.rb still open, find the to_s method. We're going to change one line, the bit that describes the body of the cell, so that it calls our new contents_of(cell) method. The line in question is highlighted in the following snippet.

```ruby
row.each do |cell|
  cell = Cell.new(-1, -1) unless cell

➤   body = " #{contents_of(cell)} "
  east_boundary = (cell.linked?(cell.east) ? " " : "|")
  top << body << east_boundary

  south_boundary = (cell.linked?(cell.south) ? "   " : "---")
  corner = "+"
  bottom << south_boundary << corner
end
```

Thanks to that quick change, we can now throw together a simple subclass of Grid, which will be able to render itself and show the distance numbers for each cell.

Create a new file, called distance_grid.rb, and put the following code in it. This will override the contents_of method to return the distance information for each cell. Remember that the Grid#to_s method calls contents_of to discover how each cell should be rendered. By returning the distance information here, we can insert that information directly into our text-formatted maze! This should give us some visibility into what's going on.

```
distance_grid.rb
require 'grid'

class DistanceGrid < Grid
  attr_accessor :distances

  def contents_of(cell)
    if distances && distances[cell]
      distances[cell].to_s(36)
    else
      super
    end
  end
end
```

Note that because we're limited to one ASCII character for the body of the cell, we format the distance as a base-36 integer. That is to say, numbers from 0 to 9 are represented as usual, but when we reach a decimal number 10, we switch to letters. The number 10 is *a*, 11 is *b*, 12 is *c*, and so forth, all the way to *z* for 35. The number 36, then, becomes a *10*, and the one's place starts all over again. This lets us represent distances up to 35 using a single character.

Now we can instantiate this DistanceGrid class and see it all come together. Put the following code in a file named dijkstra.rb.

```
dijkstra.rb
Line 1  require 'distance_grid'
     -  require 'binary_tree'
     -
     -  grid = DistanceGrid.new(5, 5)
     5  BinaryTree.on(grid)
     -
     -  start = grid[0, 0]
     -  distances = start.distances
     -
    10  grid.distances = distances
     -  puts grid
```

There's nothing special about the Binary Tree algorithm here—feel free to replace it with whatever algorithm you prefer, especially as we begin to work through more algorithms. The meat of this really starts on line 7, where we choose our starting cell. The next line calls our new Cell#distances method to compute the distances of every cell relative to that starting cell, and then we assign that to the grid's distances property on line 10. When we finally display the grid, it will use that distance information to decorate each cell.

Try running it. You should get something like the following.

```
$ ruby -I. dijkstra.rb
+---+---+---+---+---+
| 0   1   2   3   4 |
+   +   +---+   +   +
| 1 | 2 | 5   4 | 5 |
+---+---+---+---+   +
| a   9   8   7   6 |
+   +---+---+   +   +
| b | a   9   8 | 7 |
+---+   +   +   +   +
| c   b | a | 9 | 8 |
+---+---+---+---+---+
```

Voilà! There's our matrix. Our starting position—in the northwest corner—has a distance of 0, as anticipated. Other cells count their distances from 1 to 9, switching to letters at that point (courtesy of those base-36 numbers) to represent 10, 11, and so on.

Finding the Shortest Path

The whole point of this exercise is to help us find a solution to our maze, a path between any two arbitrary points, so let's tackle that next. We'll implement more or less what was described previously, walking the path backward from our goal, looking for neighboring cells with sequentially smaller distances.

We first decide where we want our path to end (let's make it the southwest corner), and work backward from there. For each cell along the path, the neighboring cell with the lowest distance will be the next step of the solution.

Remember how I said we'd be making the Distances class more useful soon? Here we go. We'll plug the following method into it. Open distances.rb and add this method at the end of the definition for the Distances class, just before that class's final end keyword.

```
Line 1  def path_to(goal)
   -      current = goal
   -
   -      breadcrumbs = Distances.new(@root)
   5      breadcrumbs[current] = @cells[current]
   -
   -      until current == @root
   -        current.links.each do |neighbor|
   -          if @cells[neighbor] < @cells[current]
  10            breadcrumbs[neighbor] = @cells[neighbor]
   -            current = neighbor
   -            break
   -          end
   -        end
```

```
15    end

      breadcrumbs
    end
```

This method takes a cell and figures out the path to that cell from the original starting point. Line 2 starts that out by indicating that the given goal is our current cell, and we'll work backward from there. Then, the breadcrumbs variable on line 4 is initialized to a new Distances instance, which will eventually include only those cells that lie on the path. We start it out with just the reference cell, @root.

The process now begins a loop, starting on line 7, which continues until we reach that @root cell. Each iteration of that loop examines all of the linked neighbors of the current cell (line 8), looking for one that is closer to the root (line 9). When it finds it, that neighbor is added to the breadcrumbs (line 10), and then the loop repeats with that neighbor as the current cell.

Notice how it returns a Distances instance (the breadcrumbs object). This means it's a cinch to display, because all we have to do is take that new mapping and hand it off to the grid. Our updated contents_of method will display values in the cells along the path (because they exist in the new mapping), and render blank spaces for all the others (because they don't exist in that mapping).

To run this, we just need to call that new path_to method. Add this to the bottom of dijkstra.rb.

dijkstra.rb
```
puts "path from northwest corner to southwest corner:"
grid.distances = distances.path_to(grid[grid.rows - 1, 0])
puts grid.to_s
```

The result? Running it now, you should see your maze twice—once with the full matrix of distance values, and once showing only the path between the northwest and southwest corners, something like the following.

```
$ ruby -I. dijkstra.rb
+---+---+---+---+---+
| 0   1   2   3   4 |
+   +---+---+---+   +
| 1 | 8   7   6   5 |
+   +---+   +---+   +
| 2 | 9   8 | 7   6 |
+   +---+   +   +   +
| 3 | a   9 | 8 | 7 |
+---+---+---+   +   +
| c   b   a   9 | 8 |
+---+---+---+---+---+
```

path from northwest corner to southwest corner:

```
+---+---+---+---+---+
| 0   1   2   3   4 |
+   +---+---+---+   +
|   |           5 |
+   +---+   +---+   +
|   |       | 7   6 |
+   +---+   +   +   +
|   |       | 8 |   |
+---+---+---+   +   +
| c   b   a   9 |   |
+---+---+---+---+---+
```

There you have it! You just used Dijkstra's algorithm to find the shortest path between two points in your maze. This is great. Now when your friends ask you for the solutions to your mazes, you no longer have to act all embarrassed. You'll just *know*.

But we're not done with Dijkstra's algorithm yet. I wasn't kidding when I called it a Swiss Army knife. Oh, no. All we've shown so far is how it helps *solve* a maze. It can also be used to make a maze more challenging, and this is a property that, as maze creators, we ought to know more about. We'll take a look at this next.

Making Challenging Mazes

There are lots of ways to make a maze more challenging, but many of them are highly subjective and difficult to quantify. Walter D. Pullen, author of the Think Labyrinth! website, lists many of the considerations of a challenging maze on his Maze Psychology page,[1] and the list is not short. We're going to focus on just one of them, here—solution length—and we'll see how Dijkstra's algorithm again saves the day.

In general, the longer the path, the more difficult the maze. Ideally, then, if we want a more challenging maze, we want to identify the longest path through it. We then put the entrance of our maze at one end of the path, and drop the goal at the other end, and we've upped the ante. Easy as that.

A general solution to the "longest path" problem—one that works for any arbitrary graph, or grid—is what mathematicians call an *NP-hard* problem. Fortunately, we can narrow our requirements a bit. If we're only looking to find the longest path through a perfect maze, there happen to be a few different ways to tackle it, and Dijkstra's is one of them.

---

1. http://www.astrolog.org/labyrnth/psych.htm

It might seem counter-intuitive that an algorithm we just used to find a *shortest* path can also be used to find a *longest* path, but remember: Dijkstra's has conveniently labeled each cell with a distance value. All we have to do is look for the largest one in the maze. That will tell us the longest path from our starting point to that cell.

Be careful, though! This is not necessarily going to be the longest path *in the maze*. If our starting cell happens to be somewhere in the middle of the actual longest path, then the longest path from that cell will be shorter than the real one. The trick is to *run the algorithm twice*. The first time, you find the most distant cell from some arbitrary starting point. The second time, you turn it around and use that most distant cell as the starting point, letting Dijkstra's tell you the most distant cell from *there*. We're basically asking Dijkstra's to tell us the most distant point relative to the most distant point.

To make this real, we need to introduce a new method to our Distances class, to tell us which cell is furthest from the root and just how far away it is. Open up distances.rb again and add the following method to the Distances class, just after the path_to method.

```
def max
  max_distance = 0
  max_cell = @root

  @cells.each do |cell, distance|
    if distance > max_distance
      max_cell = cell
      max_distance = distance
    end
  end

  [max_cell, max_distance]
end
```

This just loops over each of the cells in the hash, keeping track of which cell has the greatest distance. When it's done, it returns an array of what it found.

Now, put the following code in a file named longest_path.rb. Note that it works up similarly to dijkstra.rb, but instead of simply showing the matrix of distances, lines 7–15 implement the two passes through Dijkstra's algorithm, as just described, in order to find the longest path through the maze.

longest_path.rb
```
Line 1  require 'distance_grid'
   -    require 'binary_tree'
   -
   -    grid = DistanceGrid.new(5, 5)
```

```
 5  BinaryTree.on(grid)
 -
 -  start = grid[0,0]
 -
 -  distances = start.distances
10  new_start, distance = distances.max
 -
 -  new_distances = new_start.distances
 -  goal, distance = new_distances.max
 -
15  grid.distances = new_distances.path_to(goal)
 -  puts grid
```

Line 7 gets the ball rolling by choosing the northwest corner as our starting cell. Remember, we could choose any cell we want—the northwest corner is just easy and convenient.

Next, lines 9 and 10 run Dijkstra's algorithm from that starting point and discover the most distant cell relative to it, calling it new_start.

Distances#max returns a two-dimensional array, containing the most distant cell and its distance from the root. Ruby supports *parallel assignment* so we can directly assign the elements of that array to separate variables, although in this case the distance value is not actually used. Still, the method returns it, so we have to put it somewhere!

Once we have that most distant cell, we do it again, on lines 12 and 13, finding the most distant cell from that new starting point. We assign that new distant cell to goal.

Finally, using the new_distances mapping from new_start, we compute the path to that goal cell (line 15), and assign it to our grid's distances property.

Running this program now should show you the path it discovered.

```
$ ruby -I. longest_path.rb
+---+---+---+---+---+
|           8   7   6 |
+     +---+     +---+     +
|     |   9 |       5 |
+     +---+     +---+     +
|     | b   a |       4 |
+---+     +     +---+     +
|       c |   | 2   3 |
+---+     +---+     +     +
| e   d | 0   1 |     |
+---+---+---+---+---+
$
```

And there you have it: the longest path! Be aware, though, that this is technically only *a* longest path. There may be multiple paths through the maze that are all equally long, and thus equally *longest*.

> ## Efficiently Finding the Longest Path
>
> It bears mentioning that Dijkstra's algorithm is *not* the most efficient way to find the longest path through a maze. After all, you have to run the algorithm twice, which means every cell is going to be visited twice before you find that path.
>
> If you take advantage of a bit of graph theory, though, you can calculate the longest path more efficiently. The longest path through a *tree* (exactly what our perfect mazes are) is called its *diameter*, or *width*. Using a depth-first search, you can traverse that tree and compute the diameter. The details of the algorithm are sadly beyond the scope of this little aside, but consider it a challenge, if you like!

Before moving on to more maze algorithms, let's look at one last trick that Dijkstra's algorithm can help us with. It turns out that the matrix of numbers that we get from Dijkstra's can also be interpreted another way: as *colors*. We'll see how that's useful next.

Coloring Your Mazes

It turns out that coloring mazes in a particular way acts like an X-ray machine, letting us peer inside and get a much clearer view of the structure of a maze and of the algorithm that generated it. Dijkstra's algorithm is ideal for this, because of that matrix of numbers it generates. Every cell with the same distance value has one thing in common: they all are equidistant from the starting cell. This is just *crying* for a paint-by-number exercise.

The easiest way to do this is to treat each number as an intensity value, relative to the length of the longest path. It works even better if we invert the logic, too, treating the cells with the largest distance values as being darkest, and the cell that we started with (which has a distance of zero), as being lightest.

To make this work, we'll need to dip into our Grid class again, tweaking that to_png implementation to support coloring the cells. We'll do like we did for to_s and generalize it a bit. We'll add a background_color_for(cell) method, which will return a color value, and to_png will call that for each cell. Subclasses may override background_color_for to implement their own coloring rules.

Open up grid.rb again and we'll make the following changes, starting with adding our new background_color_for(cell) method. Put it just after contents_of, since the two have similar responsibilities.

```
def background_color_for(cell)
  nil
end
```

By default, it returns nil, meaning that cells should not be colored, but subclasses that override it should return a ChunkyPNG::Color instance instead. (We'll see how that works shortly.)

For the to_png method, we're only going to change the each_cell block within that method, replacing it with the following.

```
Line 1  [:backgrounds, :walls].each do |mode|
   -      each_cell do |cell|
   -        x1 = cell.column * cell_size
   -        y1 = cell.row * cell_size
   5        x2 = (cell.column + 1) * cell_size
   -        y2 = (cell.row + 1) * cell_size
   -
   -        if mode == :backgrounds
   -          color = background_color_for(cell)
   10           img.rect(x1, y1, x2, y2, color, color) if color
   -        else
   -          img.line(x1, y1, x2, y1, wall) unless cell.north
   -          img.line(x1, y1, x1, y2, wall) unless cell.west
   -          img.line(x2, y1, x2, y2, wall) unless cell.linked?(cell.east)
   15           img.line(x1, y2, x2, y2, wall) unless cell.linked?(cell.south)
   -        end
   -      end
   -    end
```

Line 1 wraps the old each_cell block in another loop, which iterates over two symbolic constants: :backgrounds, and :walls. The first time through the loop, we're coloring cells (line 8) by calling our background_color_for method and drawing filled rectangles. The second time, we're drawing the walls, just as we did before (lines 12–15).

Now we can subclass Grid and create a ColoredGrid class, which will implement our Dijkstra-based coloring rules.

```
        colored_grid.rb
Line 1  require 'grid'
   -    require 'chunky_png'
   -
   -    class ColoredGrid < Grid
   5      def distances=(distances)
   -        @distances = distances
```

```
-          farthest, @maximum = distances.max
-       end
-
10     def background_color_for(cell)
-          distance = @distances[cell] or return nil
-          intensity = (@maximum - distance).to_f / @maximum
-          dark = (255 * intensity).round
-          bright = 128 + (127 * intensity).round
15         ChunkyPNG::Color.rgb(dark, bright, dark)
-       end
-    end
```

Our subclass only implements two methods: a writer that we'll call distances=(distances) (line 5) and our background_color_for(cell) method (line 10).

The distances= method simply stores the distances mapping, and caches the mapping's largest distance value as @maximum (line 7). We'll use that to compute the intensity color for each cell, on lines 12–14 of background_color_for, by measuring each cell's distance value against that maximum distance. We use that intensity to compute a dark value and a bright value, and compose those to return a shade of green (line 15) by setting the color's red and blue components to dark, and green to bright. (Feel free to experiment with other colors, too! For example, setting the red and green components to bright and leaving blue at dark will give you shades of yellow. See what else you can come up with!)

Finally, coloring the maze itself becomes super easy. Put the following code in a new file named coloring.rb.

coloring.rb
```
Line 1  require 'colored_grid'
-       require 'binary_tree'
-
-       grid = ColoredGrid.new(25, 25)
5       BinaryTree.on(grid)
-
-       start = grid[grid.rows / 2, grid.columns / 2]
-
-       grid.distances = start.distances
10
-       filename = "colorized.png"
-       grid.to_png.save(filename)
-       puts "saved to #{filename}"
```

We're generating a larger maze than before, 25×25, so that the coloring is more pronounced. (It works fine on a smaller maze, too; it's just not as impressive!) Again, we generate a maze using the Binary Tree algorithm, and then, starting on line 7, we choose our starting cell to be the one right in the middle of the grid. (It really doesn't matter where we start, but beginning in the middle will usually give us an attractive pattern.) Then we run Dijkstra's from that cell, tell the grid about the resulting distances matrix, and draw it to colorized.png.

Go ahead and run it:

```
$ ruby -I. coloring.rb
saved to colorized.png
$
```

Opening up colorized.png, you should see something like this figure.

It's certainly pretty, but what is it that we're looking at? Recall that we ran Dijkstra's algorithm, starting at the center of the grid. That cell—having the smallest distance value—will be colored the lightest. As cells grow more distant from that cell, they are colored darker and darker, until the cells furthest away are darkest of all.

Aside from making some rather compelling abstract art, this also happens to show us something really interesting and potentially very useful. It lets us see, quite clearly, the structure of the maze. We're shining Dijkstra-flavored X-rays at it and seeing what's inside. It turns out that this works great for letting us visually (and subjectively) compare all kinds of different maze algorithms.

For example, the following figure shows three different mazes, all generated using different algorithms.

Binary
Tree

Sidewinder

Recursive
Backtracker

The diagonal texture of the Binary Tree maze, and the vertical texture of the Sidewinder maze, are both clearly visible. The third algorithm, Recursive

Backtracker, is not one we've covered yet (we'll get there in Chapter 5, *Adding Constraints to Random Walks*, on page 67) but it's included here to show that even when you aren't familiar with how a maze was generated, this coloring technique can give you useful insight into what to expect from the algorithm.

We'll see this technique used throughout the book for just that reason. It's a great tool for looking into the structure of a maze and understanding the behavior of the algorithm that generated it.

Your Turn

So, that's Dijkstra's algorithm. As mentioned, it's not the only way—nor even the fastest way—to solve mazes, but it's certainly a useful way. We've seen how to use it to find a path between two cells. We've also seen how it can be used to find a longer (and hopefully more challenging) path through a maze. Finally, we used Dijkstra to color mazes, allowing us to look inside and see their underlying structures.

There's a lot of room to explore, here. Take some time to fiddle with Dijkstra's algorithm. Get familiar with it. It's going to be our faithful companion throughout this book!

If you need some ideas to get started, consider some of these.

Animate Dijkstra's algorithm.
> What if you were to draw the maze at each step of Dijkstra's algorithm? You ought to be able to get a good look at how the "flood" spreads out from the starting point and fills the maze.

Adaptive cell widths.
> You might have already tried running your dijkstra.rb program with a large maze. If you haven't, you should. Make it 20×20. It looks ugly, with the grid lines all out of alignment, because the paths are longer than 35 cells long, causing our base-36 numbers to overflow. The labels that are being written to each cell are too long! Try making the grid cells wider, as needed, to account for the longer text in some cells.

Draw solution paths graphically.
> We drew the solutions to our mazes using the textual display, but what would it take to make to_png draw the solution? Consider displaying the path by drawing the background of each cell in a different color, or by drawing lines or breadcrumbs along the path.

Other color schemes.

The color scheme presented above is monochromatic, using shades of only a single color to indicate distance. How else might you do it? Consider cycling through the RGB color palette in different ways to create rainbow fills. Or blend different gradients together to create new effects.

Change the starting cell.

What if you start Dijkstra's at different positions within the maze, before coloring it? Try starting it at an intersection, or a dead end, and see how it compares. Or try it from each of the corners, or from the sides. You could even get ambitious and create an animation, where each frame shows the maze colored from a different cell along some path!

Now that we're armed with Dijkstra's, we're ready to tackle two new maze algorithms. With Dijkstra's help, we'll see evidence of what makes these algorithms so special—*they have no bias*. Read on to see what that means, and what it costs.

CHAPTER 4

Avoiding Bias with Random Walks

So far, we've looked at two different maze algorithms, and while both were straightforward to understand and implement, they also had some pretty significant biases. They could be worked around, sure, but maybe there's a better way. In this chapter we're going to try to balance the scales a bit by exploring two new algorithms, Aldous-Broder and Wilson's, both of which are guaranteed to be *absolutely unbiased*.

If that sounds too good to be true, that's because it almost is! Nothing comes without a price, so we'll also see where these two algorithms—despite their mathematical flawlessness—ultimately end up with their own set of disappointments.

To get there, though, we need to have a better understanding of what biases really are, and what it means for an algorithm to have them. Let's take a short step back and look at biases from another angle, so we can see more precisely what their absence really means.

Understanding Biases

It's easy to say "this algorithm has a bias" and "that algorithm has no bias," but so far we haven't been very specific about what we mean by that. It's more than simply identifying a long passage or a slantwise tendency in a maze. A visible texture or pattern in a maze—in the output of an algorithm—is only evidence of an algorithm's bias if a significant number of mazes generated by that algorithm exhibit that same texture.

But even that definition doesn't quite cover it. Unlike Sidewinder and Binary Tree, biases may not always be blatantly obvious. They may not even produce visible artifacts at all. To understand how that can be, let's consider an example.

> **Joe asks:**
> ## Can't Mazes Have Biases, Too?
>
> Walter Pullen, on his "Maze Classification" page,[a] uses the term "bias" to describe a specific class of texture involving passage direction. A maze with horizontal bias, for instance, will have longer east-to-west passages. So, yes, in some contexts, the word bias may be applied to mazes, as well as algorithms.
>
> However, to avoid confusion, in this book "bias" will refer strictly to algorithms, while the more general term *texture* will be used to describe mazes. That is to say, a *bias of the algorithm* may produce a *texture in the maze*.
>
> ———————
>
> a.   http://www.astrolog.org/labyrnth/algrithm.htm

Let's say we wanted to generate a perfect 2×2 maze. (Recall that "perfect" here means one with no loops in it.) The following figure shows all four of the possible perfect mazes that can fit in a 2×2 grid. By generating a 2×2 maze randomly, we're effectively choosing between these four possibilities.

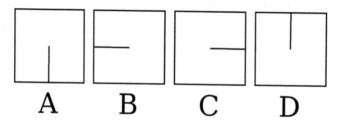

This means that, conceptually, randomly generating a maze is the same as putting all of the possible mazes into a big bag, giving them a good shake (you know—to make sure they're well shuffled), and then reaching into that bag and blindly picking one of them.

The Binary Tree algorithm is one way to do this. It lets us effectively reach into that big bag full of all possible mazes and pick one at random, but it does so *with bias*. In terms of our big bag of mazes, this means that the algorithm doesn't actually choose evenly from among all the possibilities. *It cheats.*

Consider the four perfect mazes in the preceding figure again. Ideally, we'd like the Binary Tree algorithm to be able to generate all of them, but it can't. (Or won't!) Recall what we know about its biases, revealed in the unbroken passages it always leaves on the north and east. We see right away that C is impossible because the eastern passage is broken in half by a wall. Binary Tree would never give us that one. D is similarly impossible—that passage across the north is also split by a wall. In other words, Binary Tree flatly refuses to give us anything but A and B, 50% of the possible 2×2 mazes. *It is biased against those other possibilities.*

What about Sidewinder? When we recall that Sidewinder always generates mazes with an unbroken northern passage, we immediately see that D is out, because of that wall on the north. That gives us A, B, and C, or 75% of the possible 2×2 mazes, which is better. But still—what we *want* is an algorithm that will choose from *all* of them!

And as long as we're making demands, we might as well add that we'd like to pick them *uniformly.* That is to say, we want to make sure that every maze in the bag has an equal chance of being selected. Some algorithms are *nonuniform,* which is to say that they might eventually give us every possible maze but tend to produce certain types more often (perhaps preferring longer passages, for instance). These may be subtle biases, difficult or impossible to spot by eye, but we don't want those kinds, either.

Put simply, we'd like to see what happens when we choose our mazes *uniformly* and *at random* from the set of all possible mazes. The good news is that there *are* ways to do it, and they're pretty straightforward, but, like everything, there are trade-offs.

One way is called the Aldous-Broder algorithm. Let's start there.

The Aldous-Broder Algorithm

The Aldous-Broder algorithm was developed independently by both David Aldous, a professor at UC Berkeley, and Andrei Broder, currently a Distinguished Scientist at Google. It is almost as simple to implement as the Binary Tree algorithm. The idea is just this: Start anywhere in the grid you want, and choose a random neighbor. Move to that neighbor, and if it hasn't previously been visited, link it to the prior cell. Repeat until every cell has been visited.

Easy, right? It's that *random walk*, the aimless, directionless meandering from cell to cell, that is at the root of this algorithm's ability to avoid being biased. Sadly, as we'll see it also means that it can take a long time to run.

Let's walk through it once so we can see it in action. We'll start by picking a cell at random. We'll color unvisited cells gray, and our old friend, the smiley face, will indicate which cell is current.

We need to pick a random neighbor, so let's choose east. That neighbor hasn't been visited yet, so we link the two cells together, and then we do the process again from that new cell. The following figure shows three steps in a row, each taking us to a new, unvisited cell.

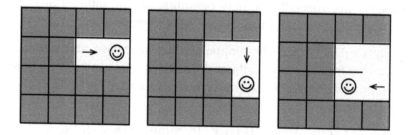

Check out this next move, though. We choose a random neighbor, going north this time, but that cell has already been visited. That's okay! It's how the algorithm works. The only difference is, this time, we don't link the two cells. We simply make the neighbor the current cell, and carry on.

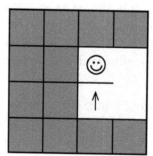

The process continues until every cell has been visited, which, for large mazes, can take a while. Go ahead and finish out this maze yourself. Assuming you're picking the neighbors randomly, you'll see that the random walk will tend to meander, visiting and revisiting some cells multiple times. By the time you're down to just one or two unvisited cells remaining, it can be downright infuriating to watch the algorithm cluelessly walk right past them!

So, have a go at it. When you're done, you should have something like this.

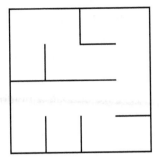

Not bad! It certainly takes a bit of time to reach those last few unvisited cells, but the process itself almost couldn't be simpler.

Next let's see how to make it real in code.

Implementing Aldous-Broder

As might be expected, that random walk forms the core of our implementation, repeatedly visiting neighboring cells until no unvisited cells remain. It comes together without any surprises, just as described.

Put the following code in a file named aldous_broder.rb. As before, we'll put the algorithm in its own class so we can reuse it more easily.

aldous_broder.rb
```
Line 1  class AldousBroder
   -
   -      def self.on(grid)
   -        cell = grid.random_cell
   5        unvisited = grid.size - 1
   -
   -        while unvisited > 0
   -          neighbor = cell.neighbors.sample
   -
  10          if neighbor.links.empty?
   -            cell.link(neighbor)
   -            unvisited -= 1
   -          end
   -
  15          cell = neighbor
   -        end
   -
   -        grid
   -      end
  20  end
```

Line 4 starts everything off by choosing one of the cells at random. The random walk will begin at that cell. To make sure the algorithm knows when everything has been visited, line 5 computes the number of unvisited cells in the grid. (We subtract one, because we treat the starting cell as having been visited already.) Each time a new cell is visited, that value will be decremented (line 12), and the loop continues until that value is zero (line 7).

On each pass through the loop, we choose a neighbor of the current cell at random (line 8) and make it the new current cell (line 15). If that cell hasn't yet been linked to any other cells (which implies that it hasn't been visited before), we link it to the current cell (line 11) before going around again.

A simple demo program will suffice for testing this. Put the following in aldous_broder_demo.rb.

```
aldous_broder_demo.rb
require 'grid'
require 'aldous_broder'

grid = Grid.new(20, 20)
AldousBroder.on(grid)

filename = "aldous_broder.png"
grid.to_png.save(filename)
puts "saved to #{filename}"
```

Feel free to display the maze using the terminal, if you prefer; this code writes the maze to a PNG simply so that we can make it larger, to better see the structure of the finished maze. Running it will save the maze to a file, like this:

```
$ ruby -I. aldous_broder_demo.rb
saved to aldous_broder.png
$
```

Opening up aldous_broder.png, we ought to see something like this figure.

Very nice. Let's go one step further and see if this algorithm produces any kind of texture that its mazes all have in common. Using our coloring.rb program from the previous chapter as a template, let's modify aldous_broder.rb to emit a colored version of the maze. In fact, let's have it generate and color several mazes at once, so we can open them all up side-by-

side to compare. Put the following code in aldous_broder_colored.rb.

```
aldous_broder_colored.rb
require 'colored_grid'
require 'aldous_broder'

6.times do |n|
  grid = ColoredGrid.new(20, 20)
  AldousBroder.on(grid)

  middle = grid[grid.rows / 2, grid.columns / 2]
  grid.distances = middle.distances

  filename = "aldous_broder_%02d.png" % n
  grid.to_png.save(filename)
  puts "saved to #{filename}"
end
```

When we run it, it will generate six different images.

```
$ ruby -I. aldous_broder_colored.rb
saved to aldous_broder_00.png
saved to aldous_broder_01.png
saved to aldous_broder_02.png
saved to aldous_broder_03.png
saved to aldous_broder_04.png
saved to aldous_broder_05.png
```

If we look at those images now, we ought to see something like these.

Remember that in general, any texture that we see is only evidence of a bias if every maze generated by the algorithm has that texture in common. Looking at this spread, you may see a few that look like they want to stretch vertically, and a couple seem to have a horizontal bridge in the middle, but there aren't any characteristics that they all seem to share. This definitely supports the claim that Aldous-Broder has no bias!

As compelling as it is, though, it doesn't mask the largest drawback of a purely random walk. All is not rosy in Aldous-Broder Land. Each individual step of the algorithm may execute quickly, but the algorithm itself can run for a long time, especially on large mazes. That aimless meandering over previously visited cells feels awfully wasteful, but we can't add a *heuristic*, or a way to give the process some intelligence, without taking away the very property of uniformity that we said we wanted.

So, we can't change Aldous-Broder itself, but maybe we can try a *different* algorithm instead. Let's see if Wilson's does any better.

Wilson's Algorithm

Wilson's algorithm was developed by David Bruce Wilson, a principle researcher at Microsoft and an affiliate associate professor of mathematics at the University of Washington. Like Aldous-Broder, this algorithm depends on the idea of a random walk, but with a twist. It performs what is called a *loop-erased* random walk, which means that as it goes, if the path it is forming happens to intersect with itself and form a loop, it *erases* that loop before continuing on.

The algorithm starts by choosing a point on the grid—any point—and marking it visited. Then it chooses any unvisited cell in the grid and does one of these loop-erased random walks until it encounters a visited cell. At that point it adds the path it followed to the maze, marking as visited each of the cells along that path, and then it goes again. The process repeats until all the cells in the grid have been visited.

That's a mouthful! Let's walk through it together, choosing some random cell to start and marking it visited. Here, the northwest corner has been marked.

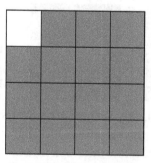

Next, we choose another cell at random. Our choice here is indicated by the smiley face. We'll call this the current cell, and it will be where we begin our loop-erased random walk. Note that we do *not* consider this cell visited!

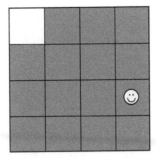

From here, we choose a random neighbor and make that neighbor the current cell, repeatedly. The following figure shows our path after four such moves. Be careful: we are not actually *carving passages*, or modifying the grid at all, here. We're just noting the path we're taking.

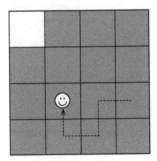

Now, here's where the "loop-erased" part of "loop-erased random walk" comes into play. In the next figure, we've (randomly) decided to move east, which causes us to intersect our current path. This creates a loop, so we erase that loop before moving on.

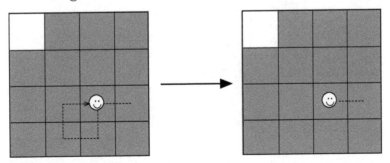

We continue in this fashion until we stumble upon a cell that has already been visited. The first time through, this means we have to find the one cell that started out visited, our needle in this haystack of cells. It can take a while, but eventually it'll find it. Our path might look like this.

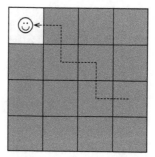

Once we have that path, we carve it into the maze by linking all the cells along that path and marking them visited.

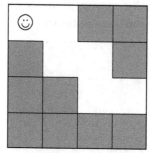

Then we do it all again: pick a random, unvisited cell from the grid, perform a loop-erased random walk until we hit a visited cell, and carve the resulting path into the maze, like this.

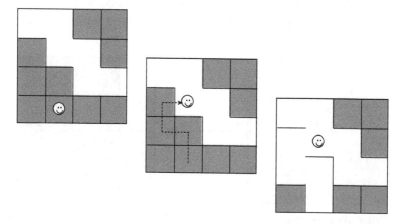

This repeats until there are no more unvisited cells in the grid. Have a go at finishing out this maze. You should be left with something like the following when you're done.

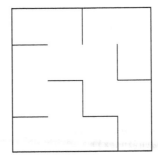

Again, not bad. We can see that Wilson's algorithm eliminates the aimless wandering at the end of the process, since the problem's been turned around: instead of looking for *unvisited* cells (which will be plentiful to start, and few at the end), we're looking for *visited* cells (which are rare to start, but common toward the end). Sadly, this also means that it has the opposite problem from Aldous-Broder. Whereas Aldous-Broder starts fast but takes progressively longer to reach the last few cells, Wilson's starts slowly, trying to find that needle in the haystack at the very beginning. Still, like Aldous-Broder, the algorithm has no bias, and perhaps that's enough to justify the price.

Let's look next at how to implement it in code.

Implementing Wilson's Algorithm

The following uses an array to keep track of all unvisited cells in the grid. Besides letting us query whether a cell has been visited or not, this also lets us quickly choose an unvisited cell from which to start our loop-erased random walk.

Put the following code in a file named wilsons.rb.

wilsons.rb
```
Line 1  class Wilsons

        def self.on(grid)
          unvisited = []
     5    grid.each_cell { |cell| unvisited << cell }

          first = unvisited.sample
          unvisited.delete(first)

    10    while unvisited.any?
            cell = unvisited.sample
            path = [cell]

            while unvisited.include?(cell)
    15        cell = cell.neighbors.sample
              position = path.index(cell)
```

```
  -            if position
  -              path = path[0..position]
  -            else
 20              path << cell
  -            end
  -          end
  -
  -          0.upto(path.length-2) do |index|
 25            path[index].link(path[index + 1])
  -            unvisited.delete(path[index])
  -          end
  -        end
  -
 30      grid
  -    end
  -
  -  end
```

This implementation really consists of three different parts: the initialization (lines 4–8), the loop-erased random walk (lines 11–22), and carving passages (lines 24–27).

In the initialization phase, we set up an empty array (line 4) to hold all of the unvisited cells. (We *could* do like we did for Aldous-Broder and just keep a counter, but using an array like this makes it easier to selected unvisited cells at random, which we need to do for our random walk phase.) We finish the initialization by choosing an unvisited cell at random (line 7) and marking it visited by removing it from the list. This will be our first goal cell, which our random walk will try to find.

The next two phases, the loop-erased random walk and passage carving, repeat for as long as our unvisited list contains any cells (as tested on line 10).

The random walk begins by choosing an unvisited cell at random (line 11) and adding it to our prospective path. This path will eventually lead to one of the visited cells in the grid, so we keep walking until this is the case (line 14). Each time we take a step on this walk, we choose a neighbor of the current cell (line 15), and then check to see if we've created a loop or not (line 16). If we've created a loop, the cell will already be present in our path, with all the cells after it forming the loop, so we remove the loop by truncating the path after that cell (line 18). Otherwise, if the cell doesn't form a loop, we append it to the path and continue (line 20).

Once the random walk finds a visited cell, that phase finishes and we move to the passage carving phase (line 24). We iterate over each cell of the path, linking it to its neighbor (line 25), and then marking it visited by removing it from our unvisited array (line 26).

Test this by creating a new program, wilsons_demo.rb.

```
wilsons_demo.rb
require 'grid'
require 'wilsons'

grid = Grid.new(20, 20)
Wilsons.on(grid)

filename = "wilsons.png"
grid.to_png.save(filename)
puts "saved to #{filename}"
```

Run it, as usual, and open up the resulting wilsons.png image. It ought to look much like what we saw in Aldous-Broder figure on page 58. We'd expect this if the two algorithms truly are without bias.

In fact, you might even want to do like we did with the Aldous-Broder algorithm and use our ColoredGrid class to colorize a few mazes, to compare. You should find the same variety as you did with Aldous-Broder—evidence that Wilson's algorithm is, indeed, biasless.

Your Turn

We've got four maze generation algorithms under our belts now. Two of them, Binary Tree and Sidewinder, are heavily biased but straightforward to implement and run very quickly to completion. The other two, Aldous-Broder and Wilson's, are perfectly unbiased, but can take much longer to generate a maze. And even between Aldous-Broder and Wilson's, we get to choose either slow-to-start or slow-to-finish. So many choices!

All these choices mean we can start trying some new ideas. We have more options to experiment with. Try some of the following suggestions, or experiment with your own ideas.

Two-in-One

Try using *two* algorithms to generate *one* maze. Instead of using a single cell to start Wilson's algorithm, what if you start with Aldous-Broder and then switch to Wilson's once it's visited some portion of the grid? Or what if you do the top half of the grid with Binary Tree, and Aldous-Broder for the rest? Be careful, though; not all combinations will work. Can you figure out why some do and others do not?

Biasing the Unbiased

We usually choose Aldous-Broder or Wilson's algorithms specifically because they are unbiased. But what would happen if you intentionally added bias to them? How might you take one of them and tweak its random walk, making it tend to move horizontally instead of vertically, or to prefer right turns over left? What other ways can you think of to introduce bias into those algorithms?

Another Way to Walk

Any change to how Aldous-Broder or Wilson's walk their paths will introduce bias. What kind of bias would you get if you were to take Aldous-Broder and give it a tendency to avoid previously visited cells? Or what if Wilson's loop-erased random walk refused to form loops in the first place?

That last experiment, in particular, leads us neatly into the next chapter, where we'll see just what happens when we add rules to a random walk. As you'd expect, it results in bias, but we'll see that not every bias is undesirable.

CHAPTER 5

Adding Constraints to Random Walks

Aimless random walking may be a good strategy if you absolutely need a perfectly unbiased algorithm, but for most purposes it's kind of overkill. An algorithm with the right kind of bias can often generate mazes that convey atmosphere, personality, or even challenge in a way that an unbiased algorithm can't. Biases aren't automatically a bad thing!

In this chapter we'll test that thesis. We'll look at two fairly similar algorithms that seem to work, superficially, much like Aldous-Broder or Wilson's, but that introduce biases by adding constraints to their random walk. These are the ominously named Hunt-and-Kill algorithm and the Recursive Backtracker.

The Hunt-and-Kill Algorithm

Hunt-and-Kill will seem, at first, very similar to the Aldous-Broder algorithm. We arbitrarily pick a cell to start, and then perform a random walk from there. The difference is that whereas Aldous-Broder allows you to step *anywhere*, even on cells that you've already visited, Hunt-and-Kill requires you to walk only on unvisited cells.

Let's go through it.

Since we can start anywhere, we'll just choose the southwest corner.

From there, we do a random walk, avoiding any cell that we've already visited. This is on purpose! Remember that the algorithm itself disallows revisiting cells during the random walk.

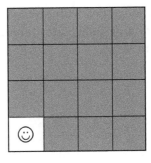

But hey, no problem. This works just fine...right up until the moment we paint ourselves into a corner, as the figure shows. We've ended at a cell surrounded by visited cells, and since we're not allowed to walk on those, we're stuck.

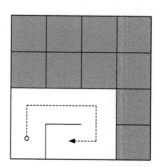

This is where we enter hunt mode. Starting at the top, we scan left-to-right until we encounter an *unvisited* cell, bordered by at least one *visited* cell. When we find it, make it our current cell, and link it to any one of its neighboring visited cells. In the figure, we've picked the first cell we encounter that fits the bill. Since it only has one visited neighbor (the cell immediately to the south)

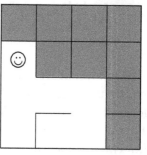

we simply link the two together; If there had been two or more, we'd have picked one at random.

We walk the random walk again, as far as we're able.

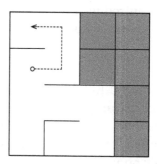

Then, once again, we scan row-by-row from the northwest corner, looking for another unvisited cell with at least one visited neighbor, and then carve another random walk from there.

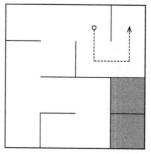

This process repeats until the hunt phase cannot find any more unvisited cells, at which point we know the maze is finished.

Piece of cake. Now let's code it.

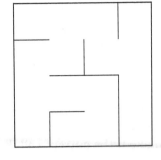

Implementing Hunt-and-Kill

There really aren't any surprises in the implementation here. As you'd expect, we start by choosing a cell at random, and then doing our random walk. In that respect, it looks a lot like our implementation of the Aldous-Broder algorithm. The similarity ends, though, when we discover we've boxed ourselves in, and there are no more unvisited neighbor cells. That triggers the hunt phase, where we'll loop over the grid, looking for unvisited cells with visited neighbors.

Put the following in hunt_and_kill.rb.

```
hunt_and_kill.rb
Line 1  class HuntAndKill
   -      def self.on(grid)
   -        current = grid.random_cell
   -
   5        while current
   -          unvisited_neighbors = current.neighbors.select { |n| n.links.empty? }
   -
   -          if unvisited_neighbors.any?
   -            neighbor = unvisited_neighbors.sample
  10            current.link(neighbor)
   -            current = neighbor
   -          else
   -            current = nil
   -
  15            grid.each_cell do |cell|
   -              visited_neighbors = cell.neighbors.select { |n| n.links.any? }
   -              if cell.links.empty? && visited_neighbors.any?
   -                current = cell
   -
  20                neighbor = visited_neighbors.sample
   -                current.link(neighbor)
   -
   -                break
   -              end
  25            end
   -          end
   -        end
   -        grid
   -      end
  30  end
```

The code has two parts, corresponding to the two phases of the algorithm: the random walk (lines 5–11) and the hunt phase (lines 12–25). Both phases alternate for as long as there is a current cell (line 5), which is initialized at the beginning by choosing one at random from the grid (line 3).

On each pass through the algorithm, we make a list of all of the unvisited neighbors of the current cell (line 6). If there are any such neighbors, we choose one at random (line 9), link it to the current cell (line 10), and then make it the current cell (line 11).

If the current cell has no unvisited neighbors, we switch to the hunt phase (line 12). Because there is no current cell during this phase, line 13 sets current to nil before proceeding. This helps us to know when the algorithm is ready to terminate, since the loop (line 5) depends on that variable.

With current reset, we now proceed to look at each cell in the grid (line 15), hunting for a promising cell to begin walking from. Line 17 codifies the criteria we're requiring: an unvisited cell (links.empty?) with at least one visited neighbor. Once we find one that passes muster, it becomes the current cell (line 18), we link it to one of its visited neighbors at random (lines 20 and 21), and we break out of hunt mode (line 23), ready to kick off another random walk.

Nice! Let's test it out. Put the following in hunt_and_kill_demo.rb.

hunt_and_kill_demo.rb
```ruby
require 'grid'
require 'hunt_and_kill'

grid = Grid.new(20, 20)
HuntAndKill.on(grid)

filename = "hunt_and_kill.png"
grid.to_png.save(filename)
puts "saved to #{filename}"
```

Running it will render our maze to hunt_and_kill.png. Open that up, and you should see something like the figure.

Tracing any of those passages, we quickly see that the paths tend to wind around quite a bit.

We can see this more clearly if we try coloring it, using the ColoredGrid class as we've done in previous chapters. Go ahead and give it a try. You ought to see something like the following.

Certainly, beauty is in the eye of the beholder, but there is just something lovely about the way those passages meander! That texture is, as you might have guessed, evidence of one of this algorithm's biases (and, depending on your taste in mazes, might be taken as proof that not all biases are bad). Another significant characteristic of this style of maze is that they have relatively fewer dead ends than mazes generated by other algorithms.

Counting Dead Ends

Let's show how the frequency of dead ends compare between algorithms. We'll add a method to our Grid class that will collect all of the dead-end cells in the entire grid—those with links to only one other cell—and return them as a list. Then we can print the size of that list to tell us how many dead ends there are. (We'll be able to use this later, too, when we start talking about braid mazes in Chapter 9, *Braiding and Weaving Your Mazes*, on page 129.)

Open up grid.rb and put this just before the last end keyword in that file.

```
grid.rb
def deadends
  list = []

  each_cell do |cell|
    list << cell if cell.links.count == 1
  end

  list
end
```

Once you've made that change, choose one of your previous programs (for example, binary_tree_demo.rb or wilsons.rb) and add a line like the following to the end.

```
deadends = grid.deadends
puts "#{deadends.count} dead-ends"
```

That should print the number of dead ends each time a maze is generated. We *could* do that to all of the programs we've written so far, run them each a few dozen times, and then try to do some analysis of the numbers we get, but that would be more than a bit tedious. Let's approach this scientifically.

Here's a program that will run each of the algorithms we've covered thus far, accumulate the number of dead ends from each run, and then display a report of the averages. Put it in deadend_counts.rb.

```ruby
deadend_counts.rb
require 'grid'
require 'binary_tree'
require 'sidewinder'
require 'aldous_broder'
require 'wilsons'
require 'hunt_and_kill'

algorithms = [BinaryTree, Sidewinder, AldousBroder, Wilsons, HuntAndKill]

tries = 100
size = 20

averages = {}
algorithms.each do |algorithm|
  puts "running #{algorithm}..."

  deadend_counts = []
  tries.times do
    grid = Grid.new(size, size)
    algorithm.on(grid)
    deadend_counts << grid.deadends.count
  end

  total_deadends = deadend_counts.inject(0) { |s,a| s + a }
  averages[algorithm] = total_deadends / deadend_counts.length
end

total_cells = size * size
puts
puts "Average dead-ends per #{size}x#{size} maze (#{total_cells} cells):"
puts

sorted_algorithms = algorithms.sort_by { |algorithm| -averages[algorithm] }

sorted_algorithms.each do |algorithm|
  percentage = averages[algorithm] * 100.0 / (size * size)
  puts "%14s : %3d/%d (%d%%)" %
    [algorithm, averages[algorithm], total_cells, percentage]
end
```

Having our algorithms in their own classes really pays off here! We simply load each of those classes and put them in an array (line 8). Lines 10 and 11 configure the number of times each algorithm will be tried and the size that each maze will be.

Then we loop over each algorithm, repeating each one tries times by instantiating a grid (line 19), applying the algorithm to it (line 20), and then accumulating the number of dead ends into a list (line 21). Once the algorithm has been run tries times, the dead-end counts are totaled and averaged (lines 24–25).

The rest of the program sorts and displays the results.

Running that ought to give us some rather interesting statistics:

```
$ ruby -I. deadend_counts.rb
running BinaryTree...
running Sidewinder...
running AldousBroder...
running Wilsons...
running HuntAndKill...

Average dead-ends per 20x20 maze (400 cells):

  AldousBroder : 115/400 (28%)
       Wilsons : 115/400 (28%)
    Sidewinder : 109/400 (27%)
    BinaryTree : 101/400 (25%)
    HuntAndKill :  40/400 (10%)
```

How about that Hunt-and-Kill algorithm, eh? On average, only 10% of the cells in the mazes it generates will be dead ends. It's essentially trading dead ends for passage length, allowing the maze to produce more winding, meandering corridors. This particular property is sometimes referred to as *river*, and Hunt-and-Kill generates mazes with a lot of it! I rather like that aesthetic, myself. If it appeals to you as much as it does to me, you might enjoy the Recursive Backtracker algorithm, too. It behaves very similarly. Let's talk about it next.

The Recursive Backtracker Algorithm

The Recursive Backtracker algorithm works very much like Hunt-and-Kill, relying on a constrained random walk to weave its rivery way across our grid. The difference is in how it recovers from dead ends; instead of hunting for another viable cell, it *backtracks*, retracing its steps until it finds a cell that has an unvisited neighbor.

Let's walk through it and see how that works in practice. We'll use a stack to keep track of the cells we've visited. A *stack* is simply a list of items, but with strict rules about how items are added to or removed from it. Adding something to the top of a stack is called *pushing*, and removing the topmost item is called *popping*. A stack can only be manipulated via these push and pop operations, which means it's great at enforcing the order in which its contents are accessed. This happens to be just what is needed for certain algorithms, like the Recursive Backtracker. Here, we'll push cells onto the stack as we visit them, and pop them off as we discover they're dead ends.

We can start anywhere we want, just like Hunt-and-Kill, so let's go ahead and start in the southwest corner (let's call it by its coordinates: *A4*). We'll push that cell onto the stack. Whatever cell is on the top of that stack will always be considered the current cell.

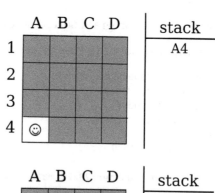

Looking at the unvisited neighbors of our current cell, we choose one at random (let's go with A3) and carve a path to it, pushing it onto our stack at the same time. Remember, this has the effect of making A3 our new current cell.

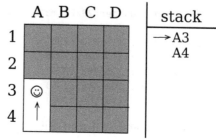

The process continues, randomly walking across the grid, as the figure demonstrates. The stack will include every cell we've visited thus far.

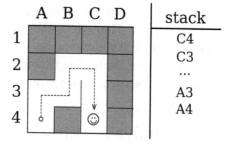

Our next random step takes us west, to B4, but B4 has no unvisited neighbors. We're boxed in!

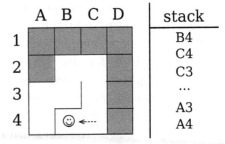

At this point, we pop that dead-end cell off the stack, which has the effect of making the previous cell—C4—our current cell again.

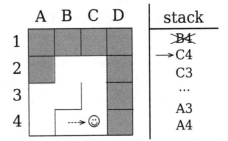

This cell has one more unvisited neighbor (D4), so we pick up our random walk by choosing that one.

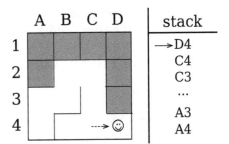

The process continues in this fashion, backtracking at every dead end, until every cell has been visited.

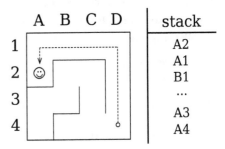

The final cell to be visited will always be a dead end, so we backtrack again. We retrace our steps, popping cells off the stack, looking for one with an unvisited neighbor. In this case, though, there *aren't* any more unvisited cells—everything has been visited—so we pop cells off the stack until we're back to where we started, at A4.

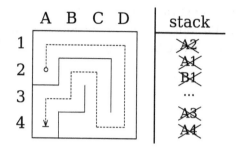

And because *that* cell doesn't have any unvisited neighbors either, we pop it off the stack as well, which leaves the stack empty.

And that, gentle reader, is how you know the algorithm is finished: the stack is empty. We're done, and what's left is our maze.

Just like that! Let's implement this in code next, and you'll see it comes together much like Hunt-and-Kill.

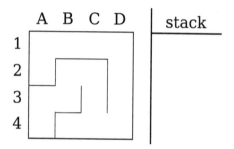

Implementing the Recursive Backtracker

We're going to implement more or less what was described in the previous section, using an explicit stack to manage the cells that have been visited. We'll use an array to represent the stack (which is easy in Ruby, since Ruby's arrays come preloaded with the standard push and pop stack operators). Put the following code in recursive_backtracker.rb.

recursive_backtracker.rb
```ruby
Line 1  class RecursiveBacktracker

     def self.on(grid, start_at: grid.random_cell)
       stack = []
   5   stack.push start_at

       while stack.any?
         current = stack.last
         neighbors = current.neighbors.select { |n| n.links.empty? }
  10
         if neighbors.empty?
           stack.pop
         else
           neighbor = neighbors.sample
```

```
15        current.link(neighbor)
          stack.push(neighbor)
        end
      end

20    grid
    end

  end
```

It all begins with lines 4 and 5, where we initialize our "stack" to be an empty array, and then push our starting location onto it. By default, that starting location is a cell chosen at random from the grid, though it can be configured by passing a different cell via the start_at parameter. The algorithm then continues for as long as the stack has any items in it (line 7).

Because the topmost cell on the stack is always the current cell, we make that explicit on line 8. Then, line 9 collects all of the current cell's unvisited neighbors into an array. (Remember: if the cell has any links to other cells at all, we know it's been visited before.)

If the cell has no unvisited neighbors, we remove that cell from the stack (line 12). This is effectively backtracking, because it makes the previous cell in the stack the current node.

On the other hand, if the cell *does* have unvisited neighbors, we choose one at random (line 14), link it to the current cell (line 15), and then push it onto the stack (line 16), implicitly making it the new current cell.

Once you've got that ready, create a test program for Recursive Backtracker:

recursive_backtracker_demo.rb
```
require 'recursive_backtracker'
require 'grid'

grid = Grid.new(20, 20)
RecursiveBacktracker.on(grid)

filename = "recursive_backtracker.png"
grid.to_png.save(filename)
puts "saved to #{filename}"
```

Running it, you should get something that looks remarkably like your Hunt-and-Kill maze, replete with twisting, meandering corridors, and few dead ends—something like the following, in fact.

Given that these two algorithms produce such similar results it might seem difficult to choose between them, but there are two points that you can consider to help you make that choice.

The first is *memory efficiency*. The Recursive Backtracker has to maintain a stack, which can potentially (worst-case) contain every cell in the grid. This suggests that the Recursive Backtracker can require up to twice as much memory as Hunt-and-Kill, because Hunt-and-Kill can get by just fine with nothing more than the grid.

The second is *speed*. Hunt-and-Kill will visit every cell *at least* twice—once while performing its random walk, and again during the hunt phase. The worst case is even worse, though, because if the hunt phase is executed many times, some cells may be visited over and over and over. Compare that to the Recursive Backtracker, which is guaranteed to visit each cell *exactly* twice (once while carving, and once while backtracking), and you can see that the Recursive Backtracker is generally going to be faster.

Memory or speed. Take your pick! Either one will give you a maze with a lot of river—twisting, meandering passages—which someday might be just the texture you need.

Your Turn

So we see that it's true: not all biases are bad! By constraining the selection of cells during the random walk—forbidding those that have already been visited, for example—we can produce mazes with a bias toward more river. We saw how Hunt-and-Kill and Recursive Backtracker both use this technique to good effect.

Once again, it's time to play with what you've acquired. What other constraints can you add to the random walks? What if you change the existing constraints somehow? The following ideas may help get you started.

Hunting Strategies

We looked at one strategy for finding cells in the hunt phase of the Hunt-and-Kill algorithm: simply looking at the cells in order until one is located. What other ways can you think of to hunt for cells? What kind of bias do they each introduce, if any?

Adding Biases

Binary Tree wants to slant, and Sidewinder wants to reach vertically. Can you tweak Hunt-and-Kill or the Recursive Backtracker to produce similar biases? Can you produce a maze with those algorithms where the passages tend to stretch horizontally?

Analyzing Dead Ends

We implemented the deadends method to help count the number of dead ends in a maze, but there are other ways to visualize this. What if you were to color the cells based on the number of cells each one links to? That is to say, a cell linked to only one other cell might be dark gray, whereas one linked to all four neighbors could be red. What other ways can you think of to visualize the dead ends and connections in a maze?

Statistical Analysis

We worked through a short program that computed the average number of dead ends for each of the algorithms we've seen so far. What other stats could you mine with it? You might look for patterns in the ratio of horizontal passages to vertical passages, or compare the number of four-way intersections to the number of dead ends.

Solving Mazes with the Recursive Backtracker

Another name for the Recursive Backtracker is *depth-first search*. This is a strategy for traversing graphs (which suggests a connection between mazes and graphs, doesn't it?). It actually works just as well for *finding solutions* to mazes as it does for *generating* them. Give it a try: instead of randomly carving passages through an empty grid, take an existing maze and follow its passages. Push newly visited cells onto a stack and pop them off again when backtracking, until you reach the goal.

A Recursive Recursive Backtracker

The implementation given here for the Recursive Backtracker uses an explicit stack, but with a bit of thought it is possible to rewrite it (quite concisely!) using an *implicit* stack. In most programming languages, when you call a method or a function, the variables in the current scope are pushed onto a stack, which is then popped to restore those variables when the function returns. Try reimplementing the Recursive Backtracker using actual *recursion*, with a function that calls itself every time a new neighbor is selected, and which returns when the current cell has no more unvisited neighbors.

Next up, we're going to take a break from learning new algorithms and instead focus on things we can do with the algorithms we have. Specifically, we're going to see how we can doctor our grids a bit to get creative with how they're shaped!

Part II

Next Steps

Right. So now we've got some algorithms under our belts. We've generated a few mazes, tried a few variations, and done a few experiments. It's time now to look beyond the algorithms themselves to what sorts of things we can do with them—aside from simply making mazes, that is. We'll see how to fit mazes to shapes, generate them in circles, and basically challenge every assumption we've made so far about what a grid is and how it's constructed.

CHAPTER 6

Fitting Mazes to Shapes

Let's take a little break from new maze algorithms and try to get a feel for what we've currently got in our toolboxes. At this point, we're pretty comfortable making rectangular mazes.

In this chapter, we're going to take it to the next level and learn how to make mazes that fit into arbitrary shapes.

The secret is a remarkably simple little technique called *masking*, which constrains a maze to fit within an arbitrary shape. It's got its own set of warts, but on the whole it's a really useful tool.

We'll begin by using masks to forbid certain areas of a grid, causing the maze algorithm to skip over those

areas you define. Then, we'll see how to use that to fit a maze into different geometric designs, and eventually to shape your maze in the form of letters and words using image templates!

But first, we need to talk about what, exactly, these masks are, and how they work.

Introducing Masking

The idea behind masking is really pretty simple. The basic metaphor is that our grid is essentially a very low-resolution image, where each cell is like a single pixel. Turning any of these pixels off marks them as off-limits, so our maze algorithm (whichever one we're using) will never try to walk there.

In the following figure, the cell in the southeast corner has been turned off. The resulting maze, then, omits that cell entirely.

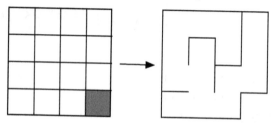

Conceptually, that's really all there is to it! In practice, though, there are some things to consider, and some consequences that follow from mucking with the geometry of our grids like this.

Consequences of Masking

Not all maze algorithms can handle the changes that masking can introduce to a grid. Consider the following, where the cell at row 3, column 4 has been turned off.

We can show pretty easily that the Binary Tree algorithm won't produce a valid maze on this grid simply by trying to generate a maze here. Let's say we start in the southwest corner again. Remember, the Binary Tree algorithm works by choosing between north and east at each point. Let's say that we make the following sequence of choices:

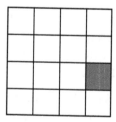

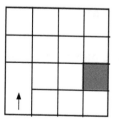 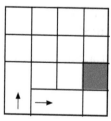 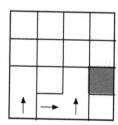

We choose north for the first cell, east for the second, and north again for the third—which brings us to the southeast corner.

Looking at the cell in that corner, we see right away that the algorithm can't go north, and it can't go east. It has no way to connect this cell to its only valid neighbor to the west—we've effectively orphaned it.

You really can't make a valid maze on this grid using Binary Tree! That algorithm will never create a dead-end cell where the only exit is west or south—which is exactly what we have in that southeast corner. (If you're having trouble believing me—give it a try. See if you can find a sequence of choices in that bottom row that doesn't orphan at least one cell!)

The Sidewinder has a similar problem. Because it will never create a dead end where the only exit is south, you can easily cause it to fail by turning off one of the cells in the middle of the northern row, creating a north-facing dead end.

The good news, though, is that any of the other algorithms we've covered so far (and many of those that we'll cover in subsequent chapters) will be just fine. The examples in this chapter will all use Recursive Backtracker, but feel free to experiment with others.

So, with those caveats out of the way, we can begin looking at how to go about manipulating our grids with masks. We'll begin in the simplest possible way: by killing cells.

Killing Cells

We can implement masking, albeit clumsily, with nothing more than the tools we've already written. Cells may be "turned off" by making their neighbors think that the cell doesn't exist. We're basically killing those cells.

The following code does this to the northwest and southeast corners by setting the appropriate attributes to nil on the neighboring cells. Put it in a file named killing_cells.rb.

killing_cells.rb
```
Line 1  require 'grid'
  -     require 'recursive_backtracker'
  -
  -     grid = Grid.new(5, 5)
  5
  -     # orphan the cell in the northwest corner...
  -     grid[0, 0].east.west = nil
  -     grid[0, 0].south.north = nil
  -
```

```
10    # ...and the one in the southeast corner
  -   grid[4, 4].west.east = nil
  -   grid[4, 4].north.south = nil
  -
  -   RecursiveBacktracker.on(grid, start_at: grid[1,1])
15
  -   puts grid
```

Lines 7 and 8 orphan the cell in the northwest corner by isolating it, removing it from its neighbors. We do this by telling the neighbor to the east of the cell that it has no western neighbor, and telling the neighbor to the south that it has no northern neighbor. We isolate the cell in the southeast corner similarly, on lines 11 and 12.

Then we run the Recursive Backtracker algorithm on the resulting grid, starting with the cell at row 1, column 1. (We can't reliably let the grid choose a random starting cell here, because it *might* choose one of those two cells we just orphaned...which would fail to generate a maze.) Finally, we dump the resulting maze to the terminal. Running it, we get something like this:

```
$ ruby -I. killing_cells.rb
+---+---+---+---+---+
|   |   |       |   |
+---+---+   +---+   +
|       |   |   |   |
+   +---+---+   +   +
|   |       |   |   |
+   +   +---+---+   +
|   |   |       |   |
+   +   +   +   +---+
|           |   |   |
+---+---+---+---+---+
```

It worked! Notice how the northwest and the southeast corners are completely walled in, disconnected from the rest of the maze, and yet the maze itself is just fine. Perfect, in fact—in the mathematical sense.

However, having to manually disconnect each cell would rapidly grow tedious. We can make this easier.

Implementing a Mask

Let's create a Mask class that will encapsulate the on-off state of each cell in our grid. That is to say, for each cell in the grid, our mask should be able to tell us whether or not it should be included in the maze. The following implementation does this by keeping a separate two-dimensional array of Boolean values, where false means the corresponding cell is "off the grid."

Create a new file named mask.rb, and start it off with the following properties and constructor.

```
mask.rb
class Mask
  attr_reader :rows, :columns

  def initialize(rows, columns)
    @rows, @columns = rows, columns
    @bits = Array.new(@rows) { Array.new(@columns, true) }
  end
```

The initialize constructor is pretty straightforward, just recording the dimensions of the mask and creating a two-dimensional array of Boolean values, indicating which cells are on (enabled) or off (disabled).

The next two methods query and modify that Boolean array.

```
def [](row, column)
  if row.between?(0, @rows - 1) && column.between?(0, @columns - 1)
    @bits[row][column]
  else
    false
  end
end

def []=(row, column, is_on)
  @bits[row][column] = is_on
end
```

The array accessor, [], accepts a (row, column) pair and says whether or not that location is enabled in the grid. The corresponding assignment method, []=, is used to indicate whether a given position is enabled or disabled by recording the value of the is_on parameter to that position in the array.

The next method, count, will tell us how many locations in the mask are enabled. This is useful for algorithms like Aldous-Broder, where we need to know how many cells are in the grid.

```
def count
  count = 0

  @rows.times do |row|
    @columns.times do |col|
      count += 1 if @bits[row][col]
    end
  end

  count
end
```

And the last method, random_location, simply reports a (*row*, *column*) pair corresponding to a random, enabled location in the grid. We'll use this for algorithms like Hunt-and-Kill or the Recursive Backtracker, which want to start at a random position.

```
def random_location
  loop do
    row = rand(@rows)
    col = rand(@columns)

    return [row, col] if @bits[row][col]
  end
end
end
```

That's our Mask class! It's only half the solution, though. Remember, we're trying to make it so that we don't have to tell the individual cells who their neighbors are and aren't. We'd rather simply hand the grid a mask and have it set up the correct connections automatically.

To make that happen, we'll subclass our Grid and provide a new constructor that accepts a Mask instance. The new grid subclass will then use that mask to determine which cells get instantiated, and which are set to nil. In fact, we might as well use the mask to inform the size of the grid, too, so that we only have to specify the dimensions once.

Put the following in masked_grid.rb.

masked_grid.rb
```
Line 1  require 'grid'
   -
   -    class MaskedGrid < Grid
   -      attr_reader :mask
   5
   -      def initialize(mask)
   -        @mask = mask
   -        super(@mask.rows, @mask.columns)
   -      end
  10
   -      def prepare_grid
   -        Array.new(rows) do |row|
   -          Array.new(columns) do |column|
   -            Cell.new(row, column) if @mask[row, column]
  15          end
   -        end
   -      end
   -
   -      def random_cell
  20        row, col = @mask.random_location
```

```
-        self[row, col]
-      end
-
-      def size
25        @mask.count
-      end
-    end
```

Notice how the constructor, initialize, no longer accepts dimensions. Instead, line 8 passes the dimensions of the mask to the superclass, so that our grid's size will always match that of the mask used to initialize it.

This class changes three other behaviors: how the grid is prepared, how random cells are found, and how the size of the grid is computed.

The prepare_grid method is almost identical to the version in the parent Grid class, but line 14 now relies on the mask to decide whether or not to instantiate a cell. If the mask reports a given location as enabled, a cell will be instantiated for it. Otherwise, that location will be nil, and the superclass will simply work around it.

The last two methods are straightforward, just delegating to the mask for the necessary computations.

With those two classes, now we can simplify our killing_cells.rb program. Put the following in simple_mask.rb.

simple_mask.rb
```
Line 1  require 'mask'
-       require 'masked_grid'
-       require 'recursive_backtracker'
-
5       mask = Mask.new(5, 5)
-
-       mask[0, 0] = false
-       mask[2, 2] = false
-       mask[4, 4] = false
10
-       grid = MaskedGrid.new(mask)
-       RecursiveBacktracker.on(grid)
-
-       puts grid
```

There! Much nicer. We can now instantiate a new mask (line 5), turn off whichever cells we want (lines 7–9), and then instantiate our new MaskedGrid using that mask (line 11). Finally, we run the Recursive Backtracker algorithm on it. (We don't need to specify the starting cell this time, because we've implemented a smarter random_cell method for MaskedGrid.)

When we run this, we should get a new maze that omits those three cells that were masked.

```
$ ruby -I. simple_mask.rb
+---+---+---+---+---+
|   |   |           |
+---+   +---+---+   +
|   |               |
+   +---+---+---+   +
|       |   |   |   |
+   +---+---+   +   +
|   |       |       |
+   +   +   +   +---+
|       |       |   |
+---+---+---+---+---+
```

Better! But it's still a bit tedious to have to manually turn cells off in the mask. Let's look at how to make that a bit more intuitive.

ASCII Masks

Imagine if we could "draw" our masks in a separate file and feed that file to our program. We could play with all kinds of designs, without having to change our program at all! Let's make that happen, using simple text files as input. The text files will be formatted something like the following, which shows one possible definition of a 10×10 grid.

mask.txt
```
X........X
....XX....
...XXXX...
....XX....
X........X
X........X
....XX....
...XXXX...
....XX....
X........X
```

Every "X" indicates an "off" cell, and anything else (the "." characters, in this case) will be an "on" cell.

We'll implement this by introducing a helper method on our Mask class. Open mask.rb and add the following just after the start of that class, before the initialize method.

```
Line 1  def self.from_txt(file)
   -      lines = File.readlines(file).map { |line| line.strip }
   -      lines.pop while lines.last.length < 1
```

```
5    rows    = lines.length
     columns = lines.first.length
     mask    = Mask.new(rows, columns)

     mask.rows.times do |row|
10     mask.columns.times do |col|
         if lines[row][col] == "X"
           mask[row, col] = false
         else
           mask[row, col] = true
15       end
       end
     end

     mask
20  end
```

This new from_txt method expects you to pass it the name of a file. Line 2 then reads the contents of that file, line-wise, stripping whitespace from each line in turn, and then line 3 removes any blank lines from the end of the file.

Now, we're going to assume that the number of rows of text in the file corresponds to the number of rows in our mask, and the number of columns of text in the first line corresponds to the number of columns in our mask. Lines 5 and 6 make that assumption real, and then we instantiate our mask.

Finally, line 9 starts looping over each character of each line of the file, setting the corresponding position in the mask to false if the character is an X or true if it is anything else. When all is said and done, the method returns the new Mask instance.

Our program now becomes the following. Put this code in ascii_mask.rb.

```
ascii_mask.rb
require 'mask'
require 'masked_grid'
require 'recursive_backtracker'

abort "Please specify a text file to use as a template" if ARGV.empty?
mask = Mask.from_txt(ARGV.first)
grid = MaskedGrid.new(mask)
RecursiveBacktracker.on(grid)

filename = "masked.png"
grid.to_png.save(filename)
puts "saved image to #{filename}"
```

Note that we're saving the resulting maze as an image, because our masks might be any size. Things would get messy if we tried to display large mazes on the terminal. We'll run this by passing the name of a file as an argument on the command line. If we use mask.txt from the beginning of this section, then we can run our program like this:

```
$ ruby -I. ascii_mask.rb mask.txt
saved image to masked.png
```

Opening up masked.png we ought to see something like this figure.

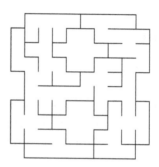

Play around with different templates, and see what you get! You might even try drawing your name and generating a maze either around the letters or inside the letters (depending on how you set up your template). If you decide to generate the maze inside the letters of a word, though, be sure you link the letters together somehow. Otherwise, the different pieces of the grid won't be connected, and the maze algorithm won't be able to connect all of them.

Once you've tried a few of these, though, you might realize that it's pretty tedious to try to design the larger templates purely in text. Let's look at a (potentially) more convenient way to define these templates.

Image Masks

These masks were previously compared to images, where each cell is like a pixel that you turn on or off. It might make sense, then, to use actual images for the templates, where pixels of a particular color (say, black) are considered off and everything else is considered on. This would let us design our templates using an image editor, which ought to make larger masks a lot easier.

Let's implement this. We're going to create a method that will accept an image in PNG format, so the first thing we'll need to do is make sure the ChunkyPNG library is loaded. Open up mask.rb again and add the following line at the very top of the file:

```
require 'chunky_png'
```

Once we have that, we can add our new method, just like we did for defining a mask from a text file. Let's call it from_png(file), and add it just after the from_txt method.

```
Line 1  def self.from_png(file)
   -      image = ChunkyPNG::Image.from_file(file)
   -      mask = Mask.new(image.height, image.width)
   -
   5      mask.rows.times do |row|
   -        mask.columns.times do |col|
   -          if image[col, row] == ChunkyPNG::Color::BLACK
   -            mask[row, col] = false
   -          else
  10            mask[row, col] = true
   -          end
   -        end
   -      end
   -
  15      mask
   -  end
```

Line 2 loads the named image from disk, and line 3 instantiates a new mask using the same dimensions as the image. Line 5 then begins looping over each pixel of the image, setting the corresponding position in the mask to false (if the pixel is black) or to true (for any other color).

With that new method, we can rework our ascii_mask.rb file to read and use PNG files as our maze templates. Copy ascii_mask.rb to image_mask.rb, and make the following changes to it.

image_mask.rb
```
require 'mask'
require 'masked_grid'
require 'recursive_backtracker'

➤  abort "Please specify a PNG image to use as a template" if ARGV.empty?
➤  mask = Mask.from_png(ARGV.first)
   grid = MaskedGrid.new(mask)
   RecursiveBacktracker.on(grid)

   filename = "masked.png"
➤  grid.to_png(cell_size: 5).save(filename)
   puts "saved image to #{filename}"
```

Note that, at the end, when we save the grid to a PNG image, we set the cell size to be 5 pixels instead of the default 10, to more easily accommodate larger mazes.

All that's left now is to come up with an image to use as a template! If you aren't sure what to use to make your own image templates, I'd recommend the GIMP,[1] an excellent, free image manipulation program, available for

---

1. http://www.gimp.org

Windows, Linux, and Mac OS X. (Be warned, though, you'll want to give yourself time to come to grips with the learning curve!) Remember: *black* is used for areas where cells should *not* be created, so if you start with a black background, you can draw on your canvas in any other color to define areas where your maze ought to exist.

On the other hand, if image manipulation isn't your thing, sample images are available online with the source code used in this book.

Let's see this in action. We'll create the following image, calling it maze_text.png.

Then, we fire up our new script much like we did before.

```
$ ruby -I. image_mask.rb maze_text.png
saved image to masked.png
```

The result? This!

It's almost magical!

Your Turn

Masking is a powerful technique that opens up many possibilities. We've only scratched the surface in this chapter. Take some time and experiment with it, and see what else you can come up with. Here are some ideas to get you started.

Geometric Designs

Our mazes so far have all been fit into grids bounded by rectangles. Experiment with using masks to shoehorn a maze into a triangle or a circle.

Multi-State Masks

In our Mask class, we used an array of Boolean values to indicate where cells can and cannot exist. If, instead of Booleans, we use integers, we end up with the possibility of *multi-state masks*, allowing us to describe multiple different regions within the grid. One use for this is to split the grid into multiple pieces, run different maze algorithms on each piece, and then link each piece together via passages to create a single maze with multiple different styles. An example: a hedge maze that surrounds a courtyard, with another maze at the center of the courtyard.

Mazes with Rooms

Another use for masks is to declare rooms within your mazes. The mask says where the maze corridors should be drawn, and when all is finished, you add corridors that link the forbidden areas to the maze itself. These forbidden regions become the rooms.

Sadly, as useful as these masks are, they do tend to create outlines with a very jagged, pixelated look, especially if the shapes you're trying for consist of any curves or diagonal lines. Circles, especially, suffer from this treatment. We'll look at a completely different technique next for generating a maze inside a circle.

CHAPTER 7

Going in Circles

At this point, if someone were to ask us for a "circle maze," we could oblige them by making a template image of a circle, and then using it as a mask to generate the corresponding maze. We'd get something like the following:

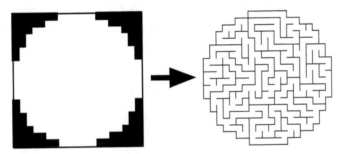

If we're perfectly honest with ourselves, though, we have to admit that while this works, it's not very attractive. The jagged, pixelated edges of the mask are merely approximating the circle we want, and are translated one-to-one onto our grid's rigid, rectangular cells. This arrangement of perpendicular rows and columns is called a *regular* or *orthogonal* grid, and though it has a lot going for it—easy to understand, easy to implement—it kind of falls down when you try to represent non-orthogonal lines like diagonals or curves.

There happens to be a class of grid that works really well for circles, though. It's called a *polar* grid, and the mazes we build with it are called *theta*, or circle mazes. In this chapter, you'll see how to use these grids to turn out circle mazes that look much like this one:

To get there, we'll begin by talking about polar grids and how they differ from what we've done so far. Then we'll introduce a new Grid subclass where we'll rewrite our to_png method to support this new way of thinking about grids, and finally we'll look at how to make the cells of the grid as evenly sized as possible.

Understanding Polar Grids

Whereas the orthogonal grids we're used to are composed of rows and columns of cells, polar grids are composed of rings of concentric circles, each divided into cells like the spokes of a wagon wheel.

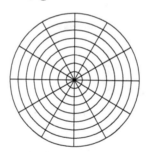

There are going to be lots of ways we could represent one of these in code, but it turns out that we can reuse our existing grid class with just a few changes. We'll work through them in stages, starting with what it will take to draw a polar grid. If we can draw one, we've got the problem more than half licked!

At the beginning, we start with a few given values. These include the height of each ring (we'll call it ring_height), and how many cells exist in the ring (or cell_count). With those, we can then define the geometry of a given cell, like this:

```
theta         = 2 * Math::PI / cell_count
inner_radius  = cell.row * ring_height
outer_radius  = (cell.row + 1) * ring_height
theta_ccw     = cell.col * theta
theta_cw      = (cell.col + 1) * theta
```

The theta variable describes the *angular size* of every cell in the ring. If a complete circle describes an angle of 2 * Math::PI radians, then we can simply divide that by the number of cells in the ring to see how many radians are covered by a single cell.

The inner_radius and outer_radius variables tell us how far the cell is from the origin, with the inner value describing the distance of the *inward* wall and the outer value describing the distance of the *outward* wall.

The last two variables are used to describe where the *counter-clockwise* and *clockwise* walls of the cell are, in radians. The counter-clockwise wall is described by theta_ccw, which is simply the angle around the circle to that wall. Likewise, theta_cw describes the angle to the clockwise wall.

Let's put these on a diagram and see if they make more sense. The following diagram zooms in on our polar grid, looking at one arbitrary cell whose corners are *A*, *B*, *C*, and *D*.

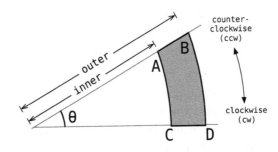

Figure 2—Describing a Cell in Polar Coordinates

We can see that θ (theta) is the angular size of the cell, and the inner and outer radii are the distances from the origin to the cell's walls. Further, the *AB* wall is the counter-clockwise one, and *CD* is the clockwise one, both being some multiple of θ radians around the circle.

Right?

Whew!

The next step, because most image libraries don't understand polar coordinates, is to convert them to *Cartesian* coordinates—the *x,y* pairs that are typically used to address locations in images. We're going to resort to triangles to help us with the conversion, measuring the *x* and *y* distances of the point from the origin of the grid. We'll need to resort to a bit of trigonometry, but don't worry if it's been awhile since you've stretched those muscles. We'll walk through this together.

Here's a diagram, in case you need a refresher of how the sides of a right triangle relate to the hypotenuse. The hypotenuse is labeled *r*:

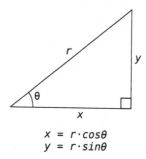

$$x = r \cdot \cos\theta$$
$$y = r \cdot \sin\theta$$

It's always helped me to remember that sine and cosine correspond alphabetically to *x* and *y*. Just as cosine comes before sine in the dictionary, so *x* comes before *y*, which suggests that we'll use cosine to compute *x*, and sine to compute *y*. Multiplying the hypotenuse by the cosine or sine of the angle *θ* will give us, respectively, the *x* or *y* distance from the origin.

Referring back to Figure 2, *Describing a Cell in Polar Coordinates*, on page 99, it's not much of a stretch to imagine a triangle superimposed, with *A* (or *B*) at the upper right and the grid origin in the lower left. If the inner and outer radii are the hypotenuse, we can use those trig formulas to get us the Cartesian coordinates we need.

Thanks to trig, then, we now know everything we need to describe the four corners of the cell, labeled *A*, *B*, *C*, and *D* in Figure 2, *Describing a Cell in Polar Coordinates*, on page 99. Assuming center_x and center_y are the coordinates of the origin of our circle, our cell's coordinates become:

```
ax = center_x + inner_radius * Math.cos(theta_ccw)
ay = center_y + inner_radius * Math.sin(theta_ccw)
bx = center_x + outer_radius * Math.cos(theta_ccw)
by = center_y + outer_radius * Math.sin(theta_ccw)
cx = center_x + inner_radius * Math.cos(theta_cw)
cy = center_y + inner_radius * Math.sin(theta_cw)
dx = center_x + outer_radius * Math.cos(theta_cw)
dy = center_y + outer_radius * Math.sin(theta_cw)
```

All that's left, then, is to draw it.

Drawing Polar Grids

The to_png method we've used to this point isn't going to help us much with polar grids, so let's just subclass Grid and rewrite to_png to be what we need it to be.

Create a new file, named polar_grid.rb. We'll start it off with the following Grid subclass and to_png implementation.

polar_grid.rb

```
Line 1  require 'grid'

        class PolarGrid < Grid
          def to_png(cell_size: 10)
    5       img_size = 2 * @rows * cell_size

            background = ChunkyPNG::Color::WHITE
            wall = ChunkyPNG::Color::BLACK

   10       img = ChunkyPNG::Image.new(img_size + 1, img_size + 1, background)
            center = img_size / 2

            each_cell do |cell|
              theta        = 2 * Math::PI / @grid[cell.row].length
   15         inner_radius = cell.row * cell_size
              outer_radius = (cell.row + 1) * cell_size
              theta_ccw    = cell.column * theta
              theta_cw     = (cell.column + 1) * theta

   20         ax = center + (inner_radius * Math.cos(theta_ccw)).to_i
              ay = center + (inner_radius * Math.sin(theta_ccw)).to_i
              bx = center + (outer_radius * Math.cos(theta_ccw)).to_i
              by = center + (outer_radius * Math.sin(theta_ccw)).to_i
              cx = center + (inner_radius * Math.cos(theta_cw)).to_i
   25         cy = center + (inner_radius * Math.sin(theta_cw)).to_i
              dx = center + (outer_radius * Math.cos(theta_cw)).to_i
              dy = center + (outer_radius * Math.sin(theta_cw)).to_i

              img.line(ax, ay, cx, cy, wall) unless cell.linked?(cell.north)
   30         img.line(cx, cy, dx, dy, wall) unless cell.linked?(cell.east)
            end

            img.circle(center, center, @rows * cell_size, wall)
            img
   35     end
        end
```

This new to_png method starts much like the old version, computing the size of our canvas. In this case, though, the canvas width and height will be the diameter of our circle, or twice the radius, which is the number of rows, times the height of each row (line 5). The center of the grid, then, will be the center of our circle, and is computed to be half the diameter (line 11).

Now, for each cell in the grid, lines 14–18 measure the inner and outer radii, and the associated angles, which are then used on lines 20–27 to compute the coordinates of each corner of the cell. (That part should look very familiar, from the previous section.) Note that we convert each coordinate to an integer, because ChunkyPNG doesn't deal well with non-integer arguments.

Once we have those coordinates, lines 29 and 30 use them to draw the inward and clockwise walls of the cell. (For now, we'll refer to those directions as north and east, respectively, since they correspond neatly to the underlying orthogonal grid. We'll get fancy soon enough and create a custom Cell subclass.)

Last of all, we draw the outer wall of the grid as a whole circle (line 33), and then return our image.

Joe asks:

Why Are We Drawing Lines Instead of Arcs?

Good catch! Ideally, we'd draw the inner wall on line 29 with an arc, to follow the curve of the circle, but as of this writing ChunkyPNG does not provide an API for drawing arcs. It turns out that straight lines do (mostly) well enough, but if you're using a different image library with your own code, maybe check to see if it supports arc drawing.

Let's check to see that this is working now. Put the following in a file called polar_grid_test.rb.

polar_grid_test.rb
```ruby
require 'polar_grid'

grid = PolarGrid.new(8, 8)

filename = "polar.png"
grid.to_png.save(filename)
puts "saved to #{filename}"
```

We create a new polar grid with eight rows (or rings), and eight columns (the spokes of the wheels), and then simply display the result. Since we're not trying to generate a maze on it, it should simply save the grid itself. Sure enough, we get the following:

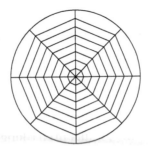

It's not great (the straight lines give it a decidedly cobweb-ish look), but it's enough to show us that we're on the right track. It's a recognizable polar grid.

At this point we could even run one of our maze algorithms, but I wouldn't recommend it—not yet, anyway. For example, here is the same grid with the Recursive Backtracker applied to it:

It's an intriguing pattern, but not really what we're going for here. The outermost cells are far too wide compared to the innermost cells, contributing to a very uneven look, and although it is technically a maze, it lacks the expected aesthetic of a maze. What we need is a way to keep the cells as evenly sized as possible, even as the concentric circles of the grid grow larger and larger.

To solve this, we need to look at a technique for dividing cells when they get too large, called *adaptive subdivision.*

Adaptively Subdividing the Grid

In order to use adaptive subdivision to make our cells more uniform in size, we need to know about what size they ought to be. Squares look pretty good in an orthogonal grid, but polar grids can't give us real squares. There are no parallel lines in a polar grid! But although we can't have squares, we *can* approximate them. We'll just say we want the length of the inner wall to be approximately the same as the height of the cell (the distance between the inner and outer walls).

With that rule in mind, look at the figure, which shows one "column" of our polar grid, and take steps to make it a bit more uniform.

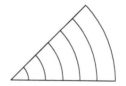

First, we look at the two innermost cells and see that they both fit the bill. Their inner walls aren't longer than the cells are tall. But the next cell...ouch. It's quite a bit wider. To fix that, we divide the cell—*and all subsequent cells*—into two, like this:

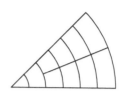

That third row now looks pretty good, and the fourth row, too (though it's definitely getting a bit wide). The fifth row, however, sounds some alarms. *Way* too wide. The answer? Subdivide again.

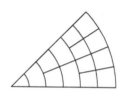

At this point, our original column has branched out to become multiple columns. The cells look much more regular now, but this comes at a cost: we've added some complexity by splitting the cells, so that some now have *two* neighbors in the outward direction, instead of just one.

Fortunately, it's not too difficult to keep under control, as we'll see in the next section when we bring it all together in code.

Implementing a Polar Grid

To implement this improved polar grid, we're going to introduce a new Cell subclass, and then walk through how these new cells will be laid out and subdivided. We'll finish it all off with one last mostly cosmetic tweak to make our final maze as tidy as possible.

The PolarCell Class

First, the new Cell subclass. We've made do so far with using the existing Cell class, but it's getting a bit unwieldy to keep referring to compass directions when they don't map very intuitively to a polar grid. Also, with adaptive subdivision, some cells may now have *two* neighbors in the outward direction, and our existing Cell class has no support for that.

So, put the following in polar_cell.rb.

```
       polar_cell.rb
Line 1  require 'cell'
   -
   -    class PolarCell < Cell
   -      attr_accessor :cw, :ccw, :inward
   5      attr_reader :outward
   -
   -      def initialize(row, column)
   -        super
   -        @outward = []
  10      end
   -
   -      def neighbors
   -        list = []
   -        list << cw if cw
  15        list << ccw if ccw
   -        list << inward if inward
   -        list += outward
   -        list
   -      end
  20    end
```

Lines 4 and 5 start things off by defining attributes for the polar directions: clockwise (cw), counter-clockwise (ccw), inward (toward the origin), and outward (toward the rim).

Refactoring the Cell Class

At this point, you might want to take some time to do a proper refactoring of Cell, so that subclasses don't inherit unnecessary baggage (like north, south, and so forth). Projects that grow organically, like ours, often go through refactoring iterations to "tidy up" as the code grows and matures. It's sadly beyond the scope of this book to do so here, but don't let that stop you!

Note that line 5 grants outward only a reader, not a writer, because we won't be assigning to it directly. Instead, in the constructor on line 9 we initialize outward to be an empty array, and we'll just append cells to it as needed.

There. With our new cell class ready, we can return to PolarGrid and start fleshing that out a bit more.

Revisiting PolarGrid

Our updated polar grid implementation will override several methods of the base class, including the constructor, prepare_grid, configure, and others. We'll open up polar_grid.rb again and make all of the following changes there.

First, let's add a dependency on our new PolarCell class.

```
require 'grid'
➤ require 'polar_cell'
```

Next, we'll create a new constructor for PolarGrid. Up to this point, we've been telling every grid how many rows and columns it has, but adaptive subdivision allows us to compute the number of columns per row. All we really need to tell our grid is the number of rows—we can get everything else from that. Put this at the top of the PolarGrid class, before the to_png method.

```
def initialize(rows)
  super(rows, 1)
end
```

The second parameter in the super call is required because the superclass needs to know how many columns the grid has (arguably a design flaw, but we'll live with it).

The next method is meaty. We're going to override prepare_grid and change it up so that instead of building a regular grid as it's been doing, we're going to prepare our adaptively subdivided polar grid. Add the following method just after the initialize method.

```
Line 1  def prepare_grid
   -      rows = Array.new(@rows)
   -
   -      row_height = 1.0 / @rows
   5      rows[0] = [ PolarCell.new(0, 0) ]
   -
   -      (1...@rows).each do |row|
   -        radius = row.to_f / @rows
   -        circumference = 2 * Math::PI * radius
  10
   -        previous_count = rows[row - 1].length
   -        estimated_cell_width = circumference / previous_count
   -        ratio = (estimated_cell_width / row_height).round
   -
  15        cells = previous_count * ratio
   -        rows[row] = Array.new(cells) { |col| PolarCell.new(row, col) }
   -      end
   -
   -      rows
  20  end
```

Even though it's a polar grid, we're still going to use arrays to represent each row. Line 2 sets that up for us.

Line 4 then computes the height of each individual row. We don't know, at this point, how large the circle will be when it's rendered, but that's okay. We can just assume that we're working with a unit circle—that is, a circle with a radius of 1—and the laws of geometry assure us that we can resize it painlessly later. This lets us simplify many of the calculations.

Next, line 5 treats the origin of our circle—row #0—as a special case. Because all the radii meet at the origin, splitting that row into more than one cell means the cells get small, fast. Instead, we'll force that innermost row to be a single cell, with coordinates $0, 0$.

Now, for each of the remaining rows, we're going to do some computation to figure out how to subdivide things. Line 8 computes the *inner* radius of the row—the distance from the origin to the row's inner wall—and then uses that to compute the circumference of that wall (line 9). Remember, we're working with a unit circle, here, so the radius of a given row is just the ratio of the row's index to the number of rows. (Isn't that convenient?) Then, line 12 divides that circumference by the number of cells in the previous row, which tells us how wide each cell would be in *this* row if we *don't* subdivide. That's the ideal condition—we don't want to subdivide unless we have to!

Recall that our ideal cell width is the same as the height of the row. Line 13 uses that ideal to see how many ideally sized cells could fit into our estimated_cell_width. This ratio variable essentially tells us how many cells in this row correspond to each cell in the previous row. If ratio is 1, then the current row will have the same number of cells as the previous row. If it is 2 (or more), then we're subdividing. The ratio will always be either 1 or 2, except for the row at index 1. The ratio there may be larger because the previous row (at index 0) always contains only a single cell.

Lastly, we take the ratio and multiply it by the number of cells in the previous row (line 15). This tells us how many cells should be in the current row, so we finish the loop off by instantiating a new array with the corresponding number of PolarCell instances (line 16).

Whew!

At this point, then, we've got our grid, but we're not yet setting up the adjacency information for the individual cells. The poor little dears have no idea who their neighbors are. For this, we need to override the configure_cells method.

```
Line 1  def configure_cells
    -     each_cell do |cell|
    -       row, col = cell.row, cell.column
    -
```

```
 5        if row > 0
 -          cell.cw  = self[row, col + 1]
 -          cell.ccw = self[row, col - 1]
 -
 -          ratio = @grid[row].length / @grid[row - 1].length
10          parent = @grid[row - 1][col / ratio]
 -          parent.outward << cell
 -          cell.inward = parent
 -        end
 -      end
15   end
```

Here, we're going to look at each cell in the grid, ignoring only the cell at the origin (line 5) because it's our special case and has no inward or clockwise neighbors.

For the other cells, we set up their clockwise (line 6) and counter-clockwise (line 7) neighbors, compute the ratio of cells in this row to the cells in the previous row (line 9), and then use that to decide which cell in the previous row is the "parent"—the cell that may or may not have been subdivided to produce the current cell (line 10). The current cell is then added as one of the outward neighbors of that parent (line 11), and the parent is set to be the inward neighbor of the current cell (line 12).

We only need to add one more new method, to help us select a random cell from the grid. This one is easy, a breath of fresh air after the previous two.

```
def random_cell
  row = rand(@rows)
  col = rand(@grid[row].length)
  @grid[row][col]
end
```

And finally, we need to make a few changes to to_png to accommodate our new neighbor names (cw, ccw, and so forth) as well as the special case around the cell at the origin. Change (or add to, as necessary) your copy of the to_png to make it match the highlighted lines in the following code.

```
each_cell do |cell|
➤   next if cell.row == 0

    # ...

➤   img.line(ax, ay, cx, cy, wall) unless cell.linked?(cell.inward)
➤   img.line(cx, cy, dx, dy, wall) unless cell.linked?(cell.cw)
end
```

Easy enough! We're almost done.

Testing and Tweaking

We're on the final stretch. All that's left is to test what we've got, then tweak one final thing so the finished product looks as good as we can make it.

Our existing polar_grid_test.rb won't work right now, because we're instantiating the PolarGrid with too many arguments. Go ahead and open that file up and change it so that we pass only a single argument to the constructor—the number of rows—and try it all again.

```
grid = PolarGrid.new(8)
```

This time around, we should get something much less cobweb-ish and much more interesting.

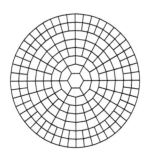

Nice! And if we then generate a maze on that grid, we ought to see a thing of beauty. Put the following in circle_maze.rb and give it a try. It uses the Recursive Backtracker algorithm, but Aldous-Broder or Wilson's ought to work equally well if you want to experiment with other algorithms.

circle_maze.rb
```
require 'polar_grid'
require 'recursive_backtracker'

grid = PolarGrid.new(8)
RecursiveBacktracker.on(grid)

filename = "circle_maze.png"
grid.to_png.save(filename)
puts "saved to #{filename}"
```

The result? Behold!
Well…but, wait. It's *almost* a thing of beauty. There's one little blemish keeping it back from blissful, circular perfection. Do you see it?

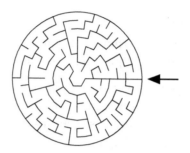

It's that radial line, marking the boundary between the clockwise and counter-clockwise edges of our grid. It may seem like a small thing, but try generating a few of these mazes. Make them bigger, with 25 rows or more. That little radial line will rapidly grow tiresome!

To fix it, we simply need to tell the grid that the cells on the clockwise boundary are adjacent to the cells on the counter-clockwise boundary. We *could* do this by further modifying the configure_cells method, but if we took that route we'd wind up having to perform the same check twice—once for the clockwise neighbor, and once for the counter-clockwise neighbor. We can avoid the duplication by moving that check into the array accessor method itself, as in the following code. Go ahead and add it to the PolarGrid class, just before the random_cell method.

```
def [](row, column)
  return nil unless row.between?(0, @rows - 1)
➤  @grid[row][column % @grid[row].count]
end
```

The highlighted line is where the magic happens. Notice that we're no longer checking the bounds on the column parameter. Instead, we're using modulus arithmetic to make sure that the column is always wrapped to fit within those bounds. In this way, the clockwise boundary and the counter-clockwise boundary effectively become adjacent.

Go ahead and save that, and try generating a maze again.

Finally, something to be proud of!

Your Turn

This chapter has been a lot to take in! We've looked at a new kind of grid—the *polar grid*—and talked about how to represent and display it. We talked about how to use adaptive subdivision to keep the cells of our new grid evenly sized, and finally showed how to use modulus arithmetic to remove seams by making opposite boundaries adjacent.

Even so, we hardly scratched the surface. Here are some things you might want to try on your own.

Tickling the Subdivision Trigger

In the earlier implementation, a cell gets subdivided when it's at least 1.5 times wider than the row is tall. (That's what the use of the round method was for, on line 13 in PolarGrid#prepare_grid.) Try adding or subtracting something, like 0.25, inside the parentheses before round gets called, to see what happens when you pull the trigger at different thresholds.

Masks on a Circle Maze

You might try putting the previous chapter to work here by applying masks to circle mazes. You'll need to find a way to map your mask to a circle, and you'll also need to make some changes to to_png, because the implementation given here assumes that every neighbor of a cell exists. Instead of having each cell draw walls only on the inward and clockwise edges, you'll need to check to see if neighbors exist in the other directions and if not, draw walls there, too.

Growing a Circular Binary Tree

Yes, Binary Tree (and Sidewinder, too) can work on a circle maze! You get a rather mesmerizing pinwheel effect, actually. You just need to make sure that your grid has a well-defined clockwise/counter-clockwise boundary, or those algorithms won't be guaranteed to produce a valid maze. Remove our customized array accessor method and give it a try!

Coloring a Circle Maze

Remember a few chapters ago, when we were playing with Dijkstra's algorithm? We implemented a method called background_color_for to support drawing cells in different colors. For clarity, I've sacrificed that method in the polar grid implementation given here, but it's not terribly hard to add back in. Give it a try! Colored circle mazes are lovely.

Once you're comfortable with the polar grids, hang on, because we're going to jump right into some other types of grids next! We'll explore how to make grids out of triangles and hexagons, and then point you at some other intriguing shape combinations.

CHAPTER 8

Exploring Other Grids

When you take a surface and divide it up into different shapes, with no gaps between them and no overlaps, you get what is called a *tessellation* of the surface. Our standard grid is one such tessellation, where we've broken up a flat area, or *plane*, into smaller squares. Another way to say this is that we've *tiled* the plane with squares.

It turns out that squares aren't the only shape that can do this for us. In this chapter, we'll look at two other grids made by tiling other geometric shapes. We'll see how hexagons come together in a honeycomb pattern and triangles form a girder-style lattice. Over the course of the chapter, we'll use these new grids to turn out mazes like the following:

Let's start with the one on the left: a maze on hexagon grid.

Implementing a Hex Grid

So far we've made regular grids and circular grids. Our next goal is to create a grid of hexagons, also called a *hex grid* for short. We'll approach this by first considering a single cell, with an eye to understanding how it relates spatially to its neighbors. From there, we'll take that information and implement the grid itself.

The cells aren't difficult to implement. The trickiest part is just understanding how they all fit together. Let's look at a simple hex grid here:

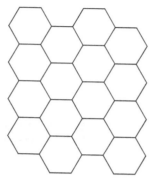

From that, we can see that each hexagon neighbors up to six other hexagons, one for each of north, south, northwest, northeast, southwest, and southeast. Right off, it's clear that our existing Cell won't cut it; it doesn't include enough neighbors! Let's take care of that now by introducing a new Cell subclass.

Put the following in hex_cell.rb.

hex_cell.rb
```ruby
require 'cell'

class HexCell < Cell
  attr_accessor :northeast, :northwest
  attr_accessor :southeast, :southwest

  def neighbors
    list = []
    list << northwest if northwest
    list << north if north
    list << northeast if northeast
    list << southwest if southwest
    list << south if south
    list << southeast if southeast
    list
  end
end
```

This simply extends the Cell class, adding new accessors for northwest, northeast, southwest, and southeast, and then updates the neighbors method to return those new directions. Note that the west and east accessors inherited from the Cell class are unused. With the hexagons in our grid oriented the way they are (flat-topped), they will never have neighbors to the east or west.

The next step is to figure out how these cells are arranged in the grid. Although they aren't necessarily laid out in clear rows, it's not too hard to find an arrangement that works well.

Looking at the previous diagram again, we can see that although vertical columns are clearly present in the grid, horizontal rows are less obvious. It's probably no surprise that there are lots of different ways to approach representing hexagons in a program, nor should it be surprising that each will have different pros and cons. We're going to choose a way to do it that maps most closely to our underlying two-dimensional array, simply because it requires the fewest changes on our end to implement.

The following figure shows how it will work, treating each row as a zig-zag path from one side of the grid to the other, whereas columns simply drop vertically through the grid.

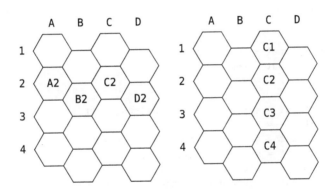

This choice has consequences for how we set up the grid. Most immediately, it means that when we set up the adjacency information for cells in some columns (for example, B and D in the previous illustration), the northwest and northeast diagonals point to the cell's *same row*, whereas southwest and southeast point to the row below. Conversely, for the other columns (for example, A and C) northwest and northeast are the ones that point to a different row.

Tricky, but not insurmountable!

Let's make a new Grid subclass. We'll override the prepare_grid method so that it instantiates our new HexCell class for cells, and we'll override configure_cells to set up the correct adjacency information for each cell.

Put the following in hex_grid.rb.

```
hex_grid.rb
Line 1  require 'grid'
   -    require 'hex_cell'
   -
   -    class HexGrid < Grid
   5      def prepare_grid
   -        Array.new(rows) do |row|
   -          Array.new(columns) do |column|
   -            HexCell.new(row, column)
   -          end
  10        end
   -      end
   -
   -      def configure_cells
   -        each_cell do |cell|
  15          row, col = cell.row, cell.column
   -
   -          if col.even?
   -            north_diagonal = row - 1
   -            south_diagonal = row
  20          else
   -            north_diagonal = row
   -            south_diagonal = row + 1
   -          end
   -
  25          cell.northwest = self[north_diagonal, col - 1]
   -          cell.north     = self[row - 1, col]
   -          cell.northeast = self[north_diagonal, col + 1]
   -          cell.southwest = self[south_diagonal, col - 1]
   -          cell.south     = self[row + 1, col]
  30          cell.southeast = self[south_diagonal, col + 1]
   -        end
   -      end
   -    end
```

Lines 17–23 set up some variables to help us deal with those zig-zagging rows.
When the column is even-numbered (col.even?), we make it so the northern
diagonals point to the preceding row, whereas the southern diagonals point
to the current row. When the column is odd-numbered, we swap it so the
northern diagonals point to the current row, and the southern ones point to
the following row.

With those variables, lines 25–30 compute the cells that abut the current
cell.

That will suffice to set up our grid, with all the cells appropriately cozy with
their neighbors. All we lack now is a way to display it, since the to_png method
on Grid itself can't handle anything but squares.

Displaying a Hex Grid

To display a hex grid, we need to be able to compute the coordinates of each of its corners, or vertices. We'll see how to compute those coordinates relative to the center of each hexagon, as well as how to compute the overall dimensions of a hex grid, and then we'll plug that all into a new to_png implementation.

We're going to assume that our grid is composed of *regular* hexagons—hexagons whose sides are all the same length. With that assumption, there is a lovely little derivation involving *equilateral* triangles (triangles whose sides are all equal) that lets us get the measurements we need. For the sake of brevity, we'll skip the derivation itself here, but if you're into geometry at all it's pleasantly straightforward.

Essentially, what we want are the lengths of a_1, a_2, and b in the following diagram:

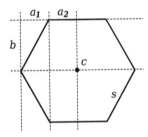

Figure 3—A Dissected Hexagon

If c is the center of our hexagon, and s is the length of a side, then it turns out that a_1 and a_2 are identical. (We'll just keep it simple, then, and call them both a.) We also find that a is half of s, and the length of b is $s\sqrt{3}/2$. From that, it follows that the width of our hexagon (from western point to eastern point) is exactly $2s$, and the height is $2b$. In code:

```
a_size = s / 2.0
b_size = s * Math.sqrt(3) / 2.0
width  = s * 2.0
height = b_size * 2.0
```

With these numbers we can compute the x- and y-coordinates of all six of the hexagon's vertices. If cx and cy represent the coordinates of the center point for some cell, and we call those vertices "far" that are farther from the center and "near" those that are nearer, we get:

```
x_far_west   = cx - s
x_near_west  = cx - a_size
x_near_east  = cx + a_size
x_far_east   = cx + s

y_north      = cy - b_size
y_mid        = cy
y_south      = cy + b_size
```

Now that we have those named coordinates we can say (for instance) that the vertex at the 3 o'clock position is at (x_far_east,y_mid).

The last bit we need before implementing our new drawing code is a way to calculate the dimensions of our canvas. It's not as straightforward as a regular grid, because adjacent cells are offset from each other. In cases like this, it's helpful to take our grid and overlay a regular grid on top of it, like the following figure.

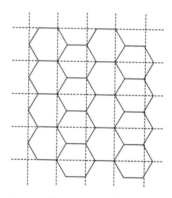

Figure 4—Measuring a Hex Grid

We know how to compute the dimensions of a regular grid, so if we can figure out how wide each cell of the overlay is, we can determine the size of our original grid.

In this case, we've got a 4×4 grid of hexagons. If you recall Figure 3, *A Dissected Hexagon*, on page 117, you can see that each of the rectangles here are three *a* lengths wide, measuring from the western point of one hex to the western point of the next neighbor. Counting the squares, then, this 4×4 canvas as a whole is as wide as four of those squares, plus one more *a* length. In code, it might come together like this:

```
canvas_width = 3 * columns * a_size + a_size
```

The height is much more straightforward. We can easily see that each square is as tall as one hexagon, and that the canvas as a whole is as tall as four of those hexes, plus another half-hex (a single *b* length). In other words:

```
canvas_height = rows * height + b_size
```

Putting this all together, we can finally write our new to_png method! Put the following in hex_grid.rb, somewhere inside the HexGrid class.

```
hex_grid.rb
Line 1  def to_png(size: 10)
   -      a_size = size / 2.0
   -      b_size = size * Math.sqrt(3) / 2.0
   -      width = size * 2
   5      height = b_size * 2

   -      img_width = (3 * a_size * columns + a_size + 0.5).to_i
   -      img_height = (height * rows + b_size + 0.5).to_i

  10      background = ChunkyPNG::Color::WHITE
   -      wall = ChunkyPNG::Color::BLACK

   -      img = ChunkyPNG::Image.new(img_width + 1, img_height + 1, background)

  15      [:backgrounds, :walls].each do |mode|
   -        each_cell do |cell|
   -          cx = size + 3 * cell.column * a_size
   -          cy = b_size + cell.row * height
   -          cy += b_size if cell.column.odd?
  20
   -          # f/n = far/near
   -          # n/s/e/w = north/south/east/west
   -          x_fw = (cx - size).to_i
   -          x_nw = (cx - a_size).to_i
  25          x_ne = (cx + a_size).to_i
   -          x_fe = (cx + size).to_i

   -          # m = middle
   -          y_n = (cy - b_size).to_i
  30          y_m = cy.to_i
   -          y_s = (cy + b_size).to_i

   -          if mode == :backgrounds
   -            color = background_color_for(cell)
  35            if color
   -              points = [[x_fw, y_m], [x_nw, y_n], [x_ne, y_n],
   -                        [x_fe, y_m], [x_ne, y_s], [x_nw, y_s]]
   -              img.polygon(points, color, color)
   -            end
  40          else
```

```
-          img.line(x_fw, y_m, x_nw, y_s, wall) unless cell.southwest
-          img.line(x_fw, y_m, x_nw, y_n, wall) unless cell.northwest
-          img.line(x_nw, y_n, x_ne, y_n, wall) unless cell.north
-          img.line(x_ne, y_n, x_fe, y_m, wall) unless cell.linked?(cell.northeast)
45         img.line(x_fe, y_m, x_ne, y_s, wall) unless cell.linked?(cell.southeast)
-          img.line(x_ne, y_s, x_nw, y_s, wall) unless cell.linked?(cell.south)
-        end
-      end
-    end
50
-    img
-  end
```

The named size parameter on line 1 is what we've called s previously—the size of a single side of the hexagon. The computations that follow (lines 2–5) use that value to determine the dimensions of our hexagons, as discussed.

The next two lines (7 and 8) compute the total width of our canvas. The extra 0.5 makes sure we always round to the nearest whole number.

The three lines starting at 17 compute the center point of the current cell, since that's what our subsequent calculations will be relative to. It all comes back to Figure 4, *Measuring a Hex Grid*, on page 118, except here we're measuring the distance of that current cell from the center of the first cells in its corresponding row and column.

Once we know the center point, we can compute the coordinates of the corners of the current cell, as we talked about earlier. Lines 23–31 take care of that.

The remaining lines work identically to our original to_png method, drawing the appropriate walls for each cell based on which neighbors exist and have been linked to the current cell.

That's it! With our new to_png, we ought to be able to draw hex grids and—by extension—mazes. Let's do that next!

Making Hexagon (Sigma) Mazes

A maze made on a hex grid is, for some perverse reason, properly called a *sigma maze*. Fortunately, it works the same regardless of what you call it: just choose a maze algorithm and let it run its course. Let's use the Recursive Backtracker algorithm to put our new to_png implementation through its paces. Put the following in a file named hex_maze.rb.

```
hex_maze.rb
require 'recursive_backtracker'
require 'hex_grid'

grid = HexGrid.new(10, 10)
RecursiveBacktracker.on(grid)

grid.to_png.save('hex.png')
```

Running it, you ought to get something like this figure. Very nice! It's
definitely working as we wanted.
Experiment a bit with some other
maze algorithms and see what you get,
but be careful with Binary Tree and
Sidewinder! These two need a bit of
babysitting.

To understand why, recall *The Binary Tree Algorithm*, on page 6. For each
cell, we choose between north and east to decide which neighbor to link, but
in the case of a hexagon grid, *cells have no eastern neighbor.* The best we have
are northeast, and southeast. Similarly, Sidewinder wants to choose an
eastern neighbor but will also be foiled by our new geometry. So what do we
do?

Well, neither of those algorithms actually wants "east." What they really want
is "the cell in the same row, in the next column over." On a regular grid, that
just happens to be *east*. For a hex grid, that will be either northeast or
southeast, depending on the current column, but we don't even need to worry
about that. We took care of the row/column assignments when we set up the
grid. To get the neighbor in the next column over, we can just use our array
accessor, like this:

```
east = grid[cell.row, cell.column+1]
```

Give it a try! Implement the Binary Tree and Sidewinder algorithms on a hex
grid, and see what you get. When you're ready, we'll move on to another style
of grid: triangles!

Implementing a Triangle Grid

A grid of triangles has a very lattice-like look the following.

As with the hexagons, there are going to be lots of ways to implement a grid like this, and each will have different strengths and weaknesses. For simplicity's sake, we'll look at one that most closely approximates the regular grid, with horizontal rows and vertical columns. We'll use equilateral triangles (mostly because it makes the math easier), 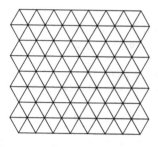 and we'll start with an examination of the cells and how they fit together. We'll see there's a pattern behind how the cell is oriented on the grid, which we'll then implement in code.

Looking at the preceding grid, you can see that some of the triangles are *upright* (point facing north) and some are *upside-down* (point facing south). In fact, this pattern repeats with every other triangle as you move across a row horizontally. Further, each row starts with a triangle in alternating orientations.

In other words, a triangle will be upright if its (base-0) row and column sum to an even number:

```
upright = (row + column).even?
```

This property is significant because an upright triangle has no northern neighbor and an upside-down triangle has no southern neighbor. If we can indicate which triangles in our grid are upright, we can then use that information when we set up the adjacency information.

Our TriangleCell winds up being pretty straightforward:

triangle_cell.rb
```
require 'cell'

class TriangleCell < Cell
  def upright?
    (row + column).even?
  end

  def neighbors
    list = []
    list << west if west
    list << east if east
    list << north if !upright? && north
    list << south if upright? && south
    list
  end
end
```

We have a method, upright?, which simply tells us whether the given cell ought to be upright or upside-down, based on the row and column. The neighbors method then gives us our usual east and west neighbors and uses upright? to decide whether the cell has a north or a south neighbor.

Let's see how this plugs into a grid. The following implementation ends up looking much like that of our hexagon grid, with overridden prepare_grid and configure_cells methods.

Put the following in triangle_grid.rb.

```
triangle_grid.rb
Line 1  require 'grid'
   -    require 'triangle_cell'
   -
   -    class TriangleGrid < Grid
   5      def prepare_grid
   -        Array.new(rows) do |row|
   -          Array.new(columns) do |column|
   -            TriangleCell.new(row, column)
   -          end
   10       end
   -      end
   -
   -      def configure_cells
   -        each_cell do |cell|
   15         row, col = cell.row, cell.column
   -
   -          cell.west = self[row, col - 1]
   -          cell.east = self[row, col + 1]
   -
   20         if cell.upright?
   -            cell.south = self[row + 1, col]
   -          else
   -            cell.north = self[row - 1, col]
   -          end
   25       end
   -      end
   -    end
```

The only part really worth pointing out here is where the north or south neighbor is configured, on lines 20–24. As we said before, if the cell is upright, then it has a southern neighbor, otherwise a northern one.

Easy enough. All that's left is for us to implement a new to_png method so we can show off our snazzy triangles.

Displaying a Triangle Grid

Displaying a grid of equilateral triangles turns out to be really straightforward. If you previously worked through the derivation of the measurements for the hexagons, then you've already worked through most of what we need for the triangles, too. Again, we won't go over the derivation itself here, but we'll walk through the resulting measurements, and then we'll implement it all in code.

Because we're working with equilateral triangles, we know that each of their sides are the same length (s). Further, geometry tells us that the height of an equilateral triangle is $s\sqrt{3}/2$. Our triangle's dimensions, then, are:

```
width = s
half_width = width / 2.0

height = s * Math.sqrt(3) / 2
half_height = height / 2.0
```

We'll let our center point be at a point halfway between the apex and the base, and halfway between the east and west vertices. If we base our coordinates on that point, then our vertices can be defined relative to it using the computed width and height values:

```
west_x = cx - half_width
mid_x  = cx
east_x = cx + half_width

if upright?
  base_y = cy + half_height
  apex_y = cy - half_height
else
  base_y = cy - half_height
  apex_y = cy + half_height
end
```

In other words, the x-coordinates are the same, regardless of whether or not the triangle is upright. The only things that change based on our triangle's orientation are the y-coordinates. If the triangle is upright, our base is below the center point; otherwise, it's above it.

Let's code this up! Put the following in triangle_grid.rb with the other methods.

```
Line 1  def to_png(size: 16)
   -      half_width = size / 2.0
   -      height = size * Math.sqrt(3) / 2.0
   -      half_height = height / 2.0
   5
   -      img_width = (size * (columns + 1) / 2.0).to_i
   -      img_height = (height * rows).to_i
```

```
   -
   -    background = ChunkyPNG::Color::WHITE
10      wall = ChunkyPNG::Color::BLACK
   -
   -    img = ChunkyPNG::Image.new(img_width + 1, img_height + 1, background)
   -
   -    [:backgrounds, :walls].each do |mode|
15        each_cell do |cell|
   -        cx = half_width + cell.column * half_width
   -        cy = half_height + cell.row * height
   -
   -        west_x = (cx - half_width).to_i
20        mid_x = cx.to_i
   -        east_x = (cx + half_width).to_i
   -
   -        if cell.upright?
   -          apex_y = (cy - half_height).to_i
25          base_y = (cy + half_height).to_i
   -        else
   -          apex_y = (cy + half_height).to_i
   -          base_y = (cy - half_height).to_i
   -        end
30
   -        if mode == :backgrounds
   -          color = background_color_for(cell)
   -          if color
   -            points = [[west_x, base_y], [mid_x, apex_y], [east_x, base_y]]
35            img.polygon(points, color, color)
   -          end
   -        else
   -          unless cell.west
   -            img.line(west_x, base_y, mid_x, apex_y, wall)
40          end
   -
   -          unless cell.linked?(cell.east)
   -            img.line(east_x, base_y, mid_x, apex_y, wall)
   -          end
45
   -          no_south = cell.upright? && cell.south.nil?
   -          not_linked = !cell.upright? && !cell.linked?(cell.north)
   -
   -          if no_south || not_linked
50            img.line(east_x, base_y, west_x, base_y, wall)
   -          end
   -        end
   -      end
   -    end
55
   -    img
  -  end
```

We use the size parameter, again, to describe the length of a single side of a triangle (line 1). Lines 2–4 then take that size value and use it to compute our triangles' dimensions.

Knowing the size of each triangle allows us to measure the size of our canvas (lines 6 and 7).

Lines 16–29 ought to look familiar—they compute the coordinates of the current triangle using the formula we described previously.

Next, let's see if this all works like we want it to.

Making Triangle (Delta) Mazes

Just as hexagon grids produce sigma mazes, so triangle grids produce *delta mazes*. (This one at least makes a little sense, since the Greek letter delta, Δ, is shaped like a triangle.) Again, though, it makes little difference what you call it, because in the end it's just another scaffolding for making mazes!

Let's copy our hex_maze.rb file to delta_maze.rb and change it to refer to our new triangle grid:

delta_maze.rb
```
  require 'recursive_backtracker'
➤ require 'triangle_grid'

➤ grid = TriangleGrid.new(10, 17)
  RecursiveBacktracker.on(grid)

➤ grid.to_png.save('delta.png')
```

The dimensions for the grid were empirically chosen to produce a roughly square canvas. Aside from that, it's just the same old deal—instantiating a grid, running a Recursive Backtracker on it, and displaying the result:

Very nice! Once again, though, you'll want to beware of Binary Tree and Sidewinder. In fact, Binary Tree in particular has real issues with these triangle grids, because it wants to choose between two perpendicular directions...but our triangle grid can only go north 50% of the time. If you aren't very careful, you'll wind up with unreachable areas of the grid. Experiment with it, if you'd like, to see what happens.

Your Turn

We've moved far beyond our early maze-making days of purely rectangular grids. In this chapter we've seen how hexagons and triangles can be tiled to create suitable settings for mazes, and we've glimpsed some of the math behind drawing these more advanced grids.

This is just the tip of the iceberg, though! There are so many ways to use and vary what was presented here. The following are just a few ideas to help you glimpse some of the possibilities when dealing with non-rectangular grids.

Coloring Non-Rectangular Mazes

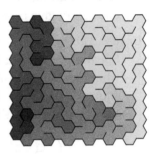

Coloring mazes always seems to add a lot of personality to them, and those done on non-rectangular grids are no exception. The to_png methods given in this chapter include the necessary code for coloring individual cells. See if you can hook up the background_color_for methods to specify the appropriate colors.

Masking

Revisit the techniques from Chapter 6, *Fitting Mazes to Shapes*, on page 83 and see what it might take to add masks to these different grids. How do you define a hexagonal mask? Or a triangular mask?

Shaping Grids

What would it take to make your triangle grid actually *triangle-shaped*? What about a hexagon-shaped hex grid?

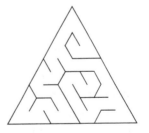

Irregular Triangles

For simplicity's sake, we used equilateral triangles for our triangle grid in this chapter. What kinds of effects would you get if you changed that assumption? It'll require a bit of math to derive the measurements, but if you're up to the challenge, see what you can do with other kinds of triangles.

Combining Grid Systems

There's absolutely no law that says grids must be homogeneous. Imagine a star-shaped grid, composed of a square-shaped regular grid in the center with triangular grids on each of its edges. Try putting different shapes together and see what happens.

Uniform Tilings and Beyond

Squares, triangles, and hexagons all tile quite neatly, but they're hardly the only shapes that do. Try researching *uniform tilings*, or *Wythoff's construction*, or even *Voronoi diagrams*, and you'll see there's an entire world of other possible grids to play with. You'll discover words like *truncated quadrille* and *rhombitrihexagonal*, which might almost be reason enough to give them a try.

Upsilon Mazes

Speaking of *truncated quadrille*, this particular tiling can be used to create what are called *upsilon mazes*. You create a tiling of regular octagons and squares, and then generate a maze on it with your choice of algorithm. You wind up with something like the following:

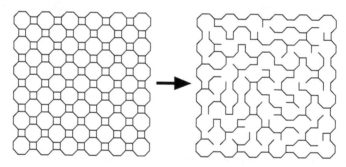

How might you approach implementing and displaying such a grid?

Next up, we're going to see what happens when we (finally!) remove the constraint that our mazes must be "perfect," or without loops. We'll also start to touch on the idea of multidimensional mazes with a kind of pseudo-3D effect that turns out to be pretty straightforward to do.

CHAPTER 9

Braiding and Weaving Your Mazes

So far, we've assumed that all of our mazes are *perfect*—that is, they have no loops in them. We've said that to get from one point in a maze to any other point there must be only a single path that is never allowed to intersect itself.

The sad fact is that most real environments are not actually perfect mazes. Whether you're navigating the stacks of a library or the streets of a town, you can generally get from one place to another via multiple possible routes. This is mirrored in video games: in Pac-Man, for instance, you can take one path into an area and return by another, cleverly escaping those ghosts on your tail. Dungeon crawlers (NetHack) and "open world" games (Zelda, Final Fantasy) give you quite a bit of freedom to move between areas using various paths. First-person shooters like Doom, Quake, and Descent use mazes with loops to enable all kinds of great tactical scenarios. From a game design perspective, allowing paths to intersect themselves can open up exciting new ways for a game to be played.

So it's time to shake things up a bit. We're going to look at two different ways to relax that "no self-intersections" rule: *braiding* by removing dead ends and thus adding loops to our mazes, and *weaving*, which allows passages to intersect by moving over and under each other.

Let's start with braiding.

Braiding Mazes

A maze with no dead ends is called a *braid maze.*

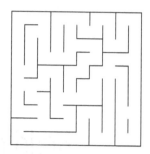

There's no reason this has to be all-or-nothing, though. Mazes may be heavily braided (with all or most dead ends removed), or lightly braided (with only a few dead ends removed), or anything in-between. The process we'll consider here, called *dead-end culling*, will let us produce a maze with any level of braiding we desire.

Recall back in *Counting Dead Ends*, on page 71, we added a method to Grid called, appropriately, deadends. We made it return a list of all the dead-end cells in the grid, and used it to compare maze algorithms based on how many dead ends they generated.

It turns out that we can use that same method here. Once it tells us where the dead ends are, the process for *culling*, or removing, them is straightforward: we just need to link each dead-end cell to one additional neighbor. This effectively erases one of its walls and adds a loop to the maze. Following that logic, it also means that a braid maze is not a perfect maze—it will always have at least one loop in it.

Let's implement this. Thanks to our deadends method, we're about halfway there already. All that's left is to loop over the cells it returns and link each one to a random neighbor. We'll make this the responsibility of a new method on Grid, so go ahead and open up grid.rb and add the following method to that class.

```
Line 1  def braid(p=1.0)
   -      deadends.shuffle.each do |cell|
   -        next if cell.links.count != 1 || rand > p
   -
   5        neighbors = cell.neighbors.reject { |n| cell.linked?(n) }
   -        best = neighbors.select { |n| n.links.count == 1 }
   -        best = neighbors if best.empty?
   -
   -        neighbor = best.sample
  10        cell.link(neighbor)
   -      end
   -   end
```

It's refreshingly direct after all that math from the previous chapter! Line 2 starts us out by fetching the list of dead ends, giving it a good shuffle, and then looping over the result. For each of the cells, we first test (on line 3) to see that it's still a dead end (as an earlier iteration of the loop may have already linked it to a neighboring dead end). We also allow for partial braid mazes by generating a random number between 0 and 1 (using the standard rand method) and comparing it with the p parameter. By default, p is 1.0, ensuring that all dead ends will be culled, but by making the number smaller (say, 0.5), fewer will be removed.

Assuming the cell is found acceptable, line 5 finds all of the neighbors to whom it is *not* linked. These form the set of potential cells that we will link to.

The next line, line 6, is a bit of an optimization. We can kill two birds with one stone and improve the aesthetics of the maze a bit by preferring to link two dead-end cells together. This line examines the set of potential neighbor cells and selects out those that are themselves dead ends. If possible, we'll choose from this set, but if that set is empty, we'll just fall back to the set of all neighbors again (line 7).

Once we've finalized our set of possible neighbors, all that's left is to choose one (line 9) and link it to the current cell.

Now it's easy to test. Choose any of the maze programs we've written so far, and add the following line just after running the maze algorithm (and before displaying the maze):

```
grid.braid(0.5)
```

That will cull roughly half the dead ends from the maze before displaying it. Assuming we add this to the program we wrote for the Recursive Backtracker (in recursive_backtracker_demo.rb), we should get something like this figure.

Just like that. Braided! And what's more, our existing implementation of Dijkstra's algorithm (from Chapter 3, *Finding Solutions*, on page 35) still works, too.

Let's give it a try. If we open up dijkstra.rb or longest_path.rb (from *Finding Solutions*) and add grid.braid in there, just after the maze is generated, we should find that the distances are all still computed correctly. The dijkstra.rb program, for example, will still show us the full distance matrix, as expected.

It just works! You can see how Dijkstra's picks out the shortest of all possible paths to each cell, like water flowing around obstacles. Our path_to method on Distances (again from *Finding Solutions*) also "just works," using the distance matrix from Dijkstra's algorithm to find the shortest path to a given cell, even successfully choosing between multiple shortest paths! Braided or not, we can still tell our friends the answers to these mazes.

```
$ ruby -I. dijkstra.rb
+---+---+---+---+---+
| 0   1 | a   b   a |
+   +   +   +---+   +
| 1 | 2 | 9   8   9 |
+   +   +---+   +   +
| 2 | 3   4 | 7 | a |
+   +---+   +   +   +
| 3   4   5   6 | 9 |
+   +---+---+   +   +
| 4   5   6   7   8 |
+---+---+---+---+---+
```

There is one particular possibility allowed by braid mazes, though, which sadly also happens to wreak havoc with our simplified Dijkstra's algorithm. When you start to ask about the relative *cost* of one path versus another, instead of just the distance, things get a little more complicated. Let's take a look at that next.

Cost versus Distance

Imagine traversing a maze, and you come to a branch in the passage. Both paths loop around and meet up again a short distance later, but the passage to the left is blocked by a pool of molten lava. The passage to the right has no lava but is much longer than the other. Which path will get you to the exit faster?

Well, it depends, of course. But for normal people with no special lava resistance, taking the path without the lava is probably going to be optimal, even though it's longer. The path with the lava, though shorter, is *more expensive*.

Costs like these are called *weights*. Distance itself is a form of weight, because if all other things are equal, a longer path will be more expensive than a shorter path. Our current implementation of Dijkstra's algorithm assumes that all cells are weighted equally, which means that the only cost being measured is distance. It'd sure be nice to be able to add lava obstacles to our braid mazes, though, so let's see what we can do to fix that.

Looking closer at our implementation of Dijkstra's algorithm, it falls down when weights are introduced because distance is no longer a reliable indicator of cost. Consider our lava example again. Our simplified Dijkstra's implementation would merrily go skipping step-by-step down both paths, adding costs along the way. The problem is that the algorithm would reach the exit via the shorter (but more expensive) passage first, and would mark its cost accordingly.

We need to approach this from an entirely different direction. Instead of working with a *frontier set*, simulating the front of a wave as it moves through the grid, each iteration of the algorithm needs to pick the cell with the lowest cost that has not yet been processed. Let's consider this visually with our lava example. When we first start, we mark our starting cell as having cost 0, and add it to a queue. Everything else is undefined.

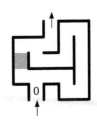

Thus, when the algorithm begins its main loop, it only has the one cell to choose from. It plucks it out of that queue, computes the cost of its only neighbor, and adds that neighbor to the queue.

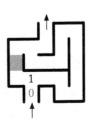

The next time around, there's still only a single cell in our queue—the one we just added. The algorithm plucks that out of the queue and computes the cost of each of its neighbors. Both neighbors go into the queue, poised and ready for the next iteration.

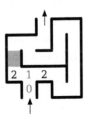

This time, the algorithm has to choose between the two cells marked 2. Either would be fine, but let's say it chooses the cell adjacent to the lava. Fine: that cell gets plucked out of the queue, the cost of its neighbor is computed, and the neighbor is added to the queue. But hot lava is hot, and crossing that gulf will be expensive. Let's say it adds fifty to the cost of that path.

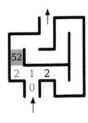

Next time around, the queue consists of one cell marked 2, and one marked 52. It's clear which cell has the lowest cost! The algorithm picks up the one marked 2, removes it from the queue, computes the cost of its neighbor (3 now), and adds that neighbor to the queue.

The lava cell is not going to be picked up by the algorithm anytime soon—that high cost is enough to scare away even the pluckiest adventurer. Eventually, the algorithm will find that the least expensive route truly is to bypass the lava entirely, even though the path is much longer.

At the very end, the only cell left in the queue will be that lava cell, and the algorithm will eventually choose it. By that time, though, all of the cells neighboring the lava will already have been processed, and all will have a lower cost than what the lava would have produced, so the cell is discarded without being used. After that, the queue is empty, and the algorithm terminates.

Let's look at it in code, and tease a few mazes with some lava pits of our own.

Implementing a Cost-Aware Dikstra's Algorithm

To make this work in code, we need two things: a cell that can be assigned a weight, and a grid composed of these weighted cells.

The cell is straightforward. We're just going to subclass Cell and add weight information to it. Also, since our Dijkstra's algorithm was implemented on Cell, we put our updated implementation in the subclass, too, by overriding the original distances method.

Put the following in weighted_cell.rb.

weighted_cell.rb

```
Line 1   require 'cell'
   -
   -     class WeightedCell < Cell
   -       attr_accessor :weight
   5
   -       def initialize(row, column)
   -         super(row, column)
   -         @weight = 1
   -       end
  10
   -       def distances
   -         weights = Distances.new(self)
   -         pending = [ self ]
   -
  15         while pending.any?
   -           cell = pending.sort_by { |c| weights[c] }.first
   -           pending.delete(cell)
   -
   -           cell.links.each do |neighbor|
  20             total_weight = weights[cell] + neighbor.weight
```

```
          if !weights[neighbor] || total_weight < weights[neighbor]
            pending << neighbor
            weights[neighbor] = total_weight
          end
25      end
      end


      weights
    end
30  end
```

Our constructor just extends the previous one by setting the default cell weight to 1. It's the new distances method, though, that is of particular interest here.

As before, we use our Distances class to track the cost of each cell, but instead of having a frontier set, we now have a pending set, which tracks which cells have yet to be processed. We initialize that on line 13 to be an array containing just self—the cell that we're asking to compute the distances. We then repeat the following steps until that array is empty (line 15).

Each pass through the loop will search that pending set, looking for the cell with the lowest cost (line 16), and then removing the cell that it finds. This cell is our *current cell.*

Priority Queues

We're using an array here for simplicity's sake, but it's not a very efficient way of doing things. We have to search that array on every iteration, which can get expensive. A much better way to do it uses a *priority queue*, which gives you a very efficient way to look up and store items by weight. It's a lovely data structure, but sadly out of scope for this book.

The next loop (line 19) looks at each of the cells that are linked to the current cell. For each one, we compute the cumulative weight of the path from the starting cell (line 20), and then check to see if that's better than any previously recorded weight for that neighbor (line 21). If so, we add the neighbor to the pending list, and update its cumulative weight.

We'll plug this new cell into a new Grid subclass, which we'll deck out with a way to actually display these weights, as well as to display the distances we're computing. For that, we'll turn to our background_color_for(cell) method.

Put the following in weighted_grid.rb. It's going to borrow bits from our colored_grid.rb implementation, from Chapter 3, *Finding Solutions*, on page 35, so don't be surprised if some of it is already a little familiar.

```
weighted_grid.rb
Line 1  require 'chunky_png'
   -    require 'grid'
   -    require 'weighted_cell'
   -
   5    class WeightedGrid < Grid
   -      attr_reader :distances
   -
   -      def distances=(distances)
   -        @distances = distances
  10        farthest, @maximum = distances.max
   -      end
   -
   -      def prepare_grid
   -        Array.new(rows) do |row|
  15          Array.new(columns) do |column|
   -            WeightedCell.new(row, column)
   -          end
   -        end
   -      end
  20
   -      def background_color_for(cell)
   -        if cell.weight > 1
   -          ChunkyPNG::Color.rgb(255, 0, 0)
   -        elsif @distances
  25          distance = @distances[cell] or return nil
   -          intensity = 64 + 191 * (@maximum - distance) / @maximum
   -          ChunkyPNG::Color.rgb(intensity, intensity, 0)
   -        end
   -      end
  30    end
```

The distances= method is used to tell the grid about the active distance matrix, to be used when coloring the grid, and prepare_grid is almost identical to the original in Grid, just instantiating our WeightedCell class for each cell (line 16).

The background_color_for(cell) method takes on a little more responsibility than we've given it in the past. We're going to have it color red any cell with a weight greater than one (line 23). This will let us see, visually, where those weighted cells are. For any cell that isn't weighted specially, we'll have it fall back to choosing a color based on the distances map, if one has been set. We'll color those distances a shade of yellow (line 27).

That's it! Now we can put together a simple program to test what we've got. Let's have it generate a maze on one of these weighted grids, and display the least expensive path from the northwest corner to the southeast corner. Then, we'll add a lava pit (that is, a heavily weighted cell) somewhere along that path, and recompute the least expensive path. Hopefully, we'll see the program route us around that gaping pit of superheated magma!

Put the following in weighted_maze.rb.

```
weighted_maze.rb
Line 1  require 'weighted_grid'
   -    require 'recursive_backtracker'
   -
   -    grid = WeightedGrid.new(10, 10)
   5    RecursiveBacktracker.on(grid)
   -
   -    grid.braid 0.5
   -    start, finish = grid[0, 0], grid[grid.rows - 1, grid.columns - 1]
   -
   10   grid.distances = start.distances.path_to(finish)
   -    filename = "original.png"
   -    grid.to_png.save(filename)
   -    puts "saved to #{filename}"
   -
   15   lava = grid.distances.cells.sample
   -    lava.weight = 50
   -
   -    grid.distances = start.distances.path_to(finish)
   -    filename = "rerouted.png"
   20   grid.to_png.save(filename)
   -    puts "saved to #{filename}"
```

The first half of the program just instantiates our WeightedGrid and performs a Recursive Backtracker on it. Line 7 removes half of the dead ends, and then lines 10–13 compute and display the shortest path between our start and finish cells, drawing the resulting maze to original.png.

Then we go all diabolical and drop some lava on it. The grid.distances property at that point already contains a map of all of the cells in the shortest (least expensive) path, so lines 15–16 choose one of those cells and set its weight to 50. (Lava is hot, remember. It's got to be worth *at least* that much.)

We finish the program off by recomputing the shortest path and writing the resulting maze to rerouted.png (lines 18–21).

Running it should generate those two images, original.png and rerouted.png, which we can then open and compare. Note, though, that because the program is blindly choosing any cell in the path, it may occasionally choose a cell (like the starting point, or the goal) that Dijkstra's algorithm cannot route around. If that happens, just run it again until it actually chooses an interesting cell to place the lava on, something like this:

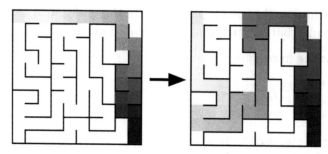

These weighted grids have potential. Aside from pits of boiling lava, you might use doors (locked and otherwise), rockfalls, piranha-filled waters, and any number of other things to change the cost of individual paths. A discussion of how best to place them randomly is beyond the scope of this book, sadly, but it's an exciting thing to experiment with!

Time's a-wasting, though. We've looked at braiding mazes, changing the assumptions we had about perfect mazes not having loops. Next, we'll look at another way to change those assumptions and allow passages to intersect by moving over or under each other.

Introducing Weaves and Insets

A *weave maze* is a maze in which passages weave over and under one another, like noodles in a bowl of spaghetti.

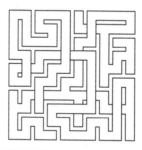

Figure 5—A Weave Maze

We can't really draw these with our existing to_png method, because our existing method does not draw any space between adjacent corridors. Without that space, there is too much ambiguity—we can't tell if a passage has dead-ended, or gone underneath another passage. The following figure shows the same maze as the previous figure, but without any gaps between corridors.

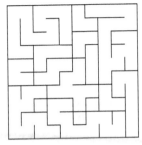

Messy! And even worse, it's not very accurate. Our existing to_png implementation only draws the east and south walls for each cell, blithely assuming that neighbors will make up the slack on the other walls. This doesn't fly with these over/under mazes. Something's got to change.

Our first order of business, then, is to level-up our to_png method in order to support gaps between corridors. Fortunately, it's not hard—it just requires a bit of extra measuring. We need to figure out how far each wall is *inset* from the original edge of the cell. Once we have this new way to draw mazes, we can look at what it takes to make the passages weave over and under one another.

Let's look at a single cell on our grid drawn using these insets. From this diagram we'll be able to infer the measurements we need in order to draw our mazes this way.

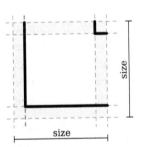

Here, the cell is linked to its neighbors to the north and east, with corresponding passages in those directions. The insets are highlighted in yellow, and the dashed lines break the cell into nine distinct regions. We're not going to worry about the four regions at the corners—those will always be dead space when we render cells this way. For the sake of discussion, let's label the remaining regions like this:

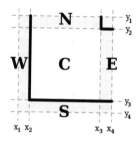

Every wall we want to draw will be on those dashed lines (x_1–x_4 and y_1–y_4), so to draw them we'll need the lines' coordinates. If the cell is size units on a side, and the northwest corner is at (x,y), and we use inset to describe the size of our gap, then the coordinates we want are

```
x1 = x
x4 = x + size
x2 = x1 + inset
x3 = x4 - inset

y1 = y
y4 = y + size
y2 = y1 + inset
y3 = y4 - inset
```

Referring to the previous diagram, we can now say (for example) that the southwest corner of C is at (x2,y3).

Let's work this up in code next. We'll keep as much of our existing to_png implementation as we can, but we'll break the core of it out into a separate method, one that will be used specifically when the inset is not specified (or zero). Then we'll add another method to compute the inset coordinates, and a third method which to_png will delegate to when an inset *has* been specified.

Open up grid.rb, and change to_png to look like the following. The highlighted lines are the ones in particular that we're changing.

```
➤ def to_png(cell_size: 10, inset: 0)
    img_width = cell_size * columns
    img_height = cell_size * rows
➤   inset = (cell_size * inset).to_i

    background = ChunkyPNG::Color::WHITE
    wall = ChunkyPNG::Color::BLACK

    img = ChunkyPNG::Image.new(img_width + 1, img_height + 1, background)

    [:backgrounds, :walls].each do |mode|
      each_cell do |cell|
```

```
➤          x = cell.column * cell_size
➤          y = cell.row * cell_size
➤
➤          if inset > 0
➤            to_png_with_inset(img, cell, mode, cell_size, wall, x, y, inset)
➤          else
➤            to_png_without_inset(img, cell, mode, cell_size, wall, x, y)
➤          end
        end
      end

      img
    end
```

On the first highlighted line, we're computing the size of the inset based on an option that is passed in. If no inset is specified, it defaults to zero, but otherwise it is interpreted as the fraction of the total size of the cell that should be given to each inset. For example, if an inset of 0.25 is given, that would cause each inset to occupy a quarter of the cell's margin, leaving half of the cell's width and height for the cell itself.

The other major change here has to do with how each cell is processed. In the second highlighted area we check to see if the computed inset is greater than zero, and if so we delegate to a new to_png_with_inset method (which will be defined shortly). Otherwise, flow falls through to the next line which invokes to_png_without_inset. Let's look at that one next; it should be added to Grid as well, below our new to_png method.

```
def to_png_without_inset(img, cell, mode, cell_size, wall, x, y)
  x1, y1 = x, y
  x2 = x1 + cell_size
  y2 = y1 + cell_size

  if mode == :backgrounds
    color = background_color_for(cell)
    img.rect(x, y, x2, y2, color, color) if color
  else
    img.line(x1, y1, x2, y1, wall) unless cell.north
    img.line(x1, y1, x1, y2, wall) unless cell.west
    img.line(x2, y1, x2, y2, wall) unless cell.linked?(cell.east)
    img.line(x1, y2, x2, y2, wall) unless cell.linked?(cell.south)
  end
end
```

This ought to be quite familiar—it's almost verbatim what was originally within the each_cell block from our old to_png method. It just computes the northwest and southeast corners of the cell and draws the corresponding walls.

Next, we'll implement our formulas from the previous section to find the x- and y-coordinates of those dashed horizontal and vertical lines.

```
Line 1  def cell_coordinates_with_inset(x, y, cell_size, inset)
   -       x1, x4 = x, x + cell_size
   -       x2 = x1 + inset
   -       x3 = x4 - inset
   5
   -       y1, y4 = y, y + cell_size
   -       y2 = y1 + inset
   -       y3 = y4 - inset
   -
   10      [x1, x2, x3, x4,
   -         y1, y2, y3, y4]
   -     end
```

We could certainly have inlined this code in the following method (to_png_with_inset), but making it a separate method turns out to be useful when we need to draw weave mazes later in the chapter.

Our last method is the bit that will consume those inset coordinates and draw the walls.

```
Line 1  def to_png_with_inset(img, cell, mode, cell_size, wall, x, y, inset)
   -       x1, x2, x3, x4, y1, y2, y3, y4 =
   -         cell_coordinates_with_inset(x, y, cell_size, inset)
   -
   5       if mode == :backgrounds
   -         # ...
   -       else
   -         if cell.linked?(cell.north)
   -           img.line(x2, y1, x2, y2, wall)
   10          img.line(x3, y1, x3, y2, wall)
   -         else
   -           img.line(x2, y2, x3, y2, wall)
   -         end
   -
   15        if cell.linked?(cell.south)
   -           img.line(x2, y3, x2, y4, wall)
   -           img.line(x3, y3, x3, y4, wall)
   -         else
   -           img.line(x2, y3, x3, y3, wall)
   20        end
   -
   -         if cell.linked?(cell.west)
   -           img.line(x1, y2, x2, y2, wall)
   -           img.line(x1, y3, x2, y3, wall)
   25        else
   -           img.line(x2, y2, x2, y3, wall)
   -         end
```

```
    if cell.linked?(cell.east)
30    img.line(x3, y2, x4, y2, wall)
      img.line(x3, y3, x4, y3, wall)
    else
      img.line(x3, y2, x3, y3, wall)
    end
35  end
  end
```

Line 3 calls our cell_coords_with_inset method to get those eight coordinates. Once armed with those, we can get to work drawing the appropriate walls of the current cell.

Implementing Background Mode

For brevity's sake, I've not included the implementation of background mode for to_png_with_inset. It's not difficult, though: essentially, it requires that you fill a rectangle for each of the labeled regions from those previous figures (N, S, E, W, and C), depending on which ones need to be drawn. Consider it an opportunity, if you like!

Drawing the walls occurs on lines 8–34. For each potential neighbor, we check to see if the neighbor has been linked, and if so, draw a corridor in that direction. Otherwise, we draw a wall.

With those changes, we ought to be able to draw a maze with gaps between the walls. Choose any of the programs we've written so far (like recursive_backtracker_demo.rb or aldous_broder_demo.rb), and change the invocation of the to_png method to include the inset specification, something like this:

```
grid.to_png(inset: 0.1).save("filename.png")
```

That will cause each gap to occupy a tenth of each cell's width and height. Assuming we change the recursive_backtracker_demo.rb program like that, the output ought to look something like this:

We're on the right track! That's good enough—now let's get back to talking about weave mazes.

Generating Weave Mazes

It turns out that generating weave mazes isn't all that different from generating normal mazes. The trick is figuring out how to represent those passages that tunnel underneath the others. Once we've got those ironed out, we'll work on a new Grid subclass with some more to_png tweaks, so we can draw these new tunneling passages.

To get an idea of how these new passages work, let's take a minute and glance back at Figure 5, *A Weave Maze*, on page 138. Pay attention to how and when the passages weave over and under each other. It's not entirely arbitrary—there are four important rules that make this work unambiguously.

A passage cannot dead-end over or under another passage.

This prevents confusion that could happen when a passage seems to disappear beneath another one.

Over- and under-passages must be perpendicular to each other.

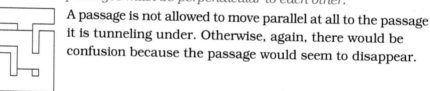

A passage is not allowed to move parallel at all to the passage it is tunneling under. Otherwise, again, there would be confusion because the passage would seem to disappear.

Passages may not change direction while above or below other passages.

A corridor can't tunnel under a cell moving north, and then exit the cell moving east. This is related to the previous rule—over/under passages must be perfectly perpendicular.

A passage may not tunnel under two consecutive passages at once.

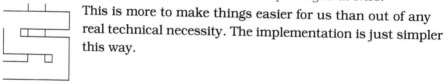

This is more to make things easier for us than out of any real technical necessity. The implementation is just simpler this way.

Rather than scrapping all that lovely code we've written so far, it would be nice if we could make this work by extending our existing grid framework.

Even better, it would be wonderful if we could just drop a new grid subclass into (for instance) our Recursive Backtracker program and have it generate weave mazes without further tweaking.

We'll approach it like this. Let's imagine that when a passage moves under another passage, it's actually moving to an invisible cell at that same location, *beneath* the other cell, like this:

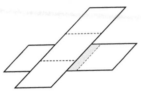

For the sake of discussion, we'll call these phantom cells *under-cells*, and the cells above them *over-cells*. If we can make our grid transparently manage these under-cells, without exposing anything about them to the outside, most of the maze algorithms we've seen so far should just work, no further changes necessary. The thing is, relatively few of these under-cells will ever actually be used in the maze, and there are some strict rules that determine which over-cells can host under-cells. For these reasons, it turns out to be simplest to just create them on-demand, when certain conditions are met. These conditions apply when deciding which neighbors exist for a given cell (either over-cell or under-cell), and are as follows:

- An under-cell cannot be placed beneath another under-cell. (If we start nesting them like that the maze gets really hard to draw clearly, and at that point we might as well be making actual 3D mazes. We'll get to those in Chapter 13, *Extending Mazes into Higher Dimensions*, on page 209.)

- When considering the neighbors to the east and west, check to see if either of those over-cells are already a *vertical passage*, that is, a passage running purely north to south. If so, we can potentially create an under-cell beneath it and tunnel one cell further in that direction.

- Similarly, when considering the neighbors to the north and south, check to see if either of them is already a *horizontal passage*, running east to west. If so, we can possibly create an under-cell there in order to tunnel that direction.

- In either case, we can only tunnel under the cell if there is actually another cell on the other side of it. Tunneling should never take us out of bounds. (We're not reenacting *The Great Escape* here!)

We'll make this real by subclassing Cell. Eventually we'll have two different cell types (one for the over-cells, and one for the under-cells), but we'll begin with the over-cells. Let's start by overriding the neighbors method to include the preceding logic.

Implementing the OverCell Class

The following is a start on our new OverCell class. Let's put it in weave_cells.rb.

```
Line 1    require 'cell'

       -  class OverCell < Cell
       -    def neighbors
       5      list = super
       -      list << north.north if can_tunnel_north?
       -      list << south.south if can_tunnel_south?
       -      list << east.east   if can_tunnel_east?
       -      list << west.west   if can_tunnel_west?
      10
       -      list
       -    end
       -  end
```

Calling super on line 5 gets us the default set of neighbors, as computed by our original Cell class. We then append to that list, adding potential targets to tunnel to. For example, on line 6 we add the northern neighbor of this cell's northern neighbor, as long as it is possible to tunnel north.

Those helper methods (can_tunnel_north? and friends) need defining next. Add these after our new neighbors method.

```
def can_tunnel_north?
  north && north.north &&
    north.horizontal_passage?
end

def can_tunnel_south?
  south && south.south &&
    south.horizontal_passage?
end

def can_tunnel_east?
  east && east.east &&
    east.vertical_passage?
end

def can_tunnel_west?
  west && west.west &&
    west.vertical_passage?
end
```

Here's where we encode the logic that decides whether or not it's even possible to tunnel in a given direction. Look at the the can_tunnel_north? method, for instance. We can only tunnel north from the current cell if a cell exists to the north, and that neighbor has a northern neighbor and is a horizontal passage (east-to-west).

We'll add those two last helper methods, horizontal_passage? and vertical_passage?, next.

```
def horizontal_passage?
  linked?(east) && linked?(west) &&
    !linked?(north) && !linked?(south)
end

def vertical_passage?
  linked?(north) && linked?(south) &&
    !linked?(east) && !linked?(west)
end
```

These aren't too tricky. A cell is a horizontal passage if it is linked to its east and west neighbors, but not to its north and south neighbors. A vertical passage is defined similarly.

There. Our OverCell now reports all potential neighbors, including those that will need an under-cell to tunnel to them, so algorithms that rely on the neighbors method (like Recursive Backtracker and Aldous-Broder) will be automatically clued in.

The next bit is to make sure that when those algorithms try to link a cell to a neighbor that needs a tunnel, we add the appropriate under-cell.

This will require a few more changes. For one, we need to make the grid itself in charge of adding the under-cell, since it needs to keep track of all cells in order to draw them. But to ask the grid to create a new under-cell, the cell needs to have a reference to the grid!

Let's give it one. Put this constructor method at the top of our OverCell class.

```
def initialize(row, column, grid)
  super(row, column)
  @grid = grid
end
```

Now that we've given the cell a handle on the grid, let's override the link(cell) method. This is where we'll check to see if the cell being linked will require a tunnel or not, and if necessary, create a new under-cell to act as a link between the two cells.

Put the following in weave_cells.rb, right after those helper methods we added.

```
Line 1  def link(cell, bidi=true)
   -      if north && north == cell.south
   -        neighbor = north
   -      elsif south && south == cell.north
   5        neighbor = south
   -      elsif east && east == cell.west
   -        neighbor = east
   -      elsif west && west == cell.east
   -        neighbor = west
   10     end
   -
   -      if neighbor
   -        @grid.tunnel_under(neighbor)
   -      else
   15       super
   -      end
   -    end
```

Don't let the length of the method fool you—there's really not much happening here. Most of it, lines 2–10, simply check if there is a neighbor in common between the current cell and the target cell. If there is, then the target requires an under-cell at that location in order to link to it. Take the first if statement as an example (line 2): if the current cell's northern neighbor is the same as the target cell's southern neighbor, we know the neighbor they have in common needs to host an under-cell to link them together.

That under-cell will be created by the call to the grid's tunnel_under(over_cell) method, on line 13. Sit tight—we'll get to that method shortly. First we need to talk about the sister class to OverCell: the much simpler UnderCell!

Implementing the UnderCell Class

The UnderCell doesn't need to manage nearly as much as the OverCell. We're only going to require it to insert itself between the appropriate cells. Everything else will be handled either by the grid or by OverCell.

Add the following to weave_cells.rb, following the definition of our OverCell class.

```
Line 1  class UnderCell < Cell
   -      def initialize(over_cell)
   -        super(over_cell.row, over_cell.column)
   -
   5        if over_cell.horizontal_passage?
   -          self.north = over_cell.north
   -          over_cell.north.south = self
   -          self.south = over_cell.south
   -          over_cell.south.north = self
```

```
10          link(north)
 -          link(south)
 -        else
 -          self.east = over_cell.east
15          over_cell.east.west = self
 -          self.west = over_cell.west
 -          over_cell.west.east = self
 -
 -          link(east)
20          link(west)
 -        end
 -      end
 -
 -      def horizontal_passage?
25        east || west
 -      end
 -
 -      def vertical_passage?
 -        north || south
30      end
 -    end
```

The constructor takes as input the over-cell that the cell will live beneath, and passes that over-cell's coordinates to the original constructor (line 3). This makes our new under-cell live at that same location in the grid. Then, depending on whether or not the over-cell is a horizontal passage, the under-cell inserts itself between the two neighbors that will be linked to it (lines 6–9 for a horizontal over-cell, and lines 14–17 otherwise). Lastly, it links itself (carving passages, so to speak) to the appropriate neighbors.

The UnderCell class also implements horizontal_passage? and vertical_passage?, so that our cells don't have to care if their neighbors are OverCell or UnderCell instances. (Isn't polymorphism wonderful?)

Implementing the WeaveGrid Class

All that's left is to implement our WeaveGrid class, which manages these two different cell types. We'll put our new class in weave_grid.rb.

weave_grid.rb
```
Line 1  require 'grid'
 -      require 'weave_cells'
 -
 -      class WeaveGrid < Grid
5         def initialize(rows, columns)
 -          @under_cells = []
 -          super
 -        end
```

```
10   def prepare_grid
       Array.new(rows) do |row|
         Array.new(columns) do |column|
           OverCell.new(row, column, self)
         end
15     end
     end

     def tunnel_under(over_cell)
       under_cell = UnderCell.new(over_cell)
20     @under_cells.push under_cell
     end

     def each_cell
       super
25
       @under_cells.each do |cell|
         yield cell
       end
     end
30   end
```

The constructor doesn't add much, just initializing a new array (line 6) that will be used to hold the under-cells that get created. The creation of those cells is managed by the tunnel_under method, on line 18. We also need to make sure that our each_cell method doesn't ignore under-cells (line 26). It needs to report every cell in the grid, including the under-cells.

That will be sufficient to *create* a weave maze, but it won't draw one yet. Our grid class may know how to render mazes with gaps between passages, but it doesn't know how to handle these new under-cells. For that, we'll override our to_png_with_inset method. We'll also make one minor tweak to to_png, so that these weave mazes are drawn with an inset by default.

Add the following to our WeaveGrid class.

```
Line 1  def to_png(cell_size: 10, inset: nil)
  -       super cell_size: cell_size, inset: (inset || 0.1)
  -     end

  5  def to_png_with_inset(img, cell, mode, cell_size, wall, x, y, inset)
  -       if cell.is_a?(OverCell)
  -         super
  -       else
  -         x1, x2, x3, x4, y1, y2, y3, y4 =
 10           cell_coordinates_with_inset(x, y, cell_size, inset)

  -         if cell.vertical_passage?
```

```
-        img.line(x2, y1, x2, y2, wall)
-        img.line(x3, y1, x3, y2, wall)
15       img.line(x2, y3, x2, y4, wall)
-        img.line(x3, y3, x3, y4, wall)
-      else
-        img.line(x1, y2, x2, y2, wall)
-        img.line(x1, y3, x2, y3, wall)
20       img.line(x3, y2, x4, y2, wall)
-        img.line(x3, y3, x4, y3, wall)
-      end
-    end
-  end
```

Line 2, in the new to_png method, simply sets the default inset size to 0.1 before calling the original to_png method on Grid. And the to_png_with_inset method isn't too much more involved—it, too, just calls the superclass's method when the cell is an OverCell (line 6). When the cell *isn't* an OverCell, though, it calls cell_coordinates_with_inset to get the x- and y-coordinates for the different walls (I *did* say that method would be useful later!) before drawing the corridors of the under-cell.

No sweat! We should now be ready to drop this into one of our other programs to see how it works. Go ahead and make a copy of recursive_backtracker_demo.rb, calling it weave_maze.rb. Then change the Grid references to WeaveGrid, like so:

weave_maze.rb
```ruby
  require 'recursive_backtracker'
➤ require 'weave_grid'

➤ grid = WeaveGrid.new(20, 20)
  RecursiveBacktracker.on(grid)

➤ filename = "weave.png"
  grid.to_png.save(filename)
  puts "saved to #{filename}"
```

Running it now, we should get a real, honest-to-goodness, spaghetti-rivaling weave maze:

Success! Now I'm hungry for some pasta...

Your Turn

It's been said that if you stick to the rules, you miss all the fun. When it comes to mazes, at least, there appears to be some truth to that. Knowing which rules to bend (or even break!) can open entire floodgates of possibility.

We focused in this chapter on breaking the rules that forbid self-intersection—that is, allowing passages to intersect themselves. We worked through braiding mazes by removing dead ends, and then further complicated things by dropping pits of molten lava in the middle of our lovely shortest path. We looked at how Dijkstra's algorithm can compensate for these traps and obstacles—these *weights*—and give you the most efficient (*least expensive*) path around them. We implemented weave mazes and a way to draw them by adding gaps between adjacent cells.

In all, a solid day's work!

It shouldn't surprise you to learn, though, that this is once again just scratching the surface of what's possible. It's your turn now. Think about some of the following suggestions, or try out some of your own.

Tweaking Dead-End Removal

Experiment with different conditions in the braid method. In the version presented in this chapter, it links to a random neighbor (though it prefers neighbors who are themselves dead ends). What if you were to make it prefer the neighbor in the direction of the cell's dead end? That is to say, if the cell's only exit is south, try to link to the cell to the north.

Further, note that by preferring to link one dead end to a neighboring dead end, this implementation skews the probability curve a bit. Linking one dead end to another actually removes *two* dead ends in one shot, which means if you're asking to remove half of all dead ends, you might be getting more than you bargained for! How might you make the braid method deal with that p parameter more accurately?

Sparse Mazes

A *sparse* maze is one that doesn't actually cover the entire grid, like the following figure.

These can be created by culling dead ends similarly to braid mazes, but instead of linking those cells to an additional neighbor, you actually remove them from the grid entirely. Experiment and see what you come up with.

Colored Braid Mazes

Here's a science experiment for you: braid a variety of mazes generated using different algorithms. Then color the resulting mazes, and compare them. Does braiding appear affect the algorithm's bias significantly? What about a partial braid? Are certain algorithms more affected than others?

Shortest Path Game

In general, braid mazes tend to be easier to solve than perfect mazes because there are more possible ways to the exit. However, adding some constraints can restore balance, and even make these braid mazes a unique challenge. What if the goal was not just to reach the exit, but to reach the exit via the shortest possible path? Design a game where the goal is to navigate a braid maze in the fewest possible steps.

Finding a Challenging Path

We've seen how to use Dijsktra's algorithm to find a path between two cells in a maze, and in this chapter we've used that information to randomly place a pit of lava on that path. However, we weren't very smart about it, and the result wasn't always very interesting. Try to do better! The goal is to take a braid maze and, by strategic placement of obstacles, create a puzzle where the player's challenge is to find an efficient path through it.

Colored Weave Mazes

For this one, you just need to fill in the missing implementation in to_png_with_inset on Grid and WeaveGrid. It's really not too hard—just a matter of drawing the rectangles that correspond to the passages.

Weaving with Different Algorithms

The Recursive Backtracker algorithm works pretty well for weave mazes, but it's not the only possibility. Experiment with some of the others that we've covered so far! Note that some won't work reliably, though: Wilson's algorithm, for instance, will require some effort because it generates a path without linking the cells, which can confuse the tunneling logic in the framework we've written. Also, as they've been presented, Binary Tree and Sidewinder won't work for weave mazes, since they don't rely on the neighbors method. How might you overcome that?

Inset Walls for Other Grids

We've implemented inset walls for regular grids here, but what about hex grids, or triangle grids? For that matter, what about the polar grids from

Chapter 7, *Going in Circles*, on page 97? Once you've got some of those working, it's a short step to thinking about actual weave mazes on those grids!

Tunnel Under Two Consecutive Corridors

One of the constraints we set for ourselves in this chapter was that a passage may not attempt to tunnel beneath two consecutive corridors at once. This was done only to keep our implementation simple, not because it isn't actually possible. How would you change our implementation to remove this constraint?

These weave mazes are a great segue to another algorithm, called Kruskal's algorithm, that can be used for generating mazes. In the next chapter we'll see how it can be used not only to generate random mazes, but also to give more control over our weave mazes, letting us specify where and how frequently passages weave.

Part III

More Algorithms

Now that you've had a chance to experiment with a few different algorithms, and potentially in some unusual settings, it's time to look at some other novel ways to generate mazes. More algorithms!

CHAPTER 10

Improving Your Weaving

You might have noticed something odd about the program you wrote in the last chapter, the one that generates weave mazes. Specifically, and especially if you were experimenting with smaller mazes, you probably saw that sometimes your program that was supposed to generate weave mazes, didn't. You set it up, you ran the program, and all that came out was a boring, old, normal maze.

The problem is that the technique described in the previous chapter is actually not very reliable. Don't get me wrong—the technique is easy to understand, straightforward to implement, and remarkably intuitive, so it has a lot going for it! But because of how it depends on random chance to determine when to tunnel under a passage, it is possible for a maze to be generated that doesn't weave at all. How embarrassing, right? That's not the kind of result you want, especially if you had just called a friend over to "see something cool."

Ideally, if we set out to generate a weave maze, we should be confident of getting one. Even better, it would be lovely if we could somehow adjust the frequency of the crossings, making them appear more or less often, and—as long as we're on the subject—we might as well mention how nice it would be if we could specify exactly *where* the crossings ought to be in the maze.

Wouldn't that be neat?

It turns out there's an algorithm for that! Or rather, there's this random maze algorithm that just happens to be great at fine-tuning these weave mazes. It's based on *Kruskal's algorithm*, and we're about to explore it. First we'll look at how Kruskal's algorithm itself works, and then see how it can be applied to maze generation. After that, you'll get to see how it can be used to make those weave mazes just about as configurable as you'd like.

Kruskal's Algorithm

Kruskal's algorithm was developed by the mathematician and computer scientist Joseph Kruskal in 1956 to construct what are called *minimum spanning trees*. Don't be put off by the crazy vocabulary—*spanning tree* is really just a fancy name for these perfect mazes we've been generating, and *minimum* simply refers to the costs and weights we discussed in the previous chapter.

Basically, Kruskal was trying to solve the following problem. Let's say you start with a graph, or grid, where every possible passage that might connect neighboring cells is given a cost. It might look something like the following figure.

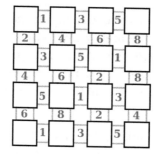

Merely constructing a spanning tree (we might say "perfect maze") from that is straightforward: you just pick passages in order to connect all of the cells without forming any loops. The algorithms we've looked at so far do essentially that, and might give you the following maze:

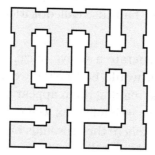

Here's the puzzle, though. How do you construct a maze from that initial grid whose passages have costs that sum to the lowest total value? *What's the cheapest tree that can be built?*

Kruskal's approach to this is quite different from that of the algorithms we've seen thus far. There's no random walking involved at all—cells are actually visited nonsequentially. And yet in spite of this, *it actually works.* Here's how.

First, we take that grid with the weighted passages and assign each cell a unique identifier. In the following figure we've given each one a letter of the alphabet, but simply numbering them would work just as well. These identifiers represent unique sets, each of which contains a single cell—but that'll change shortly!

Once those sets are all identified, the algorithm itself begins a loop in which it repeatedly chooses and processes neighboring pairs of cells. Pairs are chosen based on the weight of the passage that connects them, with smaller weights having preference. Here, all of the passages with a weight of 1 are highlighted:

In the event of a tie like this we get to pick whichever of those cells we like, so let's just choose the G,H pair. We link those two cells together, and then *merge* them into a single set. This is done by picking one of the two sets and moving all cells from the other into that one. The following figure shows that the cell in H was merged into the G set.

Then the algorithm goes around again, looking for the next passage with the lowest weight. There are still several passages left with a weight of 1, so those will all be processed next, resulting in the following configuration of cells:

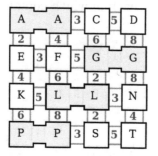

As the next figure shows, the cheapest passages at this point all have weights of 2.

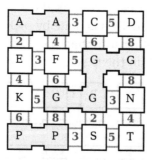

Since we get to break ties arbitrarily, let's say the algorithm picks the passage connecting the G and L sets, and see what happens. The sets of the two cells are compared and found to be different, so the cells are linked and the two sets merged together. The next figure shows that all cells in L have been merged into G now.

These merges affect *all* cells in the given set, regardless of how large that set might be, or how far from the passage the cells are. They're essentially identifying little mazes-in-embryo, subsets of the grid that are linked together!

This continues a few more times, linking together all of the cells joined by passages with weight 2, as the following figure shows.

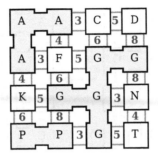

On the next few iterations, all of the passages weighted 3 will be processed, continuing to grow those little baby mazes like this:

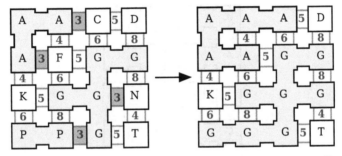

Moving on to the next pass, the cheapest passages are now all weighted 4, and we run into our first little snag. Consider the passage highlighted on the left in the following figure. If we were to select that passage and join those two cells, we'd end up connecting two cells that both belong to the same set! Since each set represents a self-contained little maze, that would mean adding a loop to that maze, which we don't want to allow.

(Although this does suggest an interesting way to generate braid mazes, doesn't it?)

We narrowly avoid catastrophe by skipping that edge entirely.

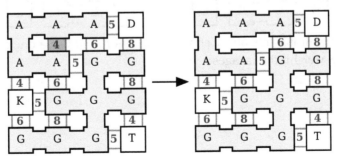

The remaining 4-weighted passages are processed without surprises, giving us the following figure:

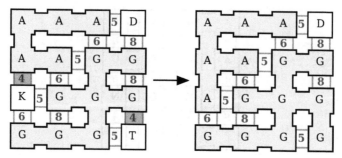

Almost there! The remaining lowest-cost passages are all 5's, highlighted in the following figure:

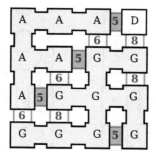

We can ignore the one in the southeast corner, as that would connect two cells that both belong to G. This leaves three more to choose from. Let's grab that cell in set D in the northeast corner and merge it into set A:

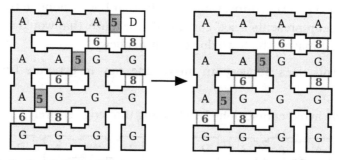

And then let's finish this off by connecting sets A and G via one of those two remaining 5-weighted passages:

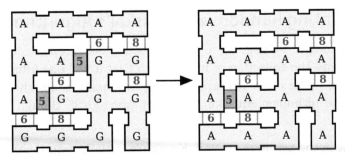

At this point, every cell in the grid belongs to the same set, A, which means we're done! The final result is a perfect maze:

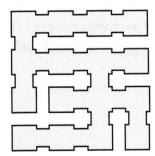

In a nutshell, then, the algorithm is:

1. Assign each cell to its own set.
2. Choose the pair of neighboring cells with the lowest cost passage between them.
3. If the two cells belong to different sets, merge them.
4. Repeat 2 and 3 until only a single set remains.

We could implement this in code exactly as described—complete with weighted passages connecting the cells—but it turns out that for our purposes, we can simplify the algorithm a bit.

While the passage weights are important in some applications (where the passages are usually referred to as *edges* and the cells as *nodes*), they aren't usually so critical when making mazes. In fact, to turn a grid into a maze using Kruskal's algorithm, we'd have to first assign random weights to all the possible passages, before we could select them in order of those weights.

That's kind of redundant. It's actually far easier to just put all the passages in a big list and select them randomly from the list. This little change converts Kruskal's algorithm into the *Randomized* Kruskal's algorithm.

Let's make it real in code.

Implementing Randomized Kruskal's Algorithm

To implement this, we're going to create a new class to represent the *state* of the algorithm—the collection of information that it will use internally. Once we've got this State class written, the rest of Kruskal's algorithm becomes almost trivial to implement. Don't take my word for it, though. Watch and see!

As you saw in the previous section, Kruskal's initially requires that each cell be associated with a unique set. This suggests that, at a minimum, our State class is going to need to track that association. We'll need a way to query the set that a particular cell belongs to, as well as the list of cells that belong to a given set. Also, the algorithm wants to select random pairs of neighboring cells on each iteration, so we could probably help things along by keeping a list of those cell pairs.

Get things started by putting the following in a new file called kruskals.rb.

```
kruskals.rb
Line 1  class Kruskals
   -
   -      class State
   -        attr_reader :neighbors
   5
   -        def initialize(grid)
   -          @grid = grid
   -          @neighbors = []
   -          @set_for_cell = {}
   10         @cells_in_set = {}
   -
   -          @grid.each_cell do |cell|
   -            set = @set_for_cell.length
   -
   15           @set_for_cell[cell] = set
   -            @cells_in_set[set] = [ cell ]
   -
   -            @neighbors << [cell, cell.south] if cell.south
   -            @neighbors << [cell, cell.east]  if cell.east
   20         end
   -        end
   -      end
   -
   -  end
```

We're nesting the State class within the Kruskals class, since it's not going to be particularly useful with any other algorithms. The initialize constructor (line 6) takes a single argument, the grid to be processed. The @neighbors array on line

8 will be used to track the pairs of neighboring cells, @set_for_cell (line 9) maps cells to their corresponding set identifiers, and @cells_in_set (line 10) does the inverse, mapping set identifiers to the cells belonging to those sets.

Then each cell is assigned to a new set (lines 13–16) and the @neighbors array is constructed, with each neighbor pair being represented as a simple two-element array.

Now, recall that the algorithm will try to merge each pair of cells as long as they aren't in the same set. To help make that decision, we'll add a can_merge?(left, right) method that will compare the sets of the two arguments. Add this immediately after the State class's initialize method.

```
def can_merge?(left, right)
  @set_for_cell[left] != @set_for_cell[right]
end
```

No surprises there—it just queries the @set_for_cell mapping for each cell and compares them, returning true if they are different (and therefore able to be merged).

This leads, then, into the merging operation itself. Add this final method to the State class, just after can_merge?.

```
Line 1  def merge(left, right)
   -      left.link(right)
   -
   -      winner = @set_for_cell[left]
   5      loser  = @set_for_cell[right]
   -      losers = @cells_in_set[loser] || [right]
   -
   -      losers.each do |cell|
   -        @cells_in_set[winner] << cell
  10        @set_for_cell[cell] = winner
   -      end
   -
   -      @cells_in_set.delete(loser)
   -  end
```

This just links the two cells together (line 2), and then loops over the cells in the loser set (the one that right belongs to). Each cell in that set is moved to the winner set (the one containing left), and then the loser set is removed (line 13).

Now, here's the best part. With that class all set to hold and maintain the state for us, Randomized Kruskal's algorithm becomes so simple it makes me giddy. Add the following method just before the final end keyword in kruskals.rb.

```
def self.on(grid, state=State.new(grid))
  neighbors = state.neighbors.shuffle

  while neighbors.any?
    left, right = neighbors.pop
    state.merge(left, right) if state.can_merge?(left, right)
  end

  grid
end
```

Seriously, that's it! Given a grid and a state object (which defaults to a new State instance if not otherwise specified), the method simply sets up a randomized list of all the neighbor pairs, and then loops over them until the list is empty. Each pass through the loop removes one pair from the list, checks to see if they can be merged and—if so—merges them.

Test that now by putting the following in kruskals_demo.rb.

kruskals_demo.rb
```
require 'kruskals'
require 'grid'

grid = Grid.new(20, 20)
Kruskals.on(grid)

filename = "kruskals.png"
grid.to_png.save(filename)
puts "saved to #{filename}"
```

Running it and opening the resulting kruskals.png, you ought to see something like the figure.

Looks random to me!

Better Weaving with Kruskal

So that's Randomized Kruskal's algorithm, and you might be wondering now what this has to do with weave mazes. That was, after all, how this chapter began, and I did promise that Kruskal's would apply. Let me assure you, it definitely does.

Recall how weave mazes were presented in the previous chapter, where the algorithm randomly attempts to move over or under passages as opportunities to do so present themselves. This certainly works, but it's not very consistent. Sometimes you may get a maze with a dozen crossing passages, and other times you might only get one or two (or none at all!). That's the nature—and consequence—of *random*.

However, what we'd like to be able to do is generate mazes with a consistent, predictable number of crossings. Different applications have different needs, so it would be nice to be able to dial back the weave density for a lightly woven maze, or dial it all the way to eleven to pack the crossings in as tightly as possible.

So what can we do?

Well, imagine if we could dictate the location of these crossings. That would let us explicitly declare how dense the weave will be, and would also let us fit the crossing passages to specific patterns and designs. The process would begin with something like this figure, where some number of these crossing passages have been placed (perhaps randomly) on the grid.

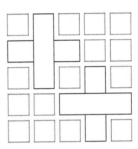

From that, then, we need to somehow generate a complete maze that *includes* the crossings at those positions. In other words, we need to take those unconnected, disjoint passages and somehow *merge* them into the final maze...

Sound familiar? It should. This is exactly the kind of thing that Kruskal's algorithm does, remember. If we were to take that grid with the crossings in the previous figure and number every contiguous grouping of cells with a unique number, we'd get this figure, a familiar configuration very much like the starting state of Kruskal's.

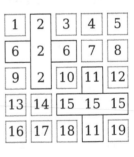

In fact, if we were to apply Kruskal's algorithm to that grid, arranging the starting sets as shown by those numbers, we would actually get a maze that incorporated those crossings, as shown.

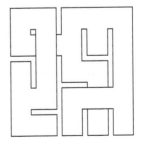

In other words, just what we wanted! We could theoretically place those crossings anywhere we wanted, pell-mell across the grid, and produce a *really* dense weave maze!

It turns out, though, that we can't quite just go nuts with this. Anytime you try to center a new crossing on a cell that is already linked to another cell, you have to tread very carefully or risk adding cycles to your maze, or worse, putting your grid into an inconsistent state. Passages can wind up being hidden by tunneling under passages moving in the same direction, for instance.

This is not to say it is impossible to make it work—you just have to go carefully. Generally, it's easiest to simply make sure that any crossing you add is centered on a cell that hasn't yet been linked to anything. This is the way we'll do it when we implement these Kruskal weave mazes, next.

Implementing Better Weaving

To make this work, we're going to add a method to our Kruskals::State class so we can install those crossings in it. That method will be supported by a simple subclass of our WeaveGrid from the previous chapter. With those changes in hand, generating the actual maze will be really straightforward.

So, first things first, open up kruskals.rb and add the following method just after the merge method in Kruskals::State.

```ruby
def add_crossing(cell)
  return false if cell.links.any? ||
    !can_merge?(cell.east, cell.west) ||
    !can_merge?(cell.north, cell.south)

  @neighbors.delete_if { |left,right| left == cell || right == cell }

  if rand(2) == 0
    merge(cell.west, cell)
    merge(cell, cell.east)

    @grid.tunnel_under(cell)
    merge(cell.north, cell.north.south)
    merge(cell.south, cell.south.north)
  else
    merge(cell.north, cell)
    merge(cell, cell.south)

    @grid.tunnel_under(cell)
    merge(cell.west, cell.west.east)
    merge(cell.east, cell.east.west)
  end

  true
end
```

This method will attempt to add a new crossing centered on the given cell, but it won't do so blindly. Line 2 makes sure that the crossing is not centered on a cell that's already been linked (as we talked about), and lines 3–4 ensure that adding the crossing won't create a loop in the maze. (This would happen, for instance, if the east and west cells of the crossing both happened to be previously connected via a path somehow.)

Once we're confident that the crossing *can* be added, the @neighbors list is checked and all pairs that include the given cell are removed (line 6). This ensures that when we eventually run our Randomized Kruskal's algorithm on the grid, the algorithm won't try to reprocess this cell that we've already processed by hand.

On line 8, we randomly determine which way the crossing should be oriented. The center cell can either be a horizontal passage, with the tunnel moving vertically beneath it, or it can be a vertical passage, with the tunnel moving horizontally. If we were to always pick just one or the other exclusively, the resulting maze would look skewed, with overpasses always going one way or the other.

Once we know how the crossing will be oriented, the cells on either side of the center cell are merged with it, forming that vertical or horizontal passage, and then the grid is called on to tunnel under it. Finally, the under-cell is merged to the two remaining cells in the crossing.

That's the hardest part of this whole thing! The rest is all downhill, requiring only two simple subclasses to help us tweak the behavior of WeaveGrid. We want *some* of the weave behavior from the previous chapter (like under-cells, and proper rendering of those tunneling passages), but we *don't* want the maze algorithm itself to try to add new tunnels. We're adding those explicitly, before the algorithm runs. To turn off that tunneling behavior, we just need to override the neighbors method of OverCell, to have it return only the immediate neighbors of the cell (and not those that can only be reached via tunneling).

Create a new file called kruskals_weave_demo.rb, and start it off with the following two lines:

kruskals_weave_demo.rb
```
require 'kruskals'
require 'weave_grid'
```

This pulls in our implementation of Kruskal's algorithm, and the WeaveGrid class (and related cell classes) that we implemented before.

Next, we'll subclass OverCell and override the neighbors method, as described. Add the following class just after those require statements.

```
class SimpleOverCell < OverCell
  def neighbors
    list = []
    list << north if north
    list << south if south
    list << east  if east
    list << west  if west
    list
  end
end
```

It's essentially just the original implementation of Cell#neighbors. (Yes, the duplication is probably indicative of a design smell, and we should really refactor this all eventually, but let's just roll with it here.)

Now that we have this cell subclass, we need to tell the grid to use it instead of the OverCell. To make that happen, we'll subclass WeaveGrid and override prepare_grid. Put this subclass in the same file, just after SimpleOverCell.

```
class PreconfiguredGrid < WeaveGrid
  def prepare_grid
    Array.new(rows) do |row|
      Array.new(columns) do |column|
        SimpleOverCell.new(row, column, self)
      end
    end
  end
end
```

And that's really the extent of the changes we have to make! Now the fun begins. We'll instantiate our grid and the Kruskals::State object, and scatter some crossings around. Add this just after the definition for PreconfiguredGrid.

```
grid = PreconfiguredGrid.new(20, 20)
state = Kruskals::State.new(grid)

grid.size.times do |i|
  row = 1 + rand(grid.rows - 2)
  column = 1 + rand(grid.columns - 2)
  state.add_crossing(grid[row, column])
end
```

This naively picks a random cell from the grid and tries to put a crossing on it, repeating over and over for as many cells as there are on the grid. In reality the number of possible crossings will be much, much lower (due to the restrictions we've placed on where these crossings can go), but grid.size gives us a convenient upper bound.

Once we've packed as many crossings into the grid as we possibly can, we get to move on to the climax of this show: generating and displaying the maze. Add this at the very end of that kruskals_weave_demo.rb file:

```
Kruskals.on(grid, state)

filename = "kruskals.png"
grid.to_png(inset:0.2).save(filename)
puts "saved to #{filename}"
```

The only bit to notice here is the inset argument passed to to_png. We *could* fall back to the default inset size of 0.1, but aesthetically, with weaves as densely packed as these will be, the maze is easier to see when the inset is slightly larger.

Go ahead and run that. You ought to get something as gloriously woven as this:

Now *that's* what I call a weave maze!

Your Turn

You've learned a new algorithm, and you've already seen one very practical application of it, in making weave mazes much more reliable and configurable than they were in the previous chapter. With this technique, you can get a weave maze every time, regardless of the size of the maze.

Where else can you take the ideas presented in this chapter? Consider the following possibilities.

Adjusting Weave Density

Now that you know how to pack those weaves in as densely as you wish, how might you dial it down to something in-between? Given some continuum moving between 0 (no weaves) and 1 (maximum weave density), what would a maze with a weave density of 0.5 look like?

Exploring Templates

The crossing pattern that we applied to the mazes in this chapter is one example of a *template*. Other possible templates include spirals, open rooms, zig-zags, and any number of other ways of arranging corridors. The following figure shows an example of a spiral template applied four times to a maze:

How would you implement a spiral template like this, using the techniques described in this chapter? What other templates can you think of?

Combining Templates

Once you've played with a few different template styles, try combining them. Mix spirals and rooms with a weave maze and see what kind of craziness you can come up with.

Applying Different Algorithms

Kruskal's algorithm was presented in this chapter as a great way to incorporate templates into a maze, but it certainly isn't the only way. Other algorithms can be adapted to this, too, like Aldous-Broder or the

Recursive Backtracker. How would you adapt those algorithms to this technique?

Tweaking the Algorithm's Bias

Kruskal's, by itself, is not strongly biased. The mazes it generates tend to have slightly more dead ends than those from the unbiased algorithms like Aldous-Broder, but it's not something that would jump out at you if you were to color the mazes. How could you change that? What could you do to the neighbor selection criteria, for instance, that would make Kruskal's generate mazes with visually obvious textures?

Super-Dense Weaves

Be warned: this one is a bit of a science project! I mentioned in passing that it's easiest to build these weave mazes if crossings are centered only on cells that have not already been linked to other cells. If you disregard that warning, you'll find that your weaves will want to overlap, with (for example) east-to-west tunnels trying to move beneath east-to-west passages. For the densest possible weave mazes, how might you overcome that?

With the Randomized Kruskal's algorithm under your belt, it's time to look at another algorithm that started life as a minimum spanning tree algorithm: Prim's.

CHAPTER 11

Growing With Prim's

The whole "minimum spanning tree" problem turns out to have lots of applications, like finding optimal ways to build out telephone lines, or the best way to structure a computer network. Kruskal's algorithm was one way to solve it, but it's not the only way, which means that we ought to be able to find yet other algorithms that we can bend to our will.

(Mwa-hahahaha!)

Sure enough, there is another algorithm, called *Prim's*, and sure enough, it adapts readily to random maze generation. We'll take a look at how this algorithm works, and then we'll see two ways that it is commonly implemented for mazes: a simplified version, and a "true" version. Lastly, we'll take a look at a closely related algorithm, called the *Growing Tree* algorithm, which can actually be configured to behave not only like Prim's, but even Recursive Backtracker!

Introducing Prim's Algorithm

Prim's algorithm was first developed in 1930 by a Czech mathematician named Vojtěch Jarník, but it gets its name from Robert C. Prim, a computer scientist who rediscovered it independently in 1957. It works similarly to Dijkstra's algorithm, starting at one point in the grid and then moving outward like water flowing, but in Prim's case it does more than just measure distances and costs. The end result of Prim's is one of those fancy minimum spanning trees—or, in our case, a maze.

As with Kruskal's algorithm, Prim's works by considering the weights on the connections between cells—passage costs—rather than on the individual cells themselves. We'll look at how this comes together, but then we'll take a step back and consider some simplifications that make it easier to implement.

So, as with Kruskal's, we start with a grid and indicate all of the costs of the potential connections between cells. Let's say our grid is set up like this, with the given passage costs:

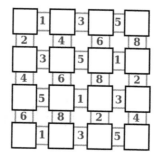

Prim's algorithm, like Dijkstra's, starts at an arbitrary cell and works outward, so our next step is to pick a starting point. Let's choose this one:

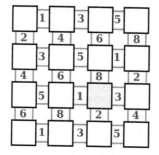

We'll color it yellow here to show that it's been added to the maze. (The white cells aren't yet in the maze—they're still waiting for their chance. By the time we're done, though, they'll all be colored yellow, too.)

Next, we look at all the possible passages from that starting cell and choose the one with the lowest cost. In this case, it's the passage with a cost of 1, heading west, so we choose that and link the current cell to its western neighbor, like this:

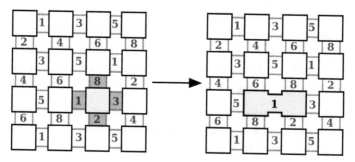

Note that we color that neighbor yellow now, too, because it's been added to the maze. We're growing the maze outward, one passage at a time.

Now we do that again, only this time we want to choose the lowest cost passage attached to *any* of our visited cells. It's like a puddle of water started at that first cell, and it can now flood outward to any cell that it's touched. It turns out that the lowest cost cell is the one marked 2, heading south from our first cell, so we choose it and link those two cells:

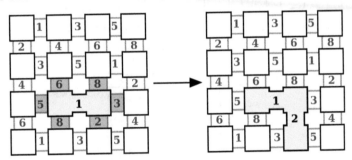

You can probably guess what the next step is—we're going to do this again, looking for the lowest cost passage attached to any of those three cells. This time, though, we've got a tie: there are *two* cells, both worth 3. In this case, we break the tie by choosing one arbitrarily, so we'll go with this one:

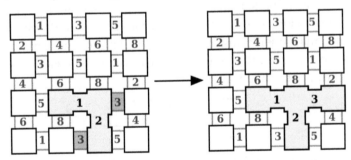

The algorithm continues like this, with each pass choosing the next passage with the lowest cost. A few more iterations and we can see the maze starting to come together:

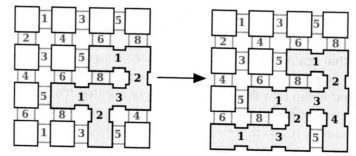

Eventually, though, we'll probably run into a situation like this one:

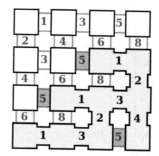

It's another tie, which is familiar enough, but notice the passage in the southeast corner. It connects two cells that are both already in the maze. If that passage were to be selected it would add a cycle, which we don't want to allow. The solution is to do like we did for Kruskal's algorithm and skip those connections, considering only those that link to a cell that isn't already in the maze. In this case, that leaves us with two more possible passages. We choose one arbitrarily, like this:

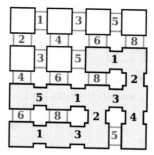

The algorithm repeats until every cell has been added to the maze, at which point you're left with something like this:

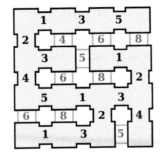

Perfect. (Literally!)

Now that we've walked through how the full algorithm works, let's look at two ways to implement it, beginning with a common variation that we'll call the "simplified" Prim's algorithm.

Simplified Prim's Algorithm

Simplified versions of Prim's algorithm are fairly common among maze generators, and are typically referred to merely as "Prim's algorithm" by many sources. However, unlike the real algorithm, these simplified versions do not actually bother with different costs and weights for passages. In fact, these algorithms tend to be similar to what you would get if you ran the real Prim's algorithm on a grid in which every passage had the same cost.

Recall how the algorithm began, after picking a cell at random as the starting point: it looked for the lowest cost passage that connected to that starting cell. But if every passage had the same weight, they'd all tie, and we'd break the tie by choosing among the candidates at random.

So if every passage in the entire grid had the same weight, Prim's would simply choose a connecting passage at random at each step. This happens to be essentially what these simplified algorithms do, with one notable difference: instead of choosing *passages*, they typically choose *cells*.

There are several possible variations that we could implement, but we'll stick with one of the simplest here. Put the following in *prims.rb*.

prims.rb

```
Line 1  class SimplifiedPrims

   -      def self.on(grid, start_at: grid.random_cell)
   -        active = []
   5        active.push(start_at)

   -        while active.any?
   -          cell = active.sample
```

```
10        available_neighbors = cell.neighbors.select { |n| n.links.empty? }

          if available_neighbors.any?
            neighbor = available_neighbors.sample
            cell.link(neighbor)
            active.push(neighbor)
15        else
            active.delete(cell)
          end
        end

20      grid
      end

    end
```

The process starts on line 4 by initializing an array, called active, and then adding our starting point to it (a random location in the grid, by default). Then, the rest of the algorithm repeats for as long as there are cells in that list.

Each time through the loop, the algorithm chooses a random cell from that active list (line 8), and then finds the neighbors of that cell that haven't yet been linked (line 9).

If there aren't any such neighbors it means the chosen cell is surrounded by the maze and won't be able to yield any more passages. In that case, the cell is removed from the active list (line 16), and the process goes around again. Otherwise, a random neighbor is selected from those available neighbors before being linked to the current cell and added to the active list (lines 12–14).

Test the algorithm with the following program:

prims_demo.rb
```ruby
require 'prims'
require 'grid'

grid = Grid.new(20, 20)
SimplifiedPrims.on(grid)

filename = "prims-simple.png"
grid.to_png.save(filename)
puts "saved to #{filename}"
```

Running that ought to generate something like the following maze:

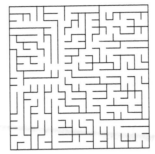

This looks pretty good, but you might detect some hints of the algorithm's bias here. This is especially clear if the maze is colored, as in the following figure. Here, Dijkstra's algorithm (as described in *Coloring Your Mazes*, on page 47) was run from the same cell that Prim's started on:

That radial texture is a consequence of the evenly weighted passages. With all other things being equal, the algorithm will try to simply spread evenly outward from the starting cell, creating that "shattered glass" pattern.

With just a little effort, though, we can do quite a bit better. All it requires is that we remain truer to the original algorithm and take cost into consideration.

True Prim's Algorithm

Although the algorithm we'll implement next is called a "true" Prim's algorithm, it's still slightly modified. Rather than assigning weights to *passages*, it assigns weights to *cells*, and then chooses cells based on those costs. This gives us mazes very similar to those from a fully passage-weighted Prim's algorithm, and for significantly less effort.

Open up prims.rb again and add the following class at the bottom of it:

```
class TruePrims

  def self.on(grid, start_at: grid.random_cell)
    active = []
    active.push(start_at)
```

```
➤        costs = {}
➤        grid.each_cell { |cell| costs[cell] = rand(100) }

        while active.any?
➤          cell = active.min { |a,b| costs[a] <=> costs[b] }
          available_neighbors = cell.neighbors.select { |n| n.links.empty? }

          if available_neighbors.any?
➤            neighbor = available_neighbors.min { |a,b| costs[a] <=> costs[b] }
            cell.link(neighbor)
            active.push(neighbor)
          else
            active.delete(cell)
          end
        end

        grid
      end

    end
```

It's nearly identical to the simplified version of the algorithm, except for the highlighted bits. For one thing, a costs mapping is created that randomly assigns a cost (0–99) to each cell. That mapping is then used to find the cell with the lowest cost via the array's min method. This is actually done up to twice on each pass through the loop—once on the active list to find the active cell with the lowest cost, and then again to find which of that cell's available neighbors has the lowest cost.

 For the sake of simplicity, the preceding code uses Ruby's Array#min method to find the cheapest cell. In practical use, though, something like a priority queue would be far more efficient!

Running that, we get a maze with a noticeably different texture:

Coloring it the same way we did for the simplified algorithm, we can see that the radial texture is gone:

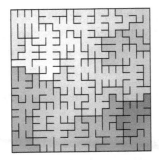

In fact, the texture of this maze is quite similar to what you'd get from Kruskal's algorithm, which shouldn't be surprising, since both algorithms are intended to generate the same kind of maze.

So, there you have two flavors of Prim's algorithm: the simplified version and the so-called true version. Each generates mazes with markedly different textures from the other, and yet the algorithms themselves are nearly identical. In fact, the only significant difference between them is the way in which cells were selected from that active list.

This simple observation turns out to be the basis of another maze algorithm, called *Growing Tree*. Let's take a look at it next.

The Growing Tree Algorithm

Let's rewind a moment and consider again those two versions of Prim's algorithm that we've looked at. Both work by starting at an arbitrary cell, and both work by then growing outward from that cell by selecting neighboring cells. In the case of the simplified version, neighboring cells are selected at random. For the "true" version, cells are selected based on their cost.

But those are hardly the only two ways to select cells from that list. What if you always tried to select the cell nearest to the starting point? Or the cell that was most recently added to the list? Or—here's a good one—what if you were to *combine multiple conditions* somehow, picking at random half the time, and picking based on weight the other half of the time?

What we have here is the basis of the Growing Tree algorithm. It works like this:

1. Choose a cell at random from the grid. Add it to the active list.
2. Select a cell from the active list.
3. Choose a random, unvisited neighbor of that cell. Link the two together, and add the neighbor to the active list.
4. Repeat steps 2 and 3 until every cell has been linked.

The magic happens in step 2, where a cell is selected. By plugging in different cell selection criteria, vastly different mazes can be constructed. In fact, the implementations of both the simplified and the true Prim's algorithms in this chapter are really just special cases of this Growing Tree algorithm!

Let's implement this. We'll use Ruby's *blocks* (anonymous functions) to define the how cells are selected.

Put the following code in growing_tree.rb.

```
growing_tree.rb
class GrowingTree

  def self.on(grid, start_at: grid.random_cell)
    active = []
    active.push(start_at)

    while active.any?
➤     cell = yield active
      available_neighbors = cell.neighbors.select { |n| n.links.empty? }

      if available_neighbors.any?
        neighbor = available_neighbors.sample
        cell.link(neighbor)
        active.push(neighbor)
      else
        active.delete(cell)
      end
    end

    grid
  end

end
```

Once again, you'll notice that it is mostly identical to the Prim's algorithm implementations we've already seen, with one significant difference. The highlighted line uses Ruby's yield keyword to invoke whatever anonymous block of code has been passed to the on(grid) method. The list of active cells is passed to that anonymous block, which is expected to return one of the cells in that list.

To see how that works in practice, take a look at the following code.

```
growing_tree_demo.rb
require 'growing_tree'
require 'grid'

def save(grid, filename)
  grid.to_png.save(filename)
```

```
    puts "saved to #{filename}"
  end

  grid = Grid.new(20, 20)
➤ GrowingTree.on(grid) { |list| list.sample }
  save(grid, "growing-tree-random.png")

  grid = Grid.new(20, 20)
➤ GrowingTree.on(grid) { |list| list.last }
  save(grid, "growing-tree-last.png")

  grid = Grid.new(20, 20)
➤ GrowingTree.on(grid) { |list| (rand(2) == 0) ? list.last : list.sample }
  save(grid, "growing-tree-mix.png")
```

This is much like all of our previous programs, but a separate method, save, has been introduced to centralize the saving of grids as images.

The interesting bits are on the highlighted lines, where the Growing Tree algorithm is applied to a grid. In the first one, a block is provided that simply returns a random element from the list passed to it (list.sample). The second one always returns the last element of the list (list.last), and the third gets tricky, choosing the last element half the time, and a random element the rest of the time.

Running that program will generate three different images. Open them up and see what you get. The following figure shows the three different mazes side-by-side, including coloration to more clearly see the different textures.

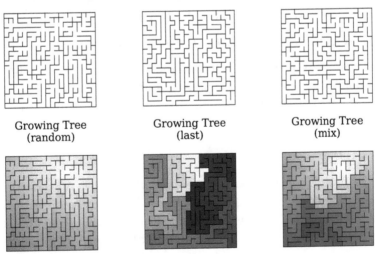

Growing Tree
(random)

Growing Tree
(last)

Growing Tree
(mix)

The image on the left is where the cells were picked at random from the active list on each iteration, and as we would expect it looks exactly like the mazes generated by the Simplified Prim's algorithm. The middle one, though—that looks familiar, too. By always choosing the *last* element from the active list, we generated a maze with long, winding passages...

It's the Recursive Backtracker!

If you need to, glance back at *The Recursive Backtracker Algorithm*, on page 73 to refresh your memory of that algorithm. Recall that it always considers the cell on the top of the stack to be the current cell, and always chooses a random unvisited neighbor of that current cell at each step.

Compare that to what Growing Tree does when you always select the last element from the active list. At each step of the algorithm, Growing Tree adds a new element to the end of the list. By choosing that newly added element again the next time around, it effectively becomes the same as the current cell in Recursive Backtracker.

In other words, with a single, ridiculously simple change, the Growing Tree algorithm can re-create either the Simplified Prim's algorithm or the Recursive Backtracker!

It gets better, though. Let's look at the third image that we generated, the one that chose the last cell half the time, and a random cell the other half of the time. Especially if you look at the colored version, you can see a vaguely radial texture, reminiscent of Simplified Prim's, but you can also see how the passages tend to wind around a bit, too. In other words, we've taken aspects of the Simplified Prim's algorithm and merged them with the Recursive Backtracker, giving us features of both algorithms.

It's like we're playing with the DNA of those two algorithms!

This is every bit as powerful as it sounds. Want more dead ends? Choose random more often. Want longer passages? Choose the last element more often. It's like we've been given a slider to control the texture of the resulting maze!

Your Turn

We added a pretty powerful tool to your toolbox just now. After looking at two simple variations on Prim's algorithm, we saw how they could be generalized into a third algorithm, Growing Tree, and further saw that Growing Tree could be configured to mimic attributes of different algorithms, simultaneously!

There are a *lot* of different places you could take this. If you're uncertain what to try next, consider some of the following ideas, but don't be afraid of jumping in completely different directions, too!

"Modified" Prim's Algorithm

As mentioned, there are several "simplified" variants of Prim's algorithm. One, usually referred to as a "modified" Prim's algorithm, gives slightly better results than the simplified version given in this chapter. It's a bit more fiddly to implement, which makes it great for a "Your Turn" challenge!

It works like this:

1. Initialize three sets: *in*, *frontier*, and *out*.

2. Place the starting cell into the *in* set, and all of its neighbors into the *frontier* set. Add all remaining cells to the *out* set.

3. For as long as there are cells in the *frontier* set, remove one at random, add it to the *in* set, and link it to a random *in* neighbor. Then move all of its *out* neighbors to the *frontier* set, and repeat.

Give it a try and see what you think!

"Truest" Prim's Algorithm

Try implementing a proper True Prim's algorithm by building and using a list of neighboring pairs, Kruskal-style. Initialize the list to contain just those pairs that include the starting cell, and at each step of the algorithm select from (and extend) that list with the pairs that include the new cell. Once you've got it working, think of ways to compare it to the True Prim's implementation presented in this chapter. Coloring mazes and counting dead ends are two ways, but what other ways can you think of to quantify how different or similar the mazes of those two algorithms are?

Other Cell Selection Methods

Growing Tree was presented in this chapter with three different cell selection methods: random, last, and a mix of the two. These only scratch the surface, though. What other cell selection methods can you think of? Here are a few possibilities to try:

- Oldest—always choose the *first* cell in the list.

- Median—always choose the cell in the middle of the list.

- Same Cell—choose at random, but once you've selected a cell once, choose it again and again until it has no more unvisited neighbors. Then choose another random cell, and repeat.

- Most Distant—always choose the cell furthest from the cell that was selected previously.

Growing Tree with Cell Costs

What if you were to track cell costs and use those to drive the cell selection of Growing Tree? What if you do a mix between last- and cost-wise selection? How does that compare to the mix between last-wise and random? What happens when you splice Simplified Prim's with True Prim's?

Passage-wise Growing Tree

Growing Tree usually keeps a list of cells, as described in this chapter, but what if you tracked passages instead? You could implement the "real" Prim's algorithm with it, for one thing, but do any of the other selection methods work differently?

Configure Neighbor Selection

Looking closely at the implementation of True Prim's given in this chapter and comparing it with the Growing Tree implementation, you might have noticed that True Prim's actually chooses neighbor cells based on weight, whereas Growing Tree just chooses them at random. What if you were to make that configurable, too? What happens when Growing Tree always wants to choose the neighbor to the west of the current cell? You could even add regional variation, where cells in the eastern half tend to go north and those in the western half prefer east.

Now that you've had a chance to explore Growing Tree and friends, we might as well finish off your repertoire of maze algorithms by exploring two particularly novel specimens. One vaguely resembles Sidewinder, but the other...well. Read on and see!

CHAPTER 12

Combining, Dividing

So many algorithms! From the Binary Tree and Sidewinder, to Kruskal's and Prim's and Growing Tree, you've learned a lot about the different methods of generating random mazes. Ten methods, to be precise—and eleven, if we're counting Dijkstra's.

There are only two more left to cover!

The first, called Eller's algorithm, is a fast, efficient, and clever technique that seems born of the unlikely union of the Sidewinder algorithm and Kruskal's.

The second is a unique algorithm called Recursive Division, which operates very differently from any of the others we've covered. Its fractal nature has some interesting consequences, which we'll exploit to produce *rooms* in our mazes.

But first, Eller's. Here we go!

Eller's Algorithm

Eller's algorithm was invented by Marlin Eller in 1982. It shares some remarkable similarities with Sidewinder (on page 12), and yet manages to avoid the striking bias of that algorithm by incorporating some of the features of Kruskal's (on page 158) as well.

Like Sidewinder, it works by considering only a single row at a time, while building up sets (Kruskal-style) to keep track of which cells are reachable from which other cells. Let's work through an example.

We'll start at the top row (for convenience's sake), and we'll highlight the current row in yellow, to keep track of where we're at.

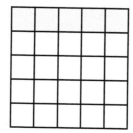

The first thing we do is assign each cell in that row a number, effectively putting each one in a set all by itself, like we did for Kruskal's (but on a smaller scale). Like this:

Then, we randomly link adjacent cells, but *only* if they aren't in the same set. As with Kruskal's algorithm, when we link adjacent cells, we also merge the two sets. Let's say we decide to link cells 1 and 2 (merging both into set 1), and cells 3 and 4 (merging into set 3). We get something like this:

The next step is to choose *at least* one cell at random from *each remaining set*, and carve passages south. We can choose more than one cell from any given set if we want to, but we must choose at least one. After choosing a few cells and carving south, we might get something like the following:

Note that carving south also adds those cells to the set of the cell that linked them, allowing us to keep track of which cells are ultimately connected between rows. (This is a key difference between this algorithm and Sidewinder!)

Carving those passages south finishes that row, and we advance to the next one:

Three cells in this row already belong to a set, because they were linked to cells in the previous row. The two other cells, though, need to be assigned new sets. These new sets can be assigned however we like, just so long as they are unique. Here, we've opted to continue counting from where the previous row left off:

And then we go around again. We:

1. Randomly link adjacent cells (as long as they don't share a set),
2. Choose at least one cell from each set to carve south, and then

3. Advance to the next row.

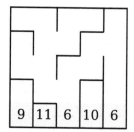

We repeat those three steps for each row, all the way to the bottom. By the time we reach the last row, our maze looks something like this:

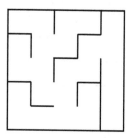

At this point we do something a bit different. Each of those sets can be thought of as a loose thread, dangling from the edge of this tapestry that we've just constructed. In order for the maze to be finished neatly, those threads have to be all tied up. That is to say, those remaining sets need to be merged together.

We do this by looking at each cell in that last row, and then linking (and merging) each with its neighbors, as long as those neighbors belong to different sets. (You never merge two cells that belong to the same set! That would introduce a loop into the maze.) The final result is this:

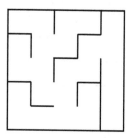

Not bad! Next let's see how it works up in code.

Implementing Eller's Algorithm

Eller's algorithm works strictly one row at a time, so our implementation will take advantage of that by leaning on a row-centric state object. Once we have that state object, the rest of the algorithm comes together quickly.

We'll start with the RowState class, which we'll place under the namespace of the Ellers class. It will all go in ellers.rb.

ellers.rb
```ruby
class Ellers

  class RowState
    def initialize(starting_set=0)
      @cells_in_set = {}
      @set_for_cell = []
      @next_set = starting_set
    end
  end

end
```

It's certainly not much yet, but it does get us started. The initialize method has a starting_set parameter (defaulting to 0), which will be used to determine what value is used for new sets. It then sets up a few instance variables that will be used for keeping track of sets within the current row.

The next three methods allow us to query and manipulate those sets. Add these just after that initialize method, within the RowState class.

```ruby
def record(set, cell)
  @set_for_cell[cell.column] = set

  @cells_in_set[set] = [] if !@cells_in_set[set]
  @cells_in_set[set].push cell
end

def set_for(cell)
  if !@set_for_cell[cell.column]
    record(@next_set, cell)
    @next_set += 1
  end

  @set_for_cell[cell.column]
end

def merge(winner, loser)
  @cells_in_set[loser].each do |cell|
    @set_for_cell[cell.column] = winner
```

```
      @cells_in_set[winner].push cell
    end

    @cells_in_set.delete(loser)
  end
```

The record method records a given set for the given cell. The set_for method checks to see if the given cell belongs to a set yet (if not, it assigns it to one) and then returns that set. And merge moves all cells from the loser set to the winner set.

The following two methods finish off the RowState class.

```
def next
  RowState.new(@next_set)
end

def each_set
  @cells_in_set.each { |set, cells| yield set, cells }
  self
end
```

The #next method returns a new RowState instance, counting sets from where the current instance left off. And the each_set method iterates over the sets in the current row, yielding each set and its collection of cells to the attached block.

All that's left, then, is to implement Eller's algorithm itself. Put the following method just after the end of the RowState class, but inside the Ellers namespace.

```
Line 1  def self.on(grid)
   -      row_state = RowState.new
   -
   -      grid.each_row do |row|
   5        row.each do |cell|
   -          next unless cell.west
   -
   -          set = row_state.set_for(cell)
   -          prior_set = row_state.set_for(cell.west)
   10
   -          should_link = set != prior_set &&
   -                        (cell.south.nil? || rand(2) == 0)
   -
   -          if should_link
   15           cell.link(cell.west)
   -            row_state.merge(prior_set, set)
   -          end
   -        end
   -
   20       if row[0].south
```

```
    -           next_row = row_state.next
    -
    -           row_state.each_set do |set, list|
    -             list.shuffle.each_with_index do |cell, index|
   25              if index == 0 || rand(3) == 0
    -                 cell.link(cell.south)
    -                 next_row.record(row_state.set_for(cell), cell.south)
    -               end
    -             end
   30          end
    -
    -           row_state = next_row
    -        end
    -      end
   35 end
```

The first thing we do is create a RowState object, and then start looping over every row in the grid. For each row that we're given, we consider its cells in sequence (line 5), skipping the west-most cell (line 6) because we're going to be trying to link each cell to its western neighbor, and it doesn't have one.

Lines 8 and 9 query the row state for the sets that the current cell and its western neighbor belong to, and then we check to see if we ought to link the two cells together (lines 11–12). Remember, we can only link them if they belong to different sets! Assuming they *are* different sets, we will always link them if we're in the last row (that is, cell.south.nil?); otherwise we decide randomly.

If things work out so that the cells need to be linked, we link them, and then *merge the two sets together* (line 16). Here, we're merging to the west so that the current cell's set disappears and is replaced by the previous cell's set.

Once we finish linking adjacent cells in the current row, we move to the second phase: choosing which cells to link *south*. We only do this if there's actually a row to the south (line 20). It works by first preparing a new RowState instance for the next row (line 21), and then looking at each set of cells in the current row (line 23). For each of those sets, we randomize the associated list of cells (line 24) and iterate across them.

Because we must carve south from at least one cell in each set, we require that the cell at index 0 be that lucky winner (line 25). (Remember, we shuffled the list on the previous line, so the "first" cell here is actually randomly selected.) If there is more than one cell in the set, subsequent cells are given a one-in-three chance of being selected as well. (There's nothing magical about those odds, by the way. Feel free to experiment with that!)

If the cell is selected, we carve south from it (line 26), and then put that southern cell in the same set as the cell we just selected (line 27).

After doing this for each of the sets in the current row, we then replace the current row state with the new row state (line 32), and do the whole thing again.

Got all that?

Let's try it out with our usual demo program. Put the following in ellers_demo.rb.

ellers_demo.rb
```ruby
require 'ellers'
require 'grid'

grid = Grid.new(20, 20)
Ellers.on(grid)

filename = "ellers.png"
grid.to_png.save(filename)
puts "saved to #{filename}"
```

Running that will produce something like the following lovely little maze:

To see how this compares to Sidewinder, we can generate and color two mazes, one using Eller's algorithm and one using Sidewinder. Putting them side by side, we get the following:

On the left is the maze generated using Eller's algorithm and on the right, Sidewinder. You can hardly miss that pronounced vertical stripe in the Sidewinder maze! As they say: you get what you pay for.

Sometimes, though, you can get *more* than you pay for. Let's look an algorithm that really is more than the sum of its parts.

Recursive Division

The Recursive Division algorithm is unique among the algorithms we've looked at, for two reasons. First of all, it treats the maze as a *fractal*—a shape whose component parts are all identical (or nearly so) to the whole. Second, instead of *carving passages* like the other algorithms have done, this one begins with a wide open space and *adds walls* until a maze is produced. Algorithms of this nature are called *wall adders* (as opposed to *passage carvers*).

It works by dividing the grid into two subgrids, adding a wall between them and a single passage linking them. The algorithm is then repeated on each side, recursively, until the passages are the desired size.

Let's walk through it.

We begin with an open grid, with no interior walls. (The grid lines are shown here in light gray, to make it easier to see where the cells are, but they're only for illustration.)

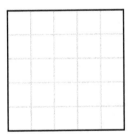

We divide the grid in half, either horizontally or vertically, along any of those grid lines. Here, we split it vertically, leaving two columns on the west side and three on the east.

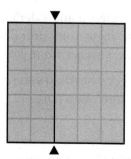

Next we add a passage through the wall, anywhere along that wall. Let's say we put it here:

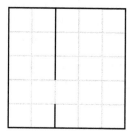

That completes one iteration of the algorithm. This process now repeats, recursively, on each of the halves. Let's process the western side next, dividing it in half horizontally and leaving a single passage to connect the two areas.

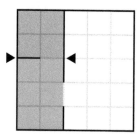

The process repeats again, here dividing the northwestern region in half:

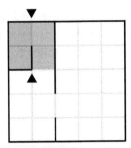

At this point, the regions that were created by the newest split are too small to divide further—we don't want to split individual cells in half—so we jump over and start processing the remaining regions.

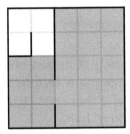

When we're all done, having processed all the regions down to the size of a single cell, we have a maze:

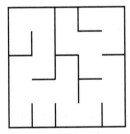

Next let's nail down an implementation.

Implementing Recursive Division

The algorithm really is as simple as described. First, we'll "blank out" the grid by linking every cell to its neighbors (effectively removing all interior walls), and then recursively split the grid in half by adding walls back in.

Unlike the other algorithms we've implemented, we're going to break this one into a few different methods to help with the recursion. It'll all start with our typical on(grid) method, though. Put the following in recursive_division.rb.

```
recursive_division.rb
Line 1  class RecursiveDivision

          def self.on(grid)
            @grid = grid
5
            @grid.each_cell do |cell|
              cell.neighbors.each { |n| cell.link(n, false) }
            end

10          divide(0, 0, @grid.rows, grid.columns)
          end


        end
```

Lines 6–8 link every cell to each of its neighbors. (We pass false to the link method to prevent it from creating a reciprocal connection. We're already iterating over every cell, after all.) Then, line 10 triggers the recursion, starting the process of dividing the grid in half.

Let's look at divide next. Go ahead and add this immediately after the on method:

```
Line 1  def self.divide(row, column, height, width)
2         return if height <= 1 || width <= 1
3
4         if height > width
5           divide_horizontally(row, column, height, width)
6         else
7           divide_vertically(row, column, height, width)
8         end
9       end
```

The condition on line 2 tests to see whether the region is too small to subdivide. If it is, then the recursion ends for this particular area. Otherwise, we decide whether to divide the area horizontally or vertically. Although this could be done randomly, dividing based on the aspect ratio of the region tends to give good results, and avoids producing areas with lots of long vertical or horizontal passages.

The last two methods are very similar to each other. Add these at the end of the RecursiveDivision class.

```
Line 1  def self.divide_horizontally(row, column, height, width)
          divide_south_of = rand(height-1)
          passage_at = rand(width)
```

```
5    width.times do |x|
       next if passage_at == x

       cell = @grid[row+divide_south_of, column+x]
       cell.unlink(cell.south)
10   end

     divide(row, column, divide_south_of+1, width)
     divide(row+divide_south_of+1, column, height-divide_south_of-1, width)
   end
15
   def self.divide_vertically(row, column, height, width)
     divide_east_of = rand(width-1)
     passage_at = rand(height)

20   height.times do |y|
       next if passage_at == y

       cell = @grid[row+y, column+divide_east_of]
       cell.unlink(cell.east)
25   end

     divide(row, column, height, divide_east_of+1)
     divide(row, column+divide_east_of+1, height, width-divide_east_of-1)
   end
```

Let's focus on divide_horizontally. (You'll see that divide_vertically is very similar.)

The first thing we do, on lines 2 and 3, is decide where to split the area and where the passage linking the two halves ought to be. We're dividing horizontally here, so the target grid line will be immediately south of whichever row is selected.

Then, for each cell along that dividing line (except for where our passage will be), we're going to *unlink* the cell from its southern neighbor (lines 8–9), effectively building a wall between the two cells.

Once that wall has been built, separating the two halves, lines 12 and 13 call divide on those new regions, recursing further into the grid.

That's it!

Let's put together our demo program so we can test it. Create recursive_division_demo.rb, and make it look like the following:

```
recursive_division_demo.rb
require 'recursive_division'
require 'grid'

grid = Grid.new(20, 20)
RecursiveDivision.on(grid)

filename = "recursive_division.png"
grid.to_png.save(filename)
puts "saved to #{filename}"
```

Running that will produce a maze via Recursive Division:

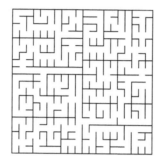

Just so!

The Recursive Division Bias

If you look at that long enough, you might begin to see evidence of one of this algorithm's biases—a certain "boxiness" to the texture caused by repeatedly halving the grid. If it seems a bit subtle, though, that's okay. We can color the grid to make the texture much more obvious.

The following figure shows a 100×100 maze generated by the Recursive Division algorithm and colored with Dijkstra's. The walls have been omitted to make the texture clearer.

The "pixelated" texture of the maze comes through much more clearly now. (It's really kind of beautiful, in a way!) But what are we seeing? What does this texture really *mean*?

Well, it suggests that there are regions of the maze that are literally boxed in—enclosed in these rectangular areas with few passages leading out. Recall that when we divided an area, we always left exactly one passage open between the two halves. This created a kind of bottleneck where any path from one side of the maze to the other *must* go through that passage.

The result is that boxy texture and a maze that is relatively straightforward to solve. All you have to do is look for the relevant bottlenecks. After all, the solution path is going to have to pass through them, one way or another!

Making Rooms with Recursion

So, it's a novel algorithm, but at this point it seems like it might have pretty limited usefulness. I mean, that colored version was pretty and all, but unless you're going for some Cubist art, it might be hard to see why you would use this algorithm.

The answer, my friend, is *rooms*.

Recall the top of our divide method, where we test the width and height of the region. The purpose there is to see if the region has grown small enough, but if you randomly force the recursion to halt before that, you can prevent some of them from ever becoming that small. This results in *open areas*—rooms, or courtyards, or parking lots, or whatever makes sense in the context of your maze.

Let's try it!

Open up recursive_division.rb again, and find the first line of the divide method, the one that returns if the height or width is too small. Try replacing that line with the following:

```
return if height <= 1 || width <= 1 ||
  height < 5 && width < 5 && rand(4) == 0
```

Running the demo program now, you ought to get a maze like the following:

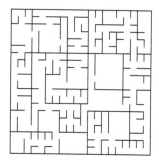

Look at that! It's a floor plan now. All that boxy texture needed was some help to masquerade as an office block.

Your Turn

There you have it: the last of those dozen algorithms you were promised. Eller's algorithm works as if it were the offspring of a marriage between Sidewinder and Kruskal's, and Recursive Division...well...Recursive Division is off doing its own thing, making fractal mazes by cutting things in half.

Play around with these and see where they take you. What ideas did you have as you read about them? Chase those down and do something about them! Maybe the following ideas can get you started.

Infinitely Eller's...

You've seen how Eller's algorithm operates on a single row at a time, clear to the last row. But what if you never give it a last row? How would you generate an arbitrarily (infinitely?) long maze using this algorithm?

Eller's Algorithm Elsewhere

Eller's, like Sidewinder, really works best on a regular grid of squares. However, with a bit of creativity it can be made to work on a grid of hexes, and even a circle grid. How would you do it?

Irregular Divisions

Here's a challenging one! As you saw, the boxiness of the Recursive Division algorithm comes from using horizontal and vertical lines to split the regions in half. What if the lines used to split those areas didn't have to be straight? How would you divide those areas into non-rectangular regions?

Mixing Algorithms

You saw the rooms that appear when the Recursive Division algorithm is forced to halt recursion early. What if, instead of leaving those rooms empty, you were to run *some other maze algorithm* in them? Each of those "rooms" are, after all, little miniature grids!

Wall Adders versus Passage Carvers

Some algorithms work best as passage carvers (like Recursive Backtracker), and some work best as wall adders (like Recursive Division). But some can be made to work using either technique. Remember that "wall adder" simply describes a process where the algorithm creates walls instead of passages. With that in mind, how would you implement the Aldous-Broder algorithm (on page 55) as a wall adder? What other algorithms can work when considered that way?

You might think you're done, now that you've learned all twelve maze algorithms. Hold on, though. The most mind-blowing bits are yet to come! We'll start by taking your mazes into higher dimensions...

Part IV

Shapes and Surfaces

That's all the algorithms, but it's hardly the end of what you can do with them. We'll wrap things up by looking at how to stretch these mazes into multiple dimensions, and how to use them to cover the surfaces of 3D objects like spheres and Möbius strips.

Part IV

Shares and Surfaces

CHAPTER 13

Extending Mazes into Higher Dimensions

All of the mazes we've generated to this point have been essentially flat, glued securely to the surface of a plane. Navigating these mazes, regardless of whether they are regular, polar, hex, or triangle grids, you only ever have the option of moving in two dimensions, north or south, east or west, or some combination of those.

It's true that weave mazes try to escape that constraint a bit, and do briefly manage to lift portions of their passages above that plane by moving over or under other passages. Still, most of a weave maze remains sadly two-dimensional. We might say that, at best, a weave maze is *two-and-a-half-dimensional*.

Now, these two-dimensional (or two-and-a-half dimensional) mazes are sufficient for many things—games like Pac-Man and Doom (to name just two) manage just fine with nothing more than two axes to constrain movement, thank-you-very-much. We've done a lot with two-dimensional mazes to this point in the book.

But there's so much *more* we can do once we add a third dimension, or even a fourth. Cave systems, office blocks, dungeons, and Death Stars, time traveling, and portal jumping are just a few.

In this chapter, we're going to look at these higher-dimensional mazes and talk about what exactly that means. We'll start with three-dimensional *regular* grids (those whose cells are rectangular in shape), going over the changes that need to be made to our Grid class to accommodate a third dimension, and we'll talk about how to apply our maze algorithms to these modified grids. Once we've got three dimensions working, we'll look briefly at what even higher dimensions do to a maze, blowing minds by considering four-dimensional grids.

Understanding Dimensions

The word "dimension" in phrases like "two-dimensional" or "three-dimensional" refers to the number of coordinates needed to specify any point within some space. In the case of our two-dimensional mazes, we've described those points (or cells) in terms of rows and columns—two coordinates, hence, two dimensions.

If you take away all dimensions, removing all coordinates, you've discovered a *zero-dimensional* space. Such spaces seem exceedingly Zen-like, having no sense of location, but only of *being*. (Whoa. Dude!) In terms of our mazes, a single cell is a zero-dimensional space because without the context of other cells, it has no concept of location. You can't *go* anywhere from such a free-standing cell. It's not very exciting by itself, but if you take a bunch of these zero-dimensional cells and stack them together, you can make a one-dimensional grid, like this:

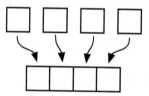

You can see that such a grid only lets you move along a single axis, like north/south or east/west. As a result, each cell in it may be addressed simply by its distance from one of the ends, like 1 or 3. One coordinate, one dimension.

A maze on such a grid would be a bit better than one in a zero-dimensional space, but not by much. There would still be no branching, no winding, and no dead ends. It would be a single, straight passage. The following figure shows a one-dimensional maze on the east/west axis.

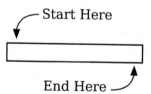

Again, not too thrilling, but if you take a few of them and stack them together, you wind up with a two-dimensional grid, like this:

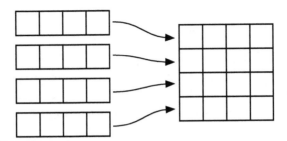

Which brings back to where we started! Each cell within such a grid must be addressed by both its *row* and its *column*—two coordinates. The grid in the preceding figure is a *regular* grid—composed of squares—but it could be a hex grid, triangle grid, polar grid, or something even more exotic. It doesn't matter—if cells are addressed by two coordinates, the grid is two-dimensional.

Let's take these to the next level. We'll take a look at grids with a third dimension.

Introducing 3D Mazes

So, zero-dimensional cells combine to form one-dimensional rows, and one-dimensional rows stack to form two-dimensional grids. It should follow, then, that *two*-dimensional grids may be stacked to form *three*-dimensional grids...which is exactly the case, as the following figure shows.

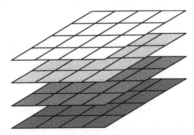

When we think of each of these separate 2D grids as *levels* within the larger 3D grid, it becomes clear that each cell in such a grid must be addressed by three coordinates: row, column, and level.

Three coordinates. Three dimensions.

Displayed like that, though, it's a bit hard to see each of the levels, so instead of rendering in perspective we generally show it as a set of floor plans, like this:

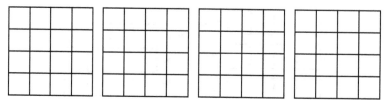

The bottom floor, or level, is on the far left, with progressively higher levels moving to the right.

So, that gives us a way to describe and display three-dimensional grids. All we need now is a way to generate a three-dimensional *maze* using a layout like this. The simplest way (if not the most flexible way) is to generate a bunch of two-dimensional mazes, stack them, and then connect adjacent levels at single point, like this:

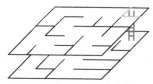

This works fine, and as long as each of the levels was originally a perfect maze the result will also be one. Remember how Kruskal's algorithm worked by linking together those little proto-mazes, one at a time? It's really just the same thing here. It's as if Kruskal's algorithm came along and linked those adjacent mazes together at that one point.

This approach could suffice for many applications. As long as there is only a single location that links adjacent levels, you can treat (and generate) each level as an independent two-dimensional maze.

However, what if you want a maze that goes up and down between levels in multiple places? What if you want a solution path that takes you all the way to the top of the tower, and then all the way back to the bottom? If you want it to remain a perfect maze, you can't just add ladders at multiple points, because as soon as you do, *you've added a loop.*

Check it out. Let's label the two cells in the previous figure that are linked by the ladder. We'll call the lower cell *A* and the upper cell *B*, like this:

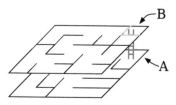

As mentioned before, as long as the two component mazes are perfect, the resulting bi-level maze is also perfect. But if we now add another link between the two, we've got problems. Let's say we add another ladder that links the two mazes as shown in the following figure, connecting point C on the lower maze to point D on the upper maze.

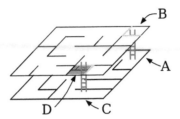

Now, because both were—by themselves—perfect mazes, we know for a fact that there is exactly one path connecting A to C via the lower maze, and exactly one path from B to D via the upper maze. But because A and B are linked, and C and D are linked, we now have *two* ways to go from A to C: through the lower maze, A to C, and via the upper maze, A to B to D to C.

A loop! We simply cannot get a perfect, three-dimensional maze by adding multiple connections between perfect two-dimensional mazes. We have to turn to other means.

Fortunately, those other means turn out to be straightforward. We need to extend our grid, adding another dimension to it, and then run our maze algorithm of choice on it.

Adding a Third Dimension

Recall back in Chapter 2, *Automating and Displaying Your Mazes*, on page 17, when we first worked on the code behind the grid, we implemented the prepare_grid method using a *two-dimensional array*. That's not just coincidence—that's exactly what determined the geometry of our grid! We'll add a third dimension to the grid by adding a third dimension to that array.

If it were that easy, this would be a very short chapter. The good news, though, is that the other changes are minor collateral damage related to that array modification. The cells need to be told about their new up/down neighbors, the grid needs to know how to iterate over cells in the other levels, and so on.

It's really not too bad, and best of all is that once we've made those changes, most of the algorithms we've looked at will automatically work. Even those that break with these changes can be brought into line with a few simple modifications. You'll see.

Let's get this implemented. For simplicity's sake, put everything—grid and cell—in the same file, called grid3d.rb. Start with the new cell class, like this:

grid3d.rb
```ruby
require 'grid'

class Cell3D < Cell
  attr_reader :level
  attr_accessor :up, :down

  def initialize(level, row, column)
    @level = level
    super(row, column)
  end

  def neighbors
    list = super
    list << up if up
    list << down if down
    list
  end
end
```

The Cell3D class simply extends our original Cell class and adds level (the third dimension, analogous to row and column), as well as accessors for the neighbors in the up and down directions. The neighbors method is also overridden to include those two new neighbors.

The grid itself is nearly as straightforward, but we need to reimplement a few of the other methods that assume the grid is only one level tall. The idea here is to change our grid so that it can represent not just a single (two-dimensional) level, but multiple levels stacked together. Put the following in grid3d.rb as well, just after the definition of Cell3D.

grid3d.rb
```ruby
class Grid3D < Grid
  attr_reader :levels

  def initialize(levels, rows, columns)
    @levels = levels
    super(rows, columns)
  end

  def prepare_grid
    Array.new(levels) do |level|
      Array.new(rows) do |row|
        Array.new(columns) do |column|
          Cell3D.new(level, row, column)
        end
```

```ruby
        end
      end
    end

    def configure_cells
      each_cell do |cell|
        level, row, col = cell.level, cell.row, cell.column

        cell.north = self[level, row - 1, col]
        cell.south = self[level, row + 1, col]
        cell.west  = self[level, row, col - 1]
        cell.east  = self[level, row, col + 1]
        cell.down  = self[level - 1, row, col]
        cell.up    = self[level + 1, row, col]
      end
    end

    def [](level, row, column)
      return nil unless level.between?(0, @levels - 1)
      return nil unless row.between?(0, @grid[level].count - 1)
      return nil unless column.between?(0, @grid[level][row].count - 1)
      @grid[level][row][column]
    end

    def random_cell
      level  = rand(@levels)
      row    = rand(@grid[level].count)
      column = rand(@grid[level][row].count)

      @grid[level][row][column]
    end

    def size
      @levels * @rows * @columns
    end

    def each_level
      @grid.each do |level|
        yield level
      end
    end

    def each_row
      each_level do |rows|
        rows.each do |row|
          yield row
        end
      end
    end
end
```

All we've done here is reimplement those methods that assume the grid is two-dimensional—prepare_grid, configure_cells, the array accessor, and so on—and make them aware of that third dimension. We've also added a new method, each_level, for iterating over every two-dimensional level of the grid.

That'll do it! With the grid made aware of the third dimension, and every cell now updated to include its "up" and "down" neighbors (those on the levels above and below), most of our algorithms ought to just work. Feel free to give it a try...but note that we don't yet have a way to draw these 3D mazes. Our current to_png requires a bit more attention.

Displaying a 3D Maze

We'll draw these mazes as sets of floor plans, with lower floors to the left and higher floors to the right. The up and down passages will be represented by red arrows drawn in the corresponding cells, indicating which of the adjacent floors each passage leads to. For example, a 3×3×3 maze might look something like this:

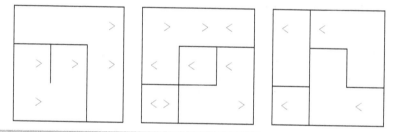

Figure 6—A 3×3×3 Maze

Arrows pointing to the right are like stairs leading to the level above them, and arrows pointing to the left are stairs leading down. If we enter the maze in the northwest corner of the bottom level (the one on the far left), we might take two steps east to the northeast corner, take the stairs up to the same corner of the middle level, go one step to the west and then up another flight of stairs, winding up on the third level.

It's a bit mind-bending!

But it works, and it's not too difficult to implement. It comes together like this. Put the following in grid3d.rb, at the end of the definition of the Grid3D class.

```
Line 1  def to_png(cell_size: 10, inset: 0, margin: cell_size/2)
   -      inset = (cell_size * inset).to_i
   -
   -      grid_width = cell_size * columns
```

```
5    grid_height = cell_size * rows

     img_width = grid_width * levels + (levels - 1) * margin
     img_height = grid_height

10   background = ChunkyPNG::Color::WHITE
     wall = ChunkyPNG::Color::BLACK
     arrow = ChunkyPNG::Color.rgb(255, 0, 0)

     img = ChunkyPNG::Image.new(img_width + 1, img_height + 1, background)
15
     [:backgrounds, :walls].each do |mode|
       each_cell do |cell|
         x = cell.level * (grid_width + margin) + cell.column * cell_size
         y = cell.row * cell_size
20
         if inset > 0
           to_png_with_inset(img, cell, mode, cell_size, wall, x, y, inset)
         else
           to_png_without_inset(img, cell, mode, cell_size, wall, x, y)
25       end

         if mode == :walls
           mid_x = x + cell_size / 2
           mid_y = y + cell_size / 2
30
           if cell.linked?(cell.down)
             img.line(mid_x-3, mid_y, mid_x-1, mid_y+2, arrow)
             img.line(mid_x-3, mid_y, mid_x-1, mid_y-2, arrow)
           end
35
           if cell.linked?(cell.up)
             img.line(mid_x+3, mid_y, mid_x+1, mid_y+2, arrow)
             img.line(mid_x+3, mid_y, mid_x+1, mid_y-2, arrow)
           end
40       end
       end
     end

     img
45 end
```

This implementation introduces a new parameter, margin, which represents the spacing between the different levels of the grid. By default, it'll be half of one cell width.

Next, we need to figure out just how large our image will be. It's easy enough to figure out the size of a single grid—that's just what we did in our first to_png implementation, and it's what we do here on lines 4 and 5. The image itself is going to remain one grid-height tall, but the width will be one grid-width wide for each level, plus that margin between adjacent pairs of levels. Line 7 computes that for us.

The last new thing we do before actually drawing the maze is to set the color for our arrows, on line 12. We're using a pure red, leaving the green and blue components of the color at zero.

Then, we do the actual drawing. We can reuse most of what we'd implemented in previous chapters—all we have to do is compute the correct position of each cell, and then have our individual cell-drawing methods do the rest. Line 18 computes the x-coordinate of the cell's northwest corner, and the next line does the same for the y-coordinate.

Once the cells are drawn, all that's left is to draw the arrows for passages going up or down. This happens on lines 27–40, drawing each arrow relative to the center of the current cell.

With that bit in place, we can try building and drawing a 3D maze. The Recursive Backtracker is a pretty safe algorithm here—it's very forgiving of changes in the grid geometry—so we'll use it here. Put the following in grid3d_demo.rb.

grid3d_demo.rb
```
require 'grid3d'
require 'recursive_backtracker'

grid = Grid3D.new(3, 3, 3)
RecursiveBacktracker.on(grid)

filename = "3d.png"
grid.to_png(cell_size: 20).save(filename)
puts "saved to #{filename}"
```

It should all be very familiar by now, though we're drawing the cells larger (20 pixels on a side) so that the up/down arrows don't get so crowded. The resulting maze ought to look very much like the one in Figure 6, *A 3x3x3 Maze*, on page 216. Experiment with different dimensions and see what you get!

You may want to experiment with other algorithms, too—and well you should!—but not all of those we've looked at will work as implemented. The ones to look out for are Kruskal's, Binary Tree, and Sidewinder—and the truth is, even those could be made to work with a 3D grid. In each case, it is our implementation at fault, and not the algorithm.

In Kruskal's case, our implementation of the State class is hard-coded to match each cell against its *south* and *east* neighbors when forming the list of neighbor pairs. Adding either *up* or *down* as an additional neighbor (in the State#initialize method) fixes that problem.

For Sidewinder, every time a run of cells is closed out, our implementation chooses one of the cells from that run and adds a passage *north*. If we were to change it so that instead of always going *north*, it chooses between *north* and *up* (or whichever one is available, if one or the other neighbor doesn't exist), then we'll get a 3D-capable Sidewinder.

And for Binary Tree, the trick is to turn it into a *trinary* tree. At each cell, instead of choosing only between *north* and *east*, try choosing between *north*, *east*, and *up* (or *down*). The resulting algorithm is perfectly happy to generate mazes on a three-dimensional grid.

Give those a try and see how it works out! When you're ready, we'll make one last, brief stop—in the fourth dimension.

Representing Four Dimensions

You've now seen how the pattern comes together. Zero-dimensional *cells* make one-dimensional *rows* (or *columns*), which come together to make two-dimensional *levels*, which stack to make three-dimensional *worlds*.

So what happens when you take those three-dimensional worlds and stack them along *another* axis, perpendicular to the three we already have? (Ignore for the moment that it's rather difficult to imagine a direction that is simultaneously perpendicular to the three axes we've already got.) You can probably guess that we're going to wind up with a *four*-dimensional grid, and you'll be exactly right.

To illustrate stacking in the fourth dimension, we can take those three-dimensional grids and line them up vertically on the page, as shown in the figure on page 220.

This grid is 2×4×4×4—two sets of three-dimensional grids (or *worlds*), each of which is composed of four two-dimensional grids (*levels*), and each of those two-dimensional grids is a 4×4 grid of cells (*rows* and *columns*). Four coordinates, four dimensions. Movement between adjacent three-dimensional grids is via the *hither/yon* axis, analogous to *up/down* but in the fourth dimension.

Adjacency works just as it did with the three-dimensional grids, but also connects the hither cells (those that are in the 3D grid above the current one) and yon cells (those that are in the 3D grid below). The following figure shows

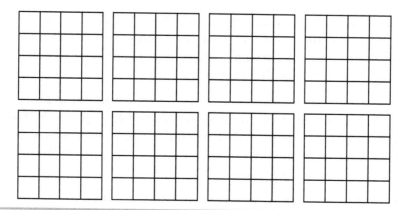

Figure 7—Representing a 4D Stack

a 3×3×3×3 grid with a single cell drawn in green, and all of the cells adjacent to it in yellow.

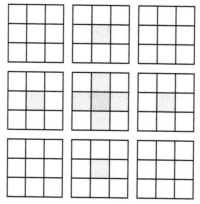

Implementing such a grid is as easy as it was for the third dimension—adding another dimension to the array that holds the cells, adding new neighbor accessors (hither and yon) to the Cell class, and updating the various Grid methods to accommodate this new dimension. Once you've made those changes, you can go truly nuts and generate mind-bending *four-dimensional* mazes, like Figure 8, *A 4D Maze*, on page 221.

Movement works just as it did with the three-dimensional mazes, with the left and right arrows acting as stairs pointing *up* and *down*. We've also added arrows pointing *hither* and *yon*. If you think of them as portals, warping you between worlds, the picture might begin to make a little more sense!

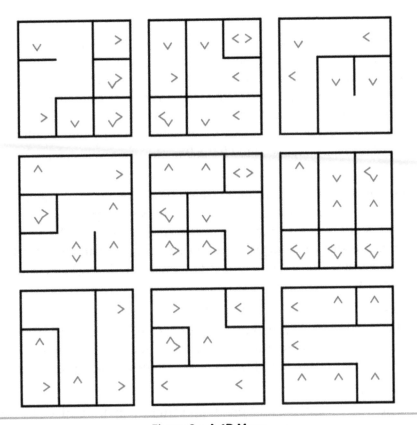

Figure 8—A 4D Maze

Your Turn

So there you have it, a whirlwind tour of the third and (briefly!) fourth dimensions. We've looked at how to modify the Grid and Cell classes to accommodate these new dimensions and saw one way to visualize mazes on these kinds of grids.

Where will you go with this knowledge? If you find yourself lacking a destination, perhaps consider some of the following:

Changing the Grid Type

The examples and illustrations in this chapter were all based on *regular* grids—grids based on square (or cubic) cells. What if you were to stack hex grids, or triangle grids instead?

Three-Dimensional Circle Mazes

Try stacking a bunch of polar grids together (from Chapter 7, *Going in Circles*, on page 97), to form a cylindrical tower maze! If you're feeling particularly adventurous, try varying the radius of the circle as the level increases, decreasing it to a point to form a cone. Even more adventurous, make a "Death Star" by changing the radius of each level so that they form a sphere. (Obi-wan might never have found the off switch for that tractor beam if you'd been in charge!)

Forcing a Level Bias

Running our maze algorithms on these three-dimensional grids, we wind up with paths that move between levels very frequently. In real life, though, a multistory building only moves between floors in a few locations. How can you modify these algorithms so that they prefer to choose cells that are adjacent north-to-south or east-to-west, before falling back to up/down neighbors?

A First-Person Perspective

Using whatever tools you prefer, implement a first-person view from inside a randomly generated three-dimensional maze. Either allow users to navigate it themselves, or just animate a fly-through of the longest path.

Cells as Polyhedra

For a *real* challenge, consider a three-dimensional grid composed of interlocking polyhedra! Rhombic dodecahedrons, for example, can be stacked to tile a three-dimensional space. If you go this route, though, say good-bye to simple floor plans; you'll need to get creative in order to visualize the result! A first-person perspective may be ideal for mazes like this...

Even Higher Dimensions

If you're feeling particularly devious, try generating a five- or six-dimensional maze! Draw it by taking sets of four-dimensional mazes and lining them up horizontally and vertically, just as we did with the two-dimensional grids when drawing three- and four-dimensional mazes. You'll need to get creative with vocabulary in order to describe neighbors in those higher dimensions, but that might just be the hardest challenge you'll face on this one!

You're getting pretty handy with these grids now, and quite comfortable building mazes on them. You can even build them out in three and four dimensions! It's time to learn a new trick: building out mazes on *non-planar surfaces*.

CHAPTER 14

Bending and Folding Your Mazes

It's been a wild ride, but we're nearly done. Maze algorithms, grids born of non-rectangular tesselations, circles, weaves, and braids, and even building those mazes out in three and four dimensions—it's all brought us to this point.

Let's go out with a bang. Let's blow some minds.

Consider those mazes you've generated up to now, all of them neatly built on flat, predictable surfaces. Even the three-dimensional ones were composed of neatly planar levels. But what would happen if you were to take one of those mazes and *bend* it a bit, warping the surface so that it curves in one or more dimensions? What if you were to even go so far as to *fold* it?

Those first-person shooters take on an entirely different feel when the corridors wrap around the surface of a sphere, or carry you around the inside of a ribbon. Picture a game where you can see your goal *above you* as the maze arches overhead, or where monsters may be lurking just down the passage, hidden by a not-so-distant horizon!

These are what are called *planair* mazes, an unusual name for an unusual kind of puzzle. Mazes on cylinders, cubes, cones, pyramids, spheres, and toruses are all examples of these planair mazes, and I'll be honest: this is a topic that could easily be an entire book in its own right. We've only got time for a brief taste, but hopefully that'll be enough to set you exploring some more on your own.

We'll look at four different surfaces in this chapter: cylinders, Möbius strips, cubes, and spheres. In each case, you'll learn how to generate a maze on that surface. For the first three, we'll use simple paper-crafting techniques to visualize the resulting mazes, and for the last we'll resort to using a 3D renderer to draw our maze on the surface of a sphere.

Cylinder Mazes

Cylinder mazes are a good place to start, because they're actually really, really easy. You can make a naive one simply by generating a rectangular maze, printing it out, and wrapping it around a soup can so that the ends touch, like this:

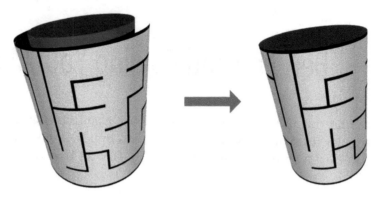

The problem with this approach is that you wind up with a seam where the maze's east and west boundaries meet:

Is this ringing any bells? You may recall that we ran into a similar issue at the end of our discussion on circle mazes on page 110. We can solve the problem here using the same trick we used there: overriding the [] method to ensure that the column parameter wraps smoothly from one side to the other. In this way, columns on the east and west boundaries are made to think they're actually adjacent to one another.

The entirety of our cylinder grid implementation looks like this:

cylinder_grid.rb
```ruby
require 'grid'

class CylinderGrid < Grid
  def [](row, column)
    return nil unless row.between?(0, @rows - 1)
    column = column % @grid[row].count
    @grid[row][column]
  end
end
```

We'll do the usual drill here and make a demo program to test it:

cylinder_demo.rb
```ruby
require 'cylinder_grid'
require 'recursive_backtracker'

grid = CylinderGrid.new(7, 16)
RecursiveBacktracker.on(grid)

filename = "cylinder.png"
grid.to_png.save(filename)
puts "saved to #{filename}"
```

The resulting maze will look a bit odd:

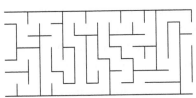

Keep in mind, though, that this maze is intended to *wrap around*, so the east and west edges are actually supposed to be adjacent. The dimensions here were chosen intentionally to give an aspect ratio similar to that of the label on a can of soup, so if you wanted, you could scale your image up to approximately 8.25" by 3.625" (21cm by 9.2cm), print it out, and disguise your least-favorite can in the pantry with it. With any luck, the chef will be so hypnotized by the seamlessness of your cylinder maze that you'll be able to propose something more palatable as an alternative!

Let's take things up a notch and consider putting a maze on a Möbius strip.

Möbius Mazes

A *Möbius strip* (sometimes spelled *Moebius*, or *Mobius*) is a novel surface with only a single side. You can make one easily by taking a strip of paper, giving one end a 180° twist, and then taping the two ends together. The result (assuming you happened to use checkered paper) would look something like this:

An ant crawling along the surface of this strip of paper would find that it had traversed both sides before returning to its starting point. Like magic!

This is begging to have a maze on it, and it turns out that we can do so with very little effort. It's actually very much like a cylinder maze, but with a twist—literally! We need to take that cylinder maze and give it a 180° twist. Therein lies the rub. A cylinder maze only needs to exist on a single side of the paper, since it has a well-defined inside and outside. Adding that twist means that our maze needs to exist on *both* sides, in such a way that when we twist it and join the ends, the edges and passages all line up correctly.

We *could* try to do this by generating two images, each corresponding to one side of the strip, and then attempt to print them back to back, but getting the printer to line up the two images correctly would be an exceedingly fiddly undertaking. We can do this much more easily.

First, we generate our maze on a long, thin grid, like the following:

Then, we split that grid in half and generate a single image with the two halves side-by-side, like this:

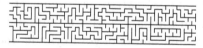

After printing the image and cutting away the extraneous paper, we fold the result in half lengthwise, so that the two halves of the maze wind up back-to-back:

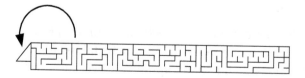

This gives us our maze on both sides of the strip, just what we need for the final act! Not only that, though: folding the paper like this also flips the two halves top-to-bottom relative to each other, which means that when we finally give the paper a half-twist and connect the ends, the edges are properly oriented. Isn't that ingenious? Go on, admit it. You're dying to try this out.

Put the following in moebius_grid.rb.

moebius_grid.rb
```
Line 1   require 'cylinder_grid'
   -
   -     class MoebiusGrid < CylinderGrid
   -       def initialize(rows, columns)
   5           super(rows, columns*2)
   -       end
   -
   -       def to_png(cell_size: 10, inset: 0)
   -         grid_height = cell_size * rows
  10         mid_point = columns / 2
   -
   -         img_width = cell_size * mid_point
   -         img_height = grid_height * 2
   -
  15         inset = (cell_size * inset).to_i
   -
   -         background = ChunkyPNG::Color::WHITE
   -         wall = ChunkyPNG::Color::BLACK
   -
  20         img = ChunkyPNG::Image.new(img_width + 1, img_height + 1, background)
   -
   -         [:backgrounds, :walls].each do |mode|
   -           each_cell do |cell|
   -             x = (cell.column % mid_point) * cell_size
  25             y = cell.row * cell_size
   -
   -             y += grid_height if cell.column >= mid_point
   -
   -             if inset > 0
  30               to_png_with_inset(img, cell, mode, cell_size, wall, x, y, inset)
   -             else
   -               to_png_without_inset(img, cell, mode, cell_size, wall, x, y)
   -             end
   -           end
  35         end
   -
   -         img
   -       end
   -     end
```

We subclass our CylinderGrid so that we get the east-to-west wrapping, and then in the constructor we do something that may seem a bit odd: line 5 tells the superclass to make our grid *twice as wide* as we specify. The purpose for this is that it lets us say how many columns long the *strip of paper* needs to be—and then automatically compensates the grid for the other side of the strip.

The rest of the implementation is just our updated to_png method. It's essentially what we've seen before, but with a few tweaks. On line 10, we compute the column at which we'll split the grid. That midpoint is used to determine the width of the image on line 12, and the next line after that sets the image height to be the height of the grid, doubled. (Recall that we're rendering both halves of the grid, one above the other.)

The midpoint value is also used to compute the position of each cell in the image. Line 24 uses modulus arithmetic to make sure both halves of the grid are rendered next to each other, with line 27 moving the second half of the grid below the first half. Everything else is just as before—calling the appropriate method for drawing each cell, and simply passing in the coordinates to ensure the cells are drawn where they ought to be.

Use the following code to test our new MoebiusGrid.

moebius_demo.rb
```ruby
require 'moebius_grid'
require 'recursive_backtracker'

grid = MoebiusGrid.new(5, 50)
RecursiveBacktracker.on(grid)

filename = "moebius.png"
grid.to_png.save(filename)
puts "saved to #{filename}"
```

The dimensions of the grid given here are empirically chosen to give a strip that twists and joins neatly, but feel free to experiment with different sizes and see what you get. Remember that the number of columns describes the width of one side of the strip—the grid itself will actually be twice as long!

Taking the image from that little program and going through the process described earlier (printing it, cutting it out, folding it, etc.), you ought to wind up with something more or less like this:

Take it to your next party! It'll make a great conversation piece.

Cube Mazes

Next up: cube mazes. We're not talking about networks of passages *inside* a cube; that would give us those 3D mazes that we covered in the previous chapter. Rather, here we're considering mazes rendered purely on the *surface* of a cube.

Compared to cylindrical mazes, these are definitely a level up. It's true that they have some in common with cylinders (an ant on a cube could walk happily all the way around it, after all), but there's more to it. To help understand the difference, we need a simple way to visualize how a cube is constructed.

Start by picturing a cube, like a big cardboard box. If you were to unfold that box, taking it apart at the seams and laying it out flat, you'd end up with six square *faces* arranged something like the following figure. We'll label the faces from zero to five, to make it easier to refer to them later.

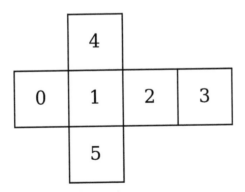

Figure 9—An Unfolded Cube

The goal here is to draw a grid on each of those faces and arrange things so that the cells on the boundaries of each face are adjacent to the cells on the shared boundaries of the adjacent faces. In other words, we want the cells on the east boundary of face #1 to be adjacent to the cells on the west boundary of face #2, and so forth.

This happens to suggest a way to represent the cube as a whole: as six separate faces. We'll do just that, storing each of those faces as distinct two-dimensional grids. Each cell will track the face, row, and column to which it belongs.

Let's go ahead and implement that much. Put the following in cube_grid.rb.

cube_grid.rb
```ruby
require 'grid'

class CubeCell < Cell
  attr_reader :face

  def initialize(face, row, column)
    @face = face
    super(row, column)
  end
end

class CubeGrid < Grid
  alias dim rows

  def initialize(dim)
    super(dim, dim)
  end

  def prepare_grid
    Array.new(6) do |face|
      Array.new(dim) do |row|
        Array.new(dim) do |column|
          CubeCell.new(face, row, column)
        end
      end
    end
  end
end
```

No real surprises here. CubeCell subclasses Cell, just adding the face attribute.

CubeGrid begins nearly as simply. It aliases the rows attribute as dim (as in "dimension"), and the constructor takes a single parameter to be used as that value (the number of rows and columns on each face). The prepare_grid method then uses dim to instantiate a 2D grid for each of those six faces.

The implementation may look very much like our three-dimensional grid from the previous chapter, but don't be fooled—the surface of a cube is actually two-dimensional! We've just added that third coordinate—face—as a convenience for organizing the subgrids.

Next, we'll override a few more methods to accommodate the six faces of this cubic geometry. Add these to the CubeGrid class as well, following the prepare_grid method.

```
def each_face
  @grid.each do |face|
    yield face
  end
end

def each_row
  each_face do |face|
    face.each do |row|
      yield row
    end
  end
end

def random_cell
  face   = rand(6)
  row    = rand(dim)
  column = rand(dim)

  @grid[face][row][column]
end

def size
  6 * dim * dim
end
```

These will let us iterate over the faces, rows, and cells of our grid, as well as choose a cell at random and compute the total number of cells in the grid.

Once we have that much, we reach the hardest part: determining cell adjacency. Specifically, we need to identify which cells are adjacent to which others at the boundaries, and there are some pretty wild edge cases here. We'll set the basics up like this, in the configure_cells and [] methods:

```
def configure_cells
  each_cell do |cell|
    face, row, column = cell.face, cell.row, cell.column

    cell.west  = self[face, row, column-1]
    cell.east  = self[face, row, column+1]
    cell.north = self[face, row-1, column]
```

```
      cell.south = self[face, row+1, column]
    end
  end

  def [](face, row, column)
    return nil if face < 0 || face >= 6
➤   face, row, column = wrap(face, row, column)
    @grid[face][row][column]
  end
```

This should all look pretty familiar, with the exception of the highlighted line in the array accessor. We're going to add a new method, wrap, which takes the given face/row/column triple and—if the row or column overflows the face it's on—figures out what the actual coordinates are on the face to which they've overflowed. This will allow the configure_cells method to work as intended, where it simply adds or subtracts one from the row or column to get the correct neighbor, even if that bleeds over to an adjacent face.

This is where the edge cases come in, but they aren't all bad. Let's start with an easy one. Consider our unfolded cube again (Figure 9, *An Unfolded Cube*, on page 229), and imagine moving from face 0, to 1, to 2, to 3, and back to 0. The transitions there are straightforward—you would go from the last column of one face, to column 0 of the next face, while remaining on the same row. Similarly, moving in reverse would take you from the first column of one face to the last column on the next. The following figure illustrates this:

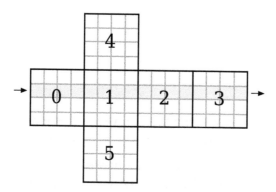

Easy enough. If only they could all be so straightforward! Let's look at a trickier one: what happens when you move east from face #4?

Ah, now things get interesting. Let's assume that we're in the last column of face #4, in some row *r*, and we want to move east. Mentally folding the cube back up, you can see that the eastern boundary of face #4 is actually adjacent to the *northern* boundary of face #2. This means that in moving to face #2 we move from row *r* to column *n-r*, and our row becomes 0. (We'll let *n* be the index of the last row or column on each face.) Check it out:

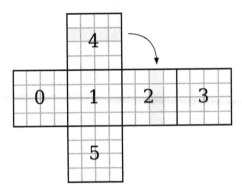

Whoa!

Take a moment and consider other transitions, like moving west from face #5, or (perhaps hardest of all to visualize) moving north from face #3. These are the kinds of transitions we need to encapsulate in our new wrap method. Once you've had a chance to give yourself a headache trying to envision these different connections, go ahead and add the following to the CubeGrid class:

```
Line 1  def wrap(face, row, column)
   -       n = dim-1
   -
   -       if row < 0
   5         return [4, column, 0]    if face == 0
   -         return [4, n, column]    if face == 1
   -         return [4, n-column, n]  if face == 2
   -         return [4, 0, n-column]  if face == 3
   -         return [3, 0, n-column]  if face == 4
  10         return [1, n, column]    if face == 5
   -       elsif row >= dim
   -         return [5, n-column, 0]  if face == 0
   -         return [5, 0, column]    if face == 1
   -         return [5, column, n]    if face == 2
  15         return [5, n, n-column]  if face == 3
   -         return [1, 0, column]    if face == 4
   -         return [3, n, n-column]  if face == 5
   -       elsif column < 0
   -         return [3, row, n]       if face == 0
  20         return [0, row, n]       if face == 1
   -         return [1, row, n]       if face == 2
   -         return [2, row, n]       if face == 3
   -         return [0, 0, row]       if face == 4
   -         return [0, n, n-row]     if face == 5
  25       elsif column >= dim
```

```
   -        return [1, row, 0]       if face == 0
   -        return [2, row, 0]       if face == 1
   -        return [3, row, 0]       if face == 2
   -        return [0, row, 0]       if face == 3
  30        return [2, 0, n-row]     if face == 4
   -        return [2, n, row]       if face == 5
   -      end
   -
   -
   -      [face, row, column]
  35   end
```

Given a face, row, and column, this method will compute and return the actual face, row, and column the coordinates correspond to. By default—if the row and column are within the bounds of the current face's grid—the method simply returns the parameter values, unaltered (line 34). But if either the row or column is less than 0, or greater than the dimensions of the grid, magic happens!

Well, not really magic. For instance, consider our simple case from before. Let's say that we're on the eastern boundary of face #1, and we move east. Our face is 1, and our column is now equal to dim. (We were in column dim-1—the last column on the face—and then moved east, which added one.) This means the wrap method takes the branch at line 25 (column >= dim), and then takes line 27 (because we're on face #1). The new coordinates are determined to be face #2, column 0, with the same row as before.

All that's left, then, is to implement a means of displaying our cube grid. We'll override to_png to generate an image with the cube's faces splayed out like in Figure 9, *An Unfolded Cube*, on page 229, which will allow us to print it, cut it out, and fold it into a neat little cube! Along with to_png, we'll also need to override to_png_without_inset (to make one little change), and we'll add a simple method for drawing faint outlines of the cube faces (to aid in folding).

We'll start with to_png. Go ahead and add the following at the end of CubeGrid.

```
Line 1  def to_png(cell_size: 10, inset: 0)
   -      inset = (cell_size * inset).to_i
   -
   -      face_width = cell_size * dim
   5      face_height = cell_size * dim
   -
   -      img_width = 4 * face_width
   -      img_height = 3 * face_height
   -
  10      offsets = [[0, 1], [1, 1], [2, 1], [3, 1], [1, 0], [1, 2]]
   -
   -      background = ChunkyPNG::Color::WHITE
   -      wall = ChunkyPNG::Color::BLACK
```

```
  -       outline = ChunkyPNG::Color.rgb(0xd0, 0xd0, 0xd0)
15
  -       img = ChunkyPNG::Image.new(img_width + 1, img_height + 1, background)
  -
  -       draw_outlines(img, face_width, face_height, outline)
  -
20        [:backgrounds, :walls].each do |mode|
  -         each_cell do |cell|
  -           x = offsets[cell.face][0] * face_width + cell.column * cell_size
  -           y = offsets[cell.face][1] * face_height + cell.row * cell_size
  -
25            if inset > 0
  -             to_png_with_inset(img, cell, mode, cell_size, wall, x, y, inset)
  -           else
  -             to_png_without_inset(img, cell, mode, cell_size, wall, x, y)
  -           end
30          end
  -       end
  -
  -       img
  -     end
```

It's remarkably similar to our original to_png method, with a few little changes. Lines 4 and 5 compute the dimensions of a single face, which is then used on lines 7 and 8 to compute the dimensions of the image as a whole.

Conceptually, we're aligning the faces to a grid of three rows and four columns, so we'll use that to make it easier to position each of the faces. The offsets variable on line 10 describes each face's position (column and row) within that larger grid. Lines 22 and 23 use those offsets to compute the position of each cell.

Also, note the call to our new draw_outlines method on line 18. Our maze would be perfectly acceptable without that call, but this will add some faint outlines around each face, helping us know better where to fold our maze after we've cut it out.

Let's look at that method next, in fact. Add the following just after our to_png method.

```
def draw_outlines(img, height, width, outline)
  # face #0
  img.rect(0, height, width, height*2, outline)

  # faces #2 & #3
  img.rect(width*2, height, width*4, height*2, outline)
  # line between faces #2 & #3
  img.line(width*3, height, width*3, height*2, outline)
```

```
  # face #4
  img.rect(width, 0, width*2, height, outline)

  # face #5
  img.rect(width, height*2, width*2, height*3, outline)
end
```

It's very simple—just drawing some rectangles and lines in our outline color (a light gray).

The last bit to look at is just our reimplementation of to_png_without_inset. The default implementation will only draw a cell's northern or western walls if the cell has no neighbors in those directions. That just won't do for our cube maze, though! A cell may have a neighbor to the north, but that neighbor could be on another face. Because of how we're drawing the maze, those two neighbors will not be drawn with a shared wall...which means that wall wouldn't get drawn. We mustn't have that!

Go ahead and add the following method just after draw_outlines.

```
def to_png_without_inset(img, cell, mode, cell_size, wall, x, y)
  x1, y1 = x, y
  x2 = x1 + cell_size
  y2 = y1 + cell_size

  if mode == :backgrounds
    color = background_color_for(cell)
    img.rect(x, y, x2, y2, color, color) if color
  else
➤   if cell.north.face != cell.face && !cell.linked?(cell.north)
➤     img.line(x1, y1, x2, y1, wall)
➤   end
➤
➤   if cell.west.face != cell.face && !cell.linked?(cell.west)
➤     img.line(x1, y1, x1, y2, wall)
➤   end

    img.line(x2, y1, x2, y2, wall) unless cell.linked?(cell.east)
    img.line(x1, y2, x2, y2, wall) unless cell.linked?(cell.south)
  end
end
```

Note the highlighted lines—that's where our new version differs from the original, ensuring that walls are drawn even if a cell has neighbors in those directions, when they happen to be on different faces.

There! Now we ought to be able to test it out by writing a simple demo program, like the following.

```
cube_demo.rb
require 'cube_grid'
require 'recursive_backtracker'

grid = CubeGrid.new(10)
RecursiveBacktracker.on(grid)

filename = "cube.png"
grid.to_png.save(filename)
puts "saved to #{filename}"
```

Running it should generate an image something like this:

Print it out, and carefully cut along the outside of the maze. Then, fold on all the gray lines, taping liberally as you go to keep it all together, and when all is said and done, you might just wind up with something as dazzling as this:

But now it's time to say farewell to paper-crafting. For our final surface, we're going to look at a way to produce an actual 3D rendering of our maze, this time on the surface of a sphere.

Sphere Mazes

Creating a maze on the surface of a sphere shares a lot in common with creating a maze inside of a circle. This shouldn't be surprising! A hemisphere, after all, is merely a circle that's been lifted up by its origin, like this:

We can create a sphere by putting two hemispheres together, which means we ought to be able to implement a spherical grid by leaning on our polar grid (from Chapter 7, *Going in Circles*, on page 97). We'll need to change a lot of the calculations behind the measuring of the cells (a hemisphere may be related to a circle, but that doesn't mean they wear the same size of shirt), and our to_png method is going to need rewriting, but it's a start.

So here's what we'll do. We'll subclass our PolarGrid to make a HemisphereGrid, and then glue two of those together to make a SphereGrid. We'll put all these in the same file, for convenience.

Let's start with the HemisphereGrid. Put the following in sphere_grid.rb:

```ruby
sphere_grid.rb
require 'polar_grid'

class HemisphereCell < PolarCell
  attr_reader :hemisphere

  def initialize(hemisphere, row, column)
    @hemisphere = hemisphere
    super(row, column)
  end
end

class HemisphereGrid < PolarGrid
  attr_reader :id

  def initialize(id, rows)
    @id = id
    super(rows)
  end

  def size(row)
    @grid[row].length
  end
```

```
     def prepare_grid
25     grid = Array.new(@rows)

       angular_height = Math::PI / (2 * @rows)

       grid[0] = [ HemisphereCell.new(id, 0, 0) ]
30
       (1...@rows).each do |row|
         theta = (row + 1) * angular_height
         radius = Math.sin(theta)
         circumference = 2 * Math::PI * radius
35
         previous_count = grid[row - 1].length
         estimated_cell_width = circumference / previous_count
         ratio = (estimated_cell_width / angular_height).round

40       cells = previous_count * ratio
         grid[row] = Array.new(cells) { |col| HemisphereCell.new(id, row, col) }
       end

       grid
45   end
   end
```

Our HemisphereCell class is simple enough—it just subclasses PolarCell and adds an attribute for keeping track of which hemisphere the cell belongs to (line 4).

The HemisphereGrid class is fairly straightforward, too—adding an id attribute to indicate which of the two hemispheres is being represented (line 13), as well as a simple method for querying the number of cells in a given row (line 20).

Our prepare_grid method is where we start busting out some math. In concept it is very similar to the same method of PolarGrid, but the computations have been adapted to a spherical surface. In particular, note the angular_height variable (line 27), which is the height *in radians* of each row. (In a curious twist of mathematical fate, this also happens to be the same as the physical distance between rows if we're building this out on a unit sphere.)

That angular_height is then used on lines 32–34 to compute the radius of the circle described by the given row, to eventually tell us how many cells that row ought to have.

There! Now that we've got a good definition of a hemispherical grid, we can use that to build our sphere. Add the following to the same file, after Hemisphere-Grid.

```
Line 1  class SphereGrid < Grid
   -      def initialize(rows)
   -        unless rows.even?
   -          raise ArgumentError, "argument must be an even number"
   5        end

   -        @equator = rows / 2
   -        super(rows, 1)
   -      end
   10

   -      def prepare_grid
   -        Array.new(2) { |id| HemisphereGrid.new(id, @equator) }
   -      end

   15     def configure_cells
   -        belt = @equator - 1
   -        size(belt).times do |index|
   -          a, b = self[0, belt, index], self[1, belt, index]
   -          a.outward << b
   20         b.outward << a
   -        end
   -      end

   -      def [](hemi, row, column)
   25       @grid[hemi][row, column]
   -      end

   -      def size(row)
   -        @grid[0].size(row)
   30     end

   -      def each_cell
   -        @grid.each do |hemi|
   -          hemi.each_cell { |cell| yield cell }
   35       end
   -      end

   -      def random_cell
   -        @grid.sample.random_cell
   40     end
   -   end
```

First off, the constructor checks to make sure that the number of rows specified for the grid is an even number (line 3). This is because we're using two hemispheres to implement the sphere as a whole, so the total number of rows needs to be evenly divisible by two. The equator line is computed next (line 7) and is used in the prepare_grid method to initialize the two hemispheres (line 12).

Remember that those HemisphereGrid instances will have already configured their own cells, but that's not quite enough. We need to tell the cells at the equator of each of those hemispheres that they are adjacent to each other as well. That's what configure_cells is doing, on lines 17–21.

The remaining methods are self-explanatory, simply providing means to query the cells of the grid.

Almost there! We're still missing the to_png method that will draw our maze, but we've left it for last for a reason. We're going to do things a bit differently here.

Instead of trying to implement a 3D renderer ourselves, we're going to rely on a third-party tool called the *Persistance of Vision Raytracer*, or *POV-Ray* for short. It excels at drawing photorealistic 3D geometry (like spheres). All we need to do is give it something to put on that geometry. (A maze, for instance!)

To understand how this is going to work, consider the following map of the world.

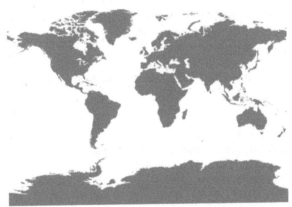

Looking at that map, you'd think that Antarctica was *enormous*. Seriously! It must comprise at least as much land as all the other continents combined! Of course, this isn't true. Antarctica is actually comparable in size to North America. So why, then, is it shown so large on the map?

The answer is that the map *distorts* it. Because the earth is a sphere, its surface cannot be drawn—or *projected*—onto a flat surface very easily, and definitely not without some amount of distortion. Our map uses what's called a *cylindrical projection*, which takes areas near the poles and stretches them out to fill a rectangular area.

Installing POV-Ray

Unless you've played with POV-Ray before, you probably won't have it installed yet. Fortunately, it's free, and pretty painless to set up. If you are on a Windows machine, you can download an installer from http://povray.org/download.

If you are on Mac OS X, you can use Homebrew:[a]

```
$ brew install povray
```

or MacPorts:[b]

```
$ sudo port install povray
```

If you're on Linux, POV-Ray will be available via your package manager of choice.

---

a. http://brew.sh
b. https://www.macports.org

We'll use this same technique to draw our maze, distorting the cells near the poles in order to fit everything in a rectangular grid. POV-Ray, then, will take that projection and apply it to a sphere, wrapping it neatly around the globe like a decal on a model airplane and fixing the distortion in one go. This lets us render a maze on a 3D surface by drawing a 2D image, a technique we're already very familiar with.

Here's how it comes together. Add the following to_png method to the end of the SphereGrid class.

```
Line 1  def to_png(ideal_size: 10)
    -     img_height = ideal_size * @rows
    -     img_width = @grid[0].size(@equator - 1) * ideal_size
    -
    5     background = ChunkyPNG::Color::WHITE
    -     wall = ChunkyPNG::Color::BLACK
    -
    -     img = ChunkyPNG::Image.new(img_width + 1, img_height + 1, background)
    -
   10     each_cell do |cell|
    -       row_size = size(cell.row)
    -       cell_width = img_width.to_f / row_size
    -
    -       x1 = cell.column * cell_width
   15       x2 = x1 + cell_width
    -
    -       y1 = cell.row * ideal_size
    -       y2 = y1 + ideal_size
    -
   20       if cell.hemisphere > 0
```

```
-        y1 = img_height - y1
-        y2 = img_height - y2
-      end
-
25      x1 = x1.round; y1 = y1.round
-      x2 = x2.round; y2 = y2.round
-
-      if cell.row > 0
-        img.line(x2, y1, x2, y2, wall) unless cell.linked?(cell.cw)
30        img.line(x1, y1, x2, y1, wall) unless cell.linked?(cell.inward)
-      end
-
-      if cell.hemisphere == 0 && cell.row == @equator - 1
-        img.line(x1, y2, x2, y2, wall) unless cell.linked?(cell.outward[0])
35      end
-    end
-
-    img
-  end
```

The ideal_size parameter (line 1) is how tall and wide an ideal cell will be—but remember the distortion we saw on that map of the world! We'll see the same kind of distortion in our maze here. The goal is not for the cells to be drawn all the same size in our projection, but for them to be roughly similar in size once we've mapped it to a sphere.

That ideal_size parameter is used to compute the size of our image on lines 2 and 3. In particular, note the line that computes the width: it takes the number of rows at the equator (the row with the greatest number of cells) and uses that to determine how wide the image ought to be. When we get to computing how wide a specific cell is (on line 12) that image width is divided by the actual number of cells in the current row. The result may be *significantly* wider than the ideal size, if there are few cells in the row. (Remember the poles in particular—they have only a single cell each!)

Once we know our cell's dimensions, we compute the x- and y-coordinates for each corner of the rectangle, and then we do something which might be a bit unexpected. Lines 20–23 *flip the y-coordinates for the southern hemisphere.*

Huh?

Remember that our sphere consists of two hemispheres, and the way our HemisphereGrid class is implemented, each hemisphere treats the pole as being at the top. However, we've flipped the southern hemisphere upside down, so that our computations there are backward. We fix it by simply subtracting the computed y-coordinate from the height of our image.

One last gotcha: we draw the "top" (or pole-ward) walls for each cell, assuming that the next row down will take care of the "bottom" (equator-facing) walls. However, when it comes to the equator itself, it happens to be the bottom of both hemispheres, and it would be omitted entirely if we failed to take it into account specially. Lines 33–35 make sure that the equator gets drawn.

Let's give it a spin. Our demo app ought to be completely unsurprising by now:

```
sphere_demo.rb
require 'sphere_grid'
require 'recursive_backtracker'

grid = SphereGrid.new(20)
RecursiveBacktracker.on(grid)

filename = "sphere-map.png"
grid.to_png.save(filename)
puts "saved to #{filename}"
```

Running that will generate our maze image and save it to sphere-map.png. Go ahead and open it up. It should look something like this:

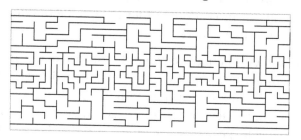

Isn't that wild? The poles are each a single cell, so those cells are stretched edge-to-edge, with the distortion growing less and less as the rows approach the equator.

It's definitely intriguing but not very useful just yet. We need to apply it to a sphere to see it in all its glory!

This is where POV-Ray comes in. POV-Ray accepts a text file describing a scene and creates the corresponding image. To be useful, our scene will need to include a camera (the location within the scene from which the image will be drawn), a light source (to illuminate our sphere), and the sphere itself.

Put the following in sphere.pov.

```
sphere.pov
#version 3.7;
#include "colors.inc"

background { color White }

camera {
  location <0,0,-2.5>
  look_at  <0,0,0>
}

light_source {
  <-50, 50, -50>
  color White
}

sphere {
  <0,0,0>, 1
  texture {
    pigment {
      image_map {
        png "sphere-map.png"
        map_type 1
      }
    }
    finish { ambient 0.3 diffuse 0.5 specular 0.2 }
  }

  rotate z*30
  rotate -x*30
}
```

Without getting too much into POV-Ray's scene description language, let me just point out what is (hopefully) obvious: the scene includes a camera, a light source, and a sphere. It then applies our sphere-map.png image as a texture to that sphere (along with some material properties, like diffuse and specular lighting), and finally rotates the sphere at a jaunty angle.

To produce an image of this scene, we just invoke POV-Ray from the command line, like this:

```
$ povray +A sphere.pov
...
POV-Ray finished
```

We pass in the scene file, sphere.pov, as one of the arguments. The other argument, +A, tells POV-Ray to perform anti-aliasing on the image so that the edges of the sphere and the lines of the maze are smoothed and made to look crisp and neat.

POV-Ray will spit out quite a bit of information while it renders, so don't be alarmed—it's working as expected. When it's all finished, the final image will be saved to sphere.png.

Voilà!

Your Turn

So we come to the end of this brief dip into the ocean of planair mazes. You've seen how to build them on surfaces like cylinders, Möbius strips, cubes, and spheres, and you've exercised your paper-crafting and 3D modeling skills by constructing some of those objects in both real and virtual space. Can you hear the possibilities calling you yet?

Try your hand at some of the following ideas, or chase some of your own. See what you come up with!

Rendering Cylinder Mazes

So you've seen how to use POV-Ray to draw a sphere with a maze on it. Doing so for a cylinder is very similar. The POV-Ray documentation[1] is fairly approachable, in spite of the fact that it claims to be "for Unix" (it actually applies to all platforms). Look it over and see if you can puzzle out how to take what you've got for the sphere maze and do the same for a cylinder.

Rectangular Prisms

A cube is just a special case of a more general shape called a *rectangular prism*. Imagine taking a cube, and stretching it along one or more axis,

---

1. http://www.povray.org/documentation

so that the faces are no longer all equal in shape or area. The result is no longer a cube, but it *is* still a prism! How would you draw a maze on such a surface?

Cone Mazes

You've done circle mazes, and cylinder mazes. What happens if you combine the two? You wind up with a *cone maze*. How would you tackle implementing a maze on the surface of such a shape?

End Caps

The cylinder maze we looked at in this chapter existed purely on the sides of the cylinder. That is to say, the cylinder was *open*, because it had no cap on the top and bottom. But these caps are circular in shape...and you just happen to know how to generate circle mazes. How would you incorporate two circle mazes into a cylinder maze, to act as the top and bottom caps on the cylinder?

An Odd Number of Rows

Our sphere maze implementation required that you give it an even number of rows, so that the two hemispheres could equally represent both halves of the sphere. You can still make that work with an odd number of rows, but you need to treat the equatorial row as a special case. How would you tackle that?

Real Walls

Painting the mazes onto these surfaces is definitely intriguing, but it's only the first step. How would you go about generating *actual geometry* for the walls? It's not as hard as it might sound, but you'll need to make sure you understand the math that was used to derive the measurements of these grids. It all boils down to two things: being able to map a point in your maze to a physical point on the surface, and being able to compute the *normal vector* at that point—that is, the direction that is perpendicular to the surface at the given location.

Four-Dimensional Objects

As if this material hadn't blown your mind enough already, what if we were to take it up a notch? Just as you can paint a 2D maze onto a 3D object, you can "paint" a 3D maze onto a 4D object. What does this even mean? It means you've got some research ahead of you! Tesseracts, duo-cylinders, and glomes are just a few of the crazy names you might encounter. See what you come up with!

There you have it, my friend. You dove deep into the sea of random maze generation, and you've come up on the other side. You found no magic there—only rules, and logic, and a vast ocean of *possibility*.

You've had a taste. You've caught glimpses of what might be done with these tools. Where will you go next?

Wherever it is, I hope there are mazes.

Summary of Maze Algorithms

Unless you use these algorithms frequently, you're bound to find your recollection of them fading over time. That's okay! You've learned them once; often all you need is a little refresher to bring them all sharply back into focus. The whole point of this appendix is to help you skip the full course and quickly recall the salient features and gotchas of each algorithm. Browse through them, skim the analyses in the next appendix, and jump right back into your own projects!

Aldous-Broder

In a nutshell: Starting at an arbitrary location in the grid, move randomly from cell to cell. If moving to a previously unvisited cell, carve a passage to it. End when all cells have been visited.

Typical features: Starts quickly but can take a very long time to finish. Significantly, it is *unbiased*, meaning it is guaranteed to generate mazes perfectly randomly, without preference to any particular texture or feature. (See also *Wilson's algorithm.*)

More information: The Aldous-Broder Algorithm, on page 55.

Binary Tree

In a nutshell: For each cell in the grid, randomly carve either north or east.

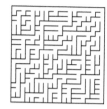 

Typical features: A strong diagonal texture, tending toward the north-east corner of the grid. Corridors run the length of the northern row and the eastern column. Difficult to use with masks and some non-rectangular grids.

Variations: The texture changes if you choose south instead of north, or west instead of east. Also, the algorithm is easily adapted to 3D (and higher) grids by adding either up or down as a choice at each cell.

More information: The Binary Tree Algorithm, on page 6, and *Implementing the Binary Tree Algorithm*, on page 22.

Eller's

In a nutshell: Consider the grid one row at a time, sequentially. Assign the unvisited cells in the current row to different sets. Randomly link adjacent cells that belong to different sets, merging the sets together as you go. For each remaining set, choose at least one cell and carve south, adding that southern cell to the set as well. Repeat for every row in the grid. On the final row, link all adjacent cells that belong to different sets.

Typical features: Final row tends to have fewer walls as a result of needing to merge multiple sets together. Difficult to use with masks and non-rectangular grids.

Variations: Render an infinitely long maze by keeping only a single row in memory at a time and never rendering a final row.

More information: Eller's Algorithm, on page 189.

Growing Tree

In a nutshell: This algorithm is a generalization of the *Prim's* algorithms. Start by creating a set and adding an arbitrary cell to it. Then, choose a cell from the set. If the cell has no unvisited neighbors, remove it from the set; otherwise choose one of the unvisited neighbors and link the two together. Add the neighbor to the set. Repeat until the set is empty.

Typical features: Depends heavily on the method used to choose the next cell from the set. Mazes may be radially textured (like *Simplified Prim's*) or twisted and snaky (like *Recursive Backtracker*), or anything in-between.

Variations: Alter the way in which cells are selected from the set. Choosing at random gives you *Simplified Prim's*. Choosing the most recently added cell gives you *Recursive Backtracker*. Weighting the cells and choosing the heaviest gives you *True Prim's*. Combine different selection methods for even greater variety, choosing (for example) randomly half the time, and most recently added the rest of the time.

More information: The Growing Tree Algorithm, on page 183.

Hunt-and-Kill

In a nutshell: Starting at an arbitrary location, perform a *random walk*, avoiding previously visited cells. When no more moves are possible, scan the grid, looking for an unvisited cell next to a visited cell. If found, connect the two, and resume the random walk. The algorithm terminates when it cannot find any unvisited cells.

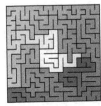

Typical features: Long, twisty passages ("high river"), with relatively few dead ends. Closely related to *Recursive Backtracker*, but potentially slower since it may scan every cell many times, though it has much lower memory requirements.

More information: The Hunt-and-Kill Algorithm, on page 67.

Kruskal's (Randomized)

In a nutshell: Begin by assigning each cell to a different set. Randomly link two adjacent cells, but only if they belong to different sets. Merge the sets of the two cells. Repeat until only a single set remains.

Typical features: Largely unbiased (see Appendix 2, *Comparison of Maze Algorithms,* on page 257, and note how similar Kruskal's mazes are to those produced by Aldous-Broder and Wilson's). Produces very regular, uniform mazes. Excels at producing mazes that are the union of disjoint subsets, where the grid is prepopulated with some cells already connected in different areas.

Variations: Template mazes (by applying template designs at different locations of the grid, and then running Kruskal's algorithm to fill in the unfinished areas), with spirals, weaves, and other patterns.

More information: Kruskal's Algorithm, on page 158.

Prim's (Simplified)

In a nutshell: Initialize a set with an arbitrary cell. Randomly choose a cell from the set. If it has no unvisited neighbors, remove it from the set. Otherwise, choose one of the cell's unvisited neighbors, link the two together, and add the neighbor to the set. Repeat until the set is empty.

Typical features: A strong radial texture centered on the starting cell. Mazes tend to have more dead ends than other algorithms, and shorter paths. Behaves identically to *Prim's (True)* if that algorithm is given a grid where every cell is weighted the same.

More information: *Simplified Prim's Algorithm*, on page 179.

Prim's (True)

In a nutshell: First, assign every cell a random weight, and initialize a set with an arbitrary cell. Choose the cell with the greatest weight from the set. If it has no unvisited neighbors, remove it from the set. Otherwise, choose one of the cell's unvisited neighbors, link the two together, and add the neighbor to the set. Repeat until the set is empty.

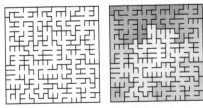

Typical features: Many, many dead ends per maze, with relatively shorter paths in general. Texture-wise, the mazes have a "jigsaw puzzle" appearance.

More information: *True Prim's Algorithm*, on page 181.

Recursive Backtracker

In a nutshell: Starting at an arbitrary location, perform a *random walk*, avoiding previously visited cells. When no more moves are possible, backtrack to the most recently visited cell and resume the random walk from there. The algorithm ends when it tries to backtrack from the cell where it started.

Typical features: Long, twisty passages ("high river"), with relatively few dead ends. Closely related to *Hunt-and-Kill*, but potentially faster, as it is guaranteed to visit every cell only twice, though it needs considerably more memory to keep track of previously visited cells.

More information: The Recursive Backtracker Algorithm, on page 73.

Recursive Division

In a nutshell: Begin with an open grid, with no internal walls. Add a wall that divides the grid in half, with a passage through it linking the two halves. Repeat on each side of the grid, recursively, until no open areas remain.

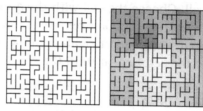

Typical features: Tends to have a boxy, rectangular texture. Solution paths are generally easy to spot due to "bottlenecks"—passages that restrict all travel between regions of the grid.

Variations: By halting the recursion early, open areas (rooms) can be created to produce mazes reminiscent of floor plans. More challenging: the grid may be divided along irregular lines to eliminate the boxy texture.

More information: Recursive Division, on page 197.

Sidewinder

In a nutshell: Consider the grid one row at a time. For each row, link random runs of adjacent cells, and then carve north from a random cell in each run. Treat the northern row specially, linking all cells into a single corridor.

Typical features: A strong vertical texture. One corridor runs the length of the northern row. Difficult to use with masks and non-rectangular grids.

Variations: The texture changes if you choose south instead of north, or if you run the algorithm by columns instead of rows and choose east or west instead of north. Also, the algorithm is easily adapted to 3D (and

higher) grids by choosing between north, and (for example) up or down
for each run.

More information: The Sidewinder Algorithm, on page 12, and *Implementing
the Sidewinder Algorithm*, on page 27.

Wilson's

In a nutshell: Choose an arbitrary cell and add it to the maze. Starting from
any other cell, perform a *loop-erased random walk* until you encounter a
cell belonging to the maze, and then add the resulting walk. Repeat until
all cells have been added.

Typical features: Slow to start but accelerates quickly as paths are added to
the maze. As with *Aldous-Broder*, it is *unbiased*, meaning it is guaranteed
to generate mazes perfectly randomly, without preference to any particular
texture or feature.

More information: Wilson's Algorithm, on page 60.

Comparison of Maze Algorithms

It's one thing to stare at a maze and try to decide whether the aesthetics of it work for you or not. It's much harder to look at the implementation of an algorithm and compare it quantitatively with other algorithms. How likely is the algorithm to generate dead ends? How does its average longest path compare with that of other algorithms? *How can we even know these things?*

For this, we turn to statistics. It's really pretty straightforward to do: you run each algorithm a set number of times, on a grid of fixed size; pick out the numbers you care about; and analyze them. It's probably not going to win you any PhDs, and the numbers by themselves certainly won't tell you the whole story, but we can still come away with some useful insights.

The graphs in this appendix were created by running each algorithm a thousand times, on a 32×32 grid. The Growing Tree algorithm was a 50/50 mix of choosing the most recently added cell and choosing a cell at random. The following data points were measured and averaged for each grid:

- Number of dead ends
- Length of longest path (the number of cells it contains)
- Number of cells with horizontal or vertical passages (east-to-west, and north-to-south)
- Number of "elbow" cells (passage enters from one side, then turns either right or left)
- Number of three-way intersections
- Number of four-way intersections

Each number was then turned into a fraction of the grid as a whole. For example, if a particular maze had a longest path of 250 cells, that was then divided by the number of cells in the grid (32×32, or 1024), to produce roughly 0.244. In other words, that path would have covered 24.4% of the cells in the grid.

Aldous-Broder and Wilson's algorithms being unbiased (and their output statistically identical to each other), their averages were used as the baseline by which all the other algorithms were compared. Keep in mind, though, that an average only tells part of the story! The numbers in these graphs may be hiding surprising things that could be exposed through more rigorous analysis. You have been warned.

Dead Ends

A dead end is defined as a cell that is linked to only a single neighbor. Fewer dead ends and a long path might suggest lengthy side roads that can take someone far astray.

The following figure shows how the number of dead ends per maze compared across algorithms.

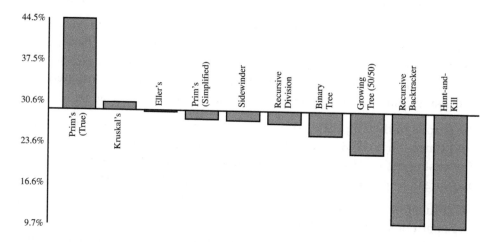

Aldous-Broder and Wilson's tend to produce mazes where around 30% of the cells are dead ends. True Prim's produces about 50% more than that, and Hunt-and-Kill and Recursive Backtracker produce significantly fewer.

Longest Path

The longest path was computed using Dijkstra's algorithm, as described in *Making Challenging Mazes*, on page 44. It is represented in the following figure as the percentage of cells in a maze that lie on that longest path.

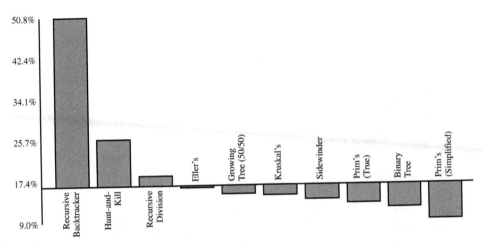

Recursive Backtracker is far-and-away the champion here, with an average of *50%* of the cells in the grid existing on the longest path. Simplified Prim's falls at the other end of the spectrum, with longest paths that cover less than 10% of the grid.

Twistiness

Twistiness is a measure of how often a passage changes direction. It is taken as the percentage of cells with a passage entering on one side, and exiting to the left or the right.

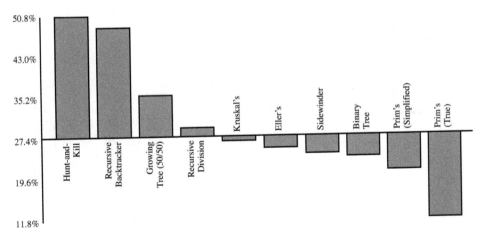

Hunt-and-Kill takes the cake here, followed closely by Recursive Backtracker, with roughly half the cells in the maze fitting this definition. True Prim's, on the other hand, turns only about 10% of the time.

Directness

Directness is the opposite of twistiness. It is a measure of how many cells in a grid go straight, either horizontally or vertically.

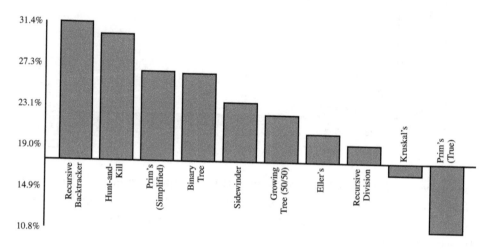

This can be broken down a bit more, though, by showing the numbers separately for horizontal passages and vertical passages. The following figure shows the relative number of horizontal passages in each maze.

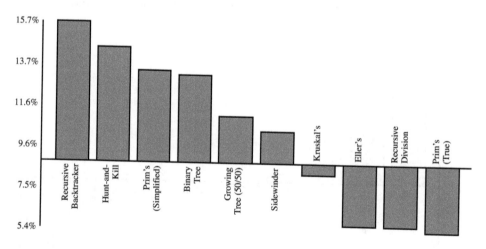

And the following gives the corresponding numbers for vertical passages.

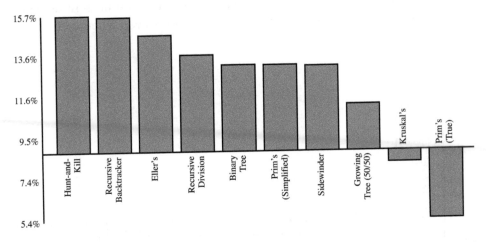

As you would expect, the baseline is pretty much the same for both horizontal and vertical passages, but two particularly interesting data points here are the Recursive Division and Eller's algorithms. Both seem to *greatly* prefer vertical passages over horizontal ones! Hunt-and-Kill and Sidewinder show some similar preference as well.

Intersections

Lastly, intersections give an indication of how often someone traversing the maze will need to make a decision. The following figure shows the relative number of three-way intersections for each algorithm.

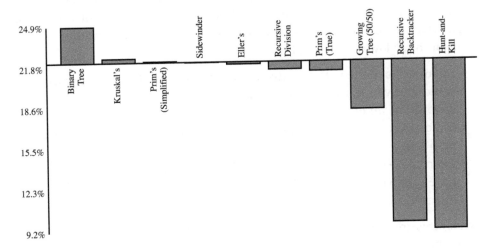

As you can see, Recursive Backtracker and Hunt-and-Kill present far fewer choices than other algorithms! This trend continues even when considering four-way intersections:

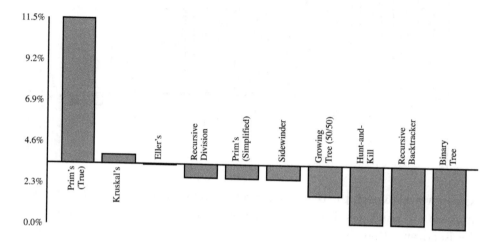

Once again, Recursive Backtracker and Hunt-and-Kill are toward the end, although Binary Tree is at the very tip of that tail with exactly zero percent of passages being four-way intersections. It's hard to get much lower than that!

Your Turn

As was pointed out, the statistics presented in this appendix are very superficial. There is a lot more that could be done. If statistics are your thing, you might want to consider analyzing other aspects of these algorithms. Maybe some of the following will inspire you!

- An analysis of the path lengths leading away from the longest path. This could give you a better idea of how far someone might go astray (though it would be an expensive number to compute!).
- Ratio of dead ends to path length. Many dead ends with a longer average path length suggests you might get very lost down a side road!
- Ratio of directness to twistiness. An algorithm with a very high ratio would have relatively few turns. Pac-Man's maze, for instance, would be more direct than twisty.

What other measurements would you like to try? See what else you can come up with!

Index

The Joy of Math and Healthy Programming

Rediscover the joy and fascinating weirdness of pure mathematics, and learn how to take a healthier approach to programming.

Good Math

Mathematics is beautiful—and it can be fun and exciting as well as practical. *Good Math* is your guide to some of the most intriguing topics from two thousand years of mathematics: from Egyptian fractions to Turing machines; from the real meaning of numbers to proof trees, group symmetry, and mechanical computation. If you've ever wondered what lay beyond the proofs you struggled to complete in high school geometry, or what limits the capabilities of the computer on your desk, this is the book for you.

Mark C. Chu-Carroll
(282 pages) ISBN: 9781937785338. $34
https://pragprog.com/book/mcmath

The Healthy Programmer

To keep doing what you love, you need to maintain your own systems, not just the ones you write code for. Regular exercise and proper nutrition help you learn, remember, concentrate, and be creative—skills critical to doing your job well. Learn how to change your work habits, master exercises that make working at a computer more comfortable, and develop a plan to keep fit, healthy, and sharp for years to come.

This book is intended only as an informative guide for those wishing to know more about health issues. In no way is this book intended to replace, countermand, or conflict with the advice given to you by your own healthcare provider including Physician, Nurse Practitioner, Physician Assistant, Registered Dietician, and other licensed professionals.

Joe Kutner
(254 pages) ISBN: 9781937785314. $36
https://pragprog.com/book/jkthp

Seven in Seven

From Web Frameworks to Concurrency Models, see what the rest of the world is doing with this introduction to seven different approaches.

Seven Web Frameworks in Seven Weeks

Whether you need a new tool or just inspiration, *Seven Web Frameworks in Seven Weeks* explores modern options, giving you a taste of each with ideas that will help you create better apps. You'll see frameworks that leverage modern programming languages, employ unique architectures, live client-side instead of server-side, or embrace type systems. You'll see everything from familiar Ruby and JavaScript to the more exotic Erlang, Haskell, and Clojure.

Jack Moffitt, Fred Daoud
(302 pages) ISBN: 9781937785635. $38
https://pragprog.com/book/7web

Seven Concurrency Models in Seven Weeks

Your software needs to leverage multiple cores, handle thousands of users and terabytes of data, and continue working in the face of both hardware and software failure. Concurrency and parallelism are the keys, and *Seven Concurrency Models in Seven Weeks* equips you for this new world. See how emerging technologies such as actors and functional programming address issues with traditional threads and locks development. Learn how to exploit the parallelism in your computer's GPU and leverage clusters of machines with MapReduce and Stream Processing. And do it all with the confidence that comes from using tools that help you write crystal clear, high-quality code.

Paul Butcher
(296 pages) ISBN: 9781937785659. $38
https://pragprog.com/book/pb7con

Put the "Fun" in Functional

Elixir puts the "fun" back into functional programming, on top of the robust, battle-tested, industrial-strength environment of Erlang.

Programming Elixir

You want to explore functional programming, but are put off by the academic feel (tell me about monads just one more time). You know you need concurrent applications, but also know these are almost impossible to get right. Meet Elixir, a functional, concurrent language built on the rock-solid Erlang VM. Elixir's pragmatic syntax and built-in support for metaprogramming will make you productive and keep you interested for the long haul. This book is *the* introduction to Elixir for experienced programmers.

Maybe you need something that's closer to Ruby, but with a battle-proven environment that's unrivaled for massive scalability, concurrency, distribution, and fault tolerance. Maybe the time is right for the Next Big Thing. Maybe it's *Elixir*.

Dave Thomas
(340 pages) ISBN: 9781937785581. $36
https://pragprog.com/book/elixir

Programming Erlang (2nd edition)

A multi-user game, web site, cloud application, or networked database can have thousands of users all interacting at the same time. You need a powerful, industrial-strength tool to handle the really hard problems inherent in parallel, concurrent environments. You need Erlang. In this second edition of the best-selling *Programming Erlang*, you'll learn how to write parallel programs that scale effortlessly on multicore systems.

Joe Armstrong
(548 pages) ISBN: 9781937785536. $42
https://pragprog.com/book/jaerlang2

Get Kids into Programming

Get your kids writing Minecraft plugins in Java, or 3D games in JavaScript. No experience required!

Learn to Program with Minecraft Plugins (2nd edition)

The bestselling, kid-tested book for Minecraft is now updated for CanaryMod! Write your own Minecraft plugins and watch your code come to life with flaming cows, flying creepers, teleportation, and interactivity. Add your own features to the Minecraft game by developing Java code that "plugs in" to the server. You'll manipulate and control elements in the 3D graphical game environment without having to write tons of code or learn huge frameworks. No previous programming experience necessary.

Andy Hunt
(284 pages) ISBN: 9781941222942. $29
https://pragprog.com/book/ahmine2

3D Game Programming for Kids

You know what's even better than playing games? Creating your own. Even if you're an absolute beginner, this book will teach you how to make your own online games with interactive examples. You'll learn programming using nothing more than a browser, and see cool, 3D results as you type. You'll learn real-world programming skills in a real programming language: JavaScript, the language of the web. You'll be amazed at what you can do as you build interactive worlds and fun games. Appropriate for ages 10-99!

Printed in full color.

Chris Strom
(308 pages) ISBN: 9781937785444. $36
https://pragprog.com/book/csjava

Pragmatic Programming

We'll show you how to be more pragmatic and effective, for new code and old.

Your Code as a Crime Scene

Jack the Ripper and legacy codebases have more in common than you'd think. Inspired by forensic psychology methods, this book teaches you strategies to predict the future of your codebase, assess refactoring direction, and understand how your team influences the design. With its unique blend of forensic psychology and code analysis, this book arms you with the strategies you need, no matter what programming language you use.

Adam Tornhill
(218 pages) ISBN: 9781680500387. $36
https://pragprog.com/book/atcrime

The Nature of Software Development

You need to get value from your software project. You need it "free, now, and perfect." We can't get you there, but we can help you get to "cheaper, sooner, and better." This book leads you from the desire for value down to the specific activities that help good Agile projects deliver better software sooner, and at a lower cost. Using simple sketches and a few words, the author invites you to follow his path of learning and understanding from a half century of software development and from his engagement with Agile methods from their very beginning.

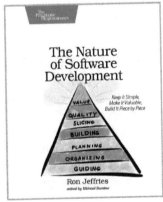

Ron Jeffries
(178 pages) ISBN: 9781941222379. $24
https://pragprog.com/book/rjnsd

The Pragmatic Bookshelf

The Pragmatic Bookshelf features books written by developers for developers. The titles continue the well-known Pragmatic Programmer style and continue to garner awards and rave reviews. As development gets more and more difficult, the Pragmatic Programmers will be there with more titles and products to help you stay on top of your game.

Visit Us Online

This Book's Home Page
https://pragprog.com/book/jbmaze
Source code from this book, errata, and other resources. Come give us feedback, too!

Register for Updates
https://pragprog.com/updates
Be notified when updates and new books become available.

Join the Community
https://pragprog.com/community
Read our weblogs, join our online discussions, participate in our mailing list, interact with our wiki, and benefit from the experience of other Pragmatic Programmers.

New and Noteworthy
https://pragprog.com/news
Check out the latest pragmatic developments, new titles and other offerings.

Save on the eBook

Save on the eBook versions of this title. Owning the paper version of this book entitles you to purchase the electronic versions at a terrific discount.

PDFs are great for carrying around on your laptop—they are hyperlinked, have color, and are fully searchable. Most titles are also available for the iPhone and iPod touch, Amazon Kindle, and other popular e-book readers.

Buy now at *https://pragprog.com/coupon*

Contact Us

Online Orders:	*https://pragprog.com/catalog*
Customer Service:	*support@pragprog.com*
International Rights:	*translations@pragprog.com*
Academic Use:	*academic@pragprog.com*
Write for Us:	*http://write-for-us.pragprog.com*
Or Call:	+1 800-699-7764